Reforming the State without Changing the Model of Power?

This book places administrative reform in post-socialist countries in a broad context of power and domination. This new perspective clarifies the reasons why reforms went awry in Russia and some other post-Soviet countries, whereas they produced positive outcomes in the Baltic States and most East European countries. The contributors analyse the idea that administrative reform cannot produce sustainable changes in the organization of the state apparatus as long as it does not touch the underpinning model of power and domination. Using an interdisciplinary and comparative approach, the essays combine elements of philosophy, sociology, political science and economics, including a wealth of primary and secondary data: surveys, in-depth interviews with state representatives and participant observation. The book focuses on Russia and analyses recent developments in this country by the way of comparison with the experience of carrying out administrative reform in Ukraine, Bulgaria, Poland, Germany and North America.

This book was published as a special issue of the *Journal of Communist Studies and Transition Politics*.

Anton Oleinik is Associate Professor of Sociology at Memorial University of Newfoundland and Senior Research Associate, Institute of Economics, Russian Academy of Sciences.

Reforming the State without Changing the Model of Power?

On Administrative Reform in Post-Socialist Countries

Edited by Anton Oleinik

Routledge
Taylor & Francis Group

LONDON AND NEW YORK

First published 2009 by Routledge
2 Park Square, Milton Park, Abingdon, Oxon, OX14 4RN

Simultaneously published in the USA and Canada
by Routledge
270 Madison Avenue, New York, NY 10016

Routledge is an imprint of the Taylor & Francis Group, an informa business

© 2009 Edited by Anton Oleinik

Typeset in Times by Techset Composition Ltd., Salisbury, UK
Printed and bound in Great Britain by Biddles Digital, Kings Lynn

British Library Cataloguing in Publication Data
A catalogue record for this book is available from the British Library

ISBN10: 0-415-46618-0
ISBN13: 978-0-415-46618-9

Contents

Notes on Contributors

Marc P. Berenson is Research Fellow at the Institute of Development Studies at the University of Sussex in Brighton, UK. In 2007–2008 he was a Max Weber Fellow at the European University Institute in Florence, Italy.

Karine Clément, Doctor of Sociology, is Research Fellow at the Institute of Sociology of the Russian Academy of Sciences in Moscow and director of the independent NGO Institute of 'Collective Action' (IKD, www.ikd.ru). She is conducting research projects in two fields of sociology: collective actions and flexible work, mostly applied to Russian society.

Oxana Gaman-Golutvina is professor at the Moscow Institute for Foreign Relations (MGIMO) and the Higher School of Economics, and specializes in political science theory, and studies of contemporary Russian politics, Russian political elites and bureaucracy, and Russian political culture.

Rumen Gechev is a Professor of Economics at the University of National and World Economy in Sofia, Bulgaria. His research interests are in the field of sustainable development and economic policy. He is former deputy prime minister and minister of economic development of Bulgaria (1995–97) and former chairman of the UN Commission on Sustainable Development (1996–97).

Valeri Ledyaev is Professor of Politics at the State University–Higher School of Economics, Moscow. His publications include *Power: A Conceptual Analysis* (1997) and a number of articles on power in the Russian context. His current research relates to power as a subject of study in political science and sociology.

William Mishler, professor of political science at the University of Arizona and visiting professor at the University of Aberdeen, specializes in the sophisticated analysis of public opinion and political participation in the United States, Canada, Europe and Asia. For a dozen years he has been publishing analyses of New Europe Barometer data in major American journals.

Neil Munro, senior research fellow at the Centre for the Study of Public Policy, concentrates on mass response to regime change in post-Communist countries and in Asia. He has co-authored three books on Russia and New European Democracies and many journal articles. Currently he is exploring how China is interpreting the implications of reforms leading to the collapse of the Soviet Union.

Richard Rose, director of the Centre for the Study of Public Policy, University of Aberdeen, created the New Europe/New Russia Barometer in 1991 to monitor mass response to transformation across 16 countries of Central and Eastern Europe and the former Soviet Union (see <http://www.abdn.ac.uk/cspp>). He is the author of more than 40 books and is a Fellow of the British Academy.

Peter H. Solomon, Jr., is Professor of Political Science, Law and Criminology at the University of Toronto and a Member of its Centre for European, Russian and Eurasian Studies. His publications include *Soviet Criminal Justice under Stalin* (1996), *Courts and Transition in Russia* (with Todd Foglesong, 2000), and articles and edited collections on governmental, legal and judicial reform in Russia and other post-Soviet states.

Introduction: Putting Administrative Reform in a Broader Context of Power

ANTON OLEINIK

The term 'post-socialist reforms' is used as a generic name for a large number of policies intended to produce political, economic and social changes in the former socialist countries of Eastern Europe and the Soviet Union. At the early stages of post-socialist reforms their expected outcomes appeared very promising and clear-cut: the market would be a substitute for a centrally planned economy; democracy for a single party political system; and an 'open' society for a 'small' society – characterized by a sharp differentiation between Us and Them, lack of control over everyday violence, the personification of relationships, and a blurred border between the private and public spheres.[1] The projection of these expected outcomes into the reality of the early 1990s explains a 'teleological' – in the term of Wladimir Andreff – orientation of reforms at that time: the point of departure was believed to count less than the point of arrival.[2] The idea of a simultaneous movement along three vectors – political (leading to full-fledged democracy), economic (leading to the full-fledged market) and social (leading to the 'open' society) – summarizes the initial design of post-socialist reforms.

However, in the second half of the 1990s it became evident that the movement along the three axes would be more difficult than expected and, nearly a decade later, reforms still have not produced the desired outcomes. In fact, in several countries, notably the successors to the Soviet Union (with a notable exception of the Baltic States), reforms 'went awry' and significantly deviated from the linear trajectory. The divergent paths of post-socialist countries ('success stories' of Poland, Slovenia and the Czech Republic contrasted with growing political, economic and social problems in Russia and Ukraine) called for theoretical explanations and corresponding adjustments in the design of reforms.

It turned out that issues related to institutions and institutional changes had been neglected in the initial blueprints of reforms. According to a broad definition, 'institutions' refer to rules of the game in political, economic and social spheres as well as mechanisms for their enforcement. 'Institutions are the humanly devised constraints that structure political, economic and social interaction'.[3] The neglect of institutions can be compared with giving cards (or, better, tokens, title deeds and paper money in the Monopoly board game) to players without telling them the rules of the game and reaching an agreement regarding their enforcement. The key novelty reflected in a new consensus among Western advisers and financial sponsors of post-socialist reforms consisted in 'bringing institutions back in'. In the economic sphere emphasis has shifted from macro-economic stabilization, price and trade liberalization and mass privatization to the case-by-case privatization of residual state property, start-up development and institution-building.[4]

The awareness of the importance of institutions and organizations as mechanisms for enforcing rules and norms questions the 'teleological' character of reforms. New institutions do not emerge 'from scratch'. Even when they are designed according to foreign templates, new formal institutions enter into a complex and contradictory relationship with informal institutions inherited from the past. Formal institutions can be changed overnight, but informal ones hardly so. 'Institutions are products of the past process, are adapted to past circumstances, and are therefore never in full accord with the requirements of the present'.[5]

Being invested with the monopoly of the legitimate use of violence, the state has a comparative advantage in enforcing norms and rules and, in doing so, in maintaining order. Max Weber explains law as order maintained with the help of physical or psychological coercion applied by state representatives in a systematic manner.[6] Hence, the introduction of new norms requires reforming the state apparatus: state servants should be motivated to implement new rules and should possess qualifications for overseeing their implementation and enforcement. That being the case, administrative reform becomes a centrepiece of post-socialist transformations: it creates favourable conditions for successfully implementing all other 'partial' policies.

In the late 1990s, administrative reform became a top item on the agenda of reforms in Russia and Ukraine: movement in all other spheres is now believed to be conditioned by progress, or the lack of it, in reforming the state apparatus. For instance, in October 1995 the Ukrainian parliament started to work on a programme of administrative reform; in July 1997 the president established a state commission on the issues of administrative reform which prepared a strategy for reforming the state service, enacted by a presidential decree in April 2000.[7] In Russia, the president initiated work on the federal programme for reforming the state service in August 2001. It was promulgated in November 2002 and its temporal scope covered the period 2003–5. In 2003 the president issued a decree aimed at implementing the programme. A strategy of administrative reform for 2006–8 was adapted by the Russian government in 2005.[8]

Most of these official documents concerning administrative reform derive from initiatives taken by the executive. It appears that administrative reform in Russia and Ukraine was initiated and carried out by those who are expected to be subject to it – state servants. This seeming paradox has an explanation deeply rooted in the Weberian approach to bureaucracy. Weber believed that the mere functional position of bureaucrats – they are appointed rather than elected and separated from ownership of the means of production or administration, and their salary depends less on performance or achievement than on status and the movement along fixed career lines – creates powerful incentives to rationalize the state service and make it predictable and 'calculable': 'Bureaucracy is *the* means of transforming social action into rationally organized action'.[9]

The results of administrative reform entrusted to state servants are far from satisfactory even according to the criteria they set for themselves. The Russian government refers to a series of indicators developed by the World Bank (the Governance Research Indicator Country Snapshot: GRICS) and Transparency International (the TI Corruption Perception Index) as measures of its progress in reforming itself.[10] Values of these indicators remain volatile and have not shown any positive dynamics since the start of administrative reform (see Figure 1). Government effectiveness refers to the quality of public services, the quality of the civil service and its degree of independence from political pressures, the quality of policy formulation and implementation, and the credibility of the government's commitment to such policies. Regulatory quality refers to the ability of the government to formulate and implement sound policies and regulations that permit and promote private sector development.[11] Values of both indicators vary from −2.5 (the lowest relative score) to + 2.5 (the highest). Scores of the TI corruption perception index range from 0 (highly corrupt) to 10 (highly clean). All three indicators are built on the basis of regular surveys conducted on a sample of experts and business people.

The failure of administrative reform in Ukraine took even more manifest forms. Even though administrative reform here started earlier than in Russia, the lack of progress led to public unrest in November 2004. The participation in mass protests of various socio-economic groups such as business people and retired persons suggests that common dissatisfaction with the government (the immediate cause of the 'Orange' revolution consisted in electoral fraud and manipulations during the presidential elections) temporarily relegated conflicting interests to a backstage position. It is worth mentioning that the level of trust in the government – the share of those who believed that the government can be 'completely' or 'to some degree' trusted – during the ten years preceding the November 2004 mass protests never exceeded 16 per cent, and during the past three years it has dipped below 10 per cent.[12]

FIGURE 1
OUTCOMES OF ADMINISTRATIVE REFORM IN RUSSIA AND UKRAINE, SELECTED
INDICATORS, 1996–2007

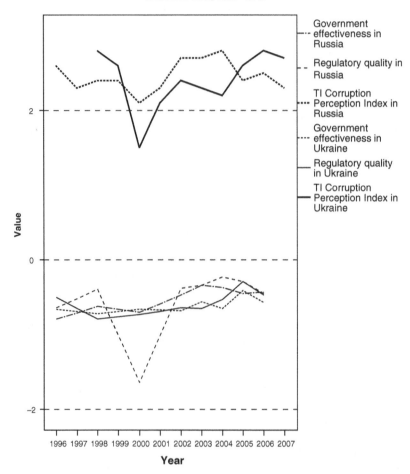

Source: The World Bank at <http://go.worldbank.org/ATJXPHZMH0>, accessed 18 January
2008, and Transparency International at <http://www.transparency.org/policy_
research/surveys_indices/global/cpi>, accessed 18 January 2008. Government effectiveness and regulatory quality were not assessed in 1997, 1999 and 2001. Values for
these years were substituted for mean scores of the preceding and following years.

Preliminary outcomes of administrative reform highlight a paradox. On
the one hand, encompassing reforms call for the active involvement of the
government as an *agens movens*[13] of change. The catch-up modernization
reshaping the institutional landscape necessitates the resources and potential

for violence that only the state possesses. On the other hand, in order to transform into an actor propelling changes, the government must first reform itself. Administrative reform, like most other post-socialist reforms, has a teleological character: models of civil service in developed countries determine its vector. For instance, administrative reform derives from a belief in rational bureaucracy grounded in the theory developed by Max Weber. The Russian government evaluates its performance in carrying out administrative reform by referring to the experience of developed countries (GRICS indicators have an explicitly relative, not absolute, nature). Since the very beginning of administrative reform, the Ukrainian executive has extensively relied on advice and templates provided by Western governments and organizations, specifically the World Bank.[14]

However, hopes that the state apparatus can be reformed *from within* appear to be vain in the case of Russia, and also in Ukraine before November 2004. The present situation in the state apparatus reflects less a 'radiant future' than a 'neither–nor' combination of one vector going from the future to the present and the other going from the past to the present. History matters here, too: informal institutions embedded in a particular bureaucratic culture and patterns of interaction between citizens and state servants keep reproducing, and they block movement toward the 'radiant' Weberian future: 'The state bureaucracy appears to be one big continuing phenomenon flowing through modern Russian history from the tsars to Putin'.[15] Like other post-socialist reforms that necessitate an external 'push', administrative reform evidently needs it as well: without an outside lever and an outside 'place to stand' there are few chances to move the Earth – the state apparatus. The epithet 'outside' refers here not exclusively to things foreign, but to anything external to the state apparatus. The concept of conservative modernization understood as efforts by the ruling elite to keep its own hold on power in the process of reforms (applied by Bertrand Badie to a large number of developing countries) suggests that the deadlock associated with reforming the government from within is far from country specific.[16]

For the reasons outlined above, a comprehensive analysis of administrative reform as a centrepiece of post-socialist reforms should not be reduced to the study of administrative processes. Administrative processes take place in an environment composed of formal and informal institutions. Some of them might provide a 'place to stand' in changing the state apparatus; others, by contrast, contribute to its continuing reproduction. A triple-layer research design seems appropriate (see Figure 2).

Its first layer corresponds to studies of particular administrative processes, documents and policies, for instance, programmes of electronic governance (e-governance) actively debated by academics and state officials. At the second layer the state apparatus as a whole becomes the subject of analysis.

FIGURE 2
A TRIPLE-LAYER ANALYSIS OF ADMINISTRATIVE REFORM

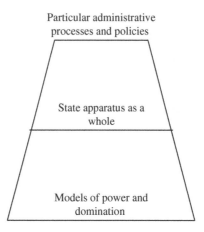

Particular administrative
processes and policies

State apparatus as a
whole

Models of power and
domination

The research question of how e-governance fits current patterns of interaction between state servants illustrates the new analytical focus. The third layer refers to formal and informal institutions in which the state apparatus is embedded. These institutions derive from particular models of power and domination that structure relationships between state servants and citizens, businesses, foreign governments and other external actors. Issues of the compatibility or incompatibility of e-governance with a prevailing model of power emerge at this stage of analysis. The bias of informal institutions in which the predominant model of power is embedded can have a significant impact on how e-governance functions. Steven Lukes speaks in this regard of the 'bias of the system' and attempts by various actors to mobilize and reinforce it to their own advantage.[17]

Because the bias of the system lies at the deepest layer of the analysis, experts on the issues of administrative reform, like policy-makers, often omit it from their calculations. The divide between formal and partial theories increasingly characterizes research in the social sciences. Yet it has especially important implications in the case of administrative reform. This collection of essays aims at making some initial steps toward narrowing this distance. The contributors attempted to relate studies of power and domination to practical issues of implementing administrative reform. Its relative failure in the Russian case can then be attributed to a deficit of change in the prevailing model of power and domination. This hypothesis guides the structure of the collection: it opens with a theoretical discussion of power and domination. A selection of texts on the state apparatus in Russia represents the next step in the movement from the abstract to the concrete. Particular administrative processes and policies are also considered by several contributors, namely state environmental policies and tax collection.

The concept of power represents the starting point in the proposed reading of administrative reform. According to a standard definition, power is 'the probability that one actor within a social relationship will be in a position to carry out his own will despite resistance, regardless of the basis on which this probability rests'.[18] In other words, power refers to the imposition of will, and consequently has a compulsory character. From this perspective, power relationships are structured by available techniques to impose will. 'Coercion and violence are two constitutive characteristics of power differentiating it from other relationships based on will'.[19] In contrast to the consumption of goods and services subject to the 'law of diminishing marginal utility',[20] power does not seem to have any 'in-built' constraints. Does this mean that power has only one attribute, namely violent techniques for imposing will?

A variety of forms of power suggest a negative answer to this question. For instance, authority does not exclude violent techniques yet it makes their use conditioned and subject to some rules respected by both the actor vested in power and the actor subordinated to it. 'In authority, it is ... a *source* [of will], that is, the perceived status, resources or personal attributes of the communicator, which induces compliance'.[21] The list of attributes of power in a pure form (it would be called 'imposed' if this characteristic did not sound redundant) includes at least the following:

1. *Purpose*: it is power as an end in itself in contrast to power as a means to achieve other ends. Domination implies a conflict of interests. The actor vested in power imposes will at the expense of the subordinate's interests. Domination over other actors becomes the sole purpose of power as an end in itself, which contrasts with an instrumental character of power as a means to achieve other ends.[22] Power transforming into a terminal value (power as an end in itself) aims to reproduce and expand itself, and contributes only tangentially to the achievement of any other results.
2. *Self-justifiable character*: power in a pure form does not need justification by reference to any external or superior principles, be it law or age-old traditions. The mere fact of exercising power justifies it. David Beetham speaks in this regard of illegitimacy of power not bounded by rules endorsed by all parties involved in a power relationship. He opposed illegitimate power to legitimate power which conforms to established rules; the rules can be justified by reference to beliefs shared by both the dominant and the subordinate, and there is evidence of consent by the subordinate to the particular power relationship.[23]

3. *Asymmetry*: all power relationships are asymmetrical in that the actor invested with power gives orders and pursues his or her agenda whereas the subordinate is expected to obey. However, power in a pure form makes the asymmetry extreme. There are several ways to operationalize and measure the asymmetry of a power relationship. One is to compare the scope of the subordinate's actions under control of the power-holder with that remaining under his or her own control. James Coleman indicates in this connection a tendency toward the power holder's 'extension of control beyond the domain covered in the relation'.[24]
4. *Absence of feedback loops*: the subordinate has no say in decisions taken by the actor vested in power, let alone influence over them. Power in a pure form implicates the idea of causality as a unidirectional relationship between a cause and an effect: 'A in some way affects B'.[25]
5. *Violent techniques for imposing will*: power in a pure form rests on violence. The repertoire of violent techniques includes force as the infliction of physical pain; coercion as the threat of applying force; manipulation as the calculated distortion of the information available to the subordinate; and domination by virtue of a constellation of interests as the deliberate restriction of his or her choices.[26]

All five attributes appear closely interrelated (see Figure 3). The 'mechanics' of power as an end in itself exclude references to external principles as irrelevant and extends the scope of actions under the power-holder's control: 'The most universal interest of those invested with power consists in expanding the scope of their control'.[27] In these circumstances there is no need to take into

FIGURE 3
FIVE ATTRIBUTES OF POWER IN A PURE FORM

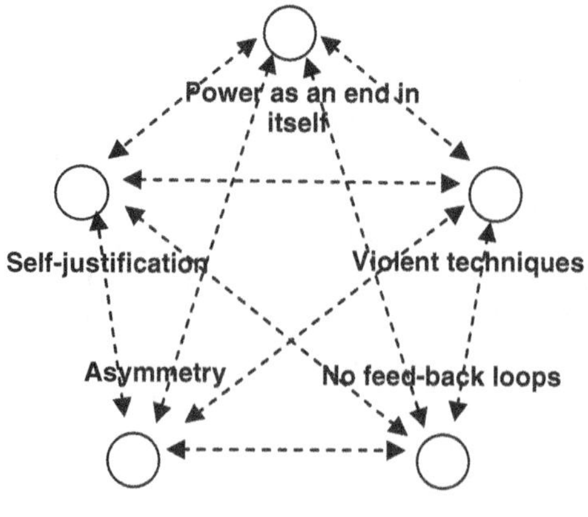

consideration the subordinate's interests or to give him or her a voice. Finally, the lack of a moral dimension in a power relationship leaves the power-holder no choice but to use violent techniques: 'When legitimacy is eroded or absent ... coercion has to be much more extensive and omnipresent'.[28] In its turn, violence limits the effectiveness of power in achieving any other objective except its own reproduction (for example, slave labour was effective only in performing a restricted number of simple tasks). In a similar manner, one can draw other links between the five elements: a self-justifiable character of power (2) renders the expression of consent by the subordinate unnecessary (4), and so on.

Power in a pure form represents a good starting point in the analysis of administrative reform. This research strategy allows avoidance of 'heroic' hypotheses about a 'natural' interest of bureaucrats in rationalization of their service or their concern with the common good. Nevertheless it can give rise, both analytically and practically, to other forms of power which involve changes of one or several attributes. Weberian bureaucracy can represent a point of arrival – if a number of conditions are met – but not a starting point. The key research and practical question then consists in indicating circumstances under which such transformation can take place. The specification of conditions under which authority as power subject to external validation and legitimation replaces power in a pure form helps redesign the strategy of administrative reform. It allows finding a 'place to stand', a bearing from which to push the state apparatus. If power in a pure form has no in-built constraints, it can be limited from the outside by creating conditions favourable for its transformation into a 'modest' and instrumental power. These conditions should be carefully maintained as there is always a risk of a reverse motion from authority to power in a pure form. The choice of the latter as a starting point in the analysis serves as a reminder of this eventuality even in countries where the market, democracy and the open society seem to be taken for granted.

The analysis of potential constraints of power necessitates the adoption of an *inter-disciplinary* approach. These constraints are varied. Some of them refer to economic processes: for instance, the repertoire of violent techniques for imposing will largely depends on military technology, on the relative prices of economic resources, and on the organization of industries (monopoly facilitates domination by virtue of a constellation of interests). The constraints related to justification derive from ideologies. The distribution of rights and obligations between the power-holder and the subordinate influences the degree of asymmetry in their relationships, which calls for legal studies. Elections represent one of the feedback loops and give the subordinate a say in a power relationship. Political science extensively studies electoral processes. In the final account, no comprehensive analysis of constraints of power seems feasible without combining political, juridical, philosophical, sociological and economic approaches.

The task of testing the hypothesis about the transformation of power – under certain conditions – from a major constraint of development into its driving force requires the adoption of a *comparative* approach. To verify the impact of various constraints of power one needs to look at their possible configurations and to compare the situation when a particular constraint is present with that when it is missing. The comparative approach helps 'deconstruct' a country-specific situation in the state service by analytically separating universal elements of the institutional environments and indicating their presence or absence. The metaphor of the mosaic seems appropriate: the same pieces of coloured glass produce various pictures portraying the state service – and underpinning models of power – across countries. The present collection contains elements of several 'mosaics' – Russian (the most complete piece: Marc Berenson, Karine Clément, Oxana Gaman-Golutvina, Valeri Ledyaev, Anton Oleinik, Richard Rose *et al.*, Peter Solomon and Joachim Zweynert contributed to its construction), Bulgarian (Rumen Gechev), Polish (Marc Berenson and – to a lesser extend – Natalia Pohorila), Ukrainian (Natalia Pohorila), German (Joachim Zweynert) and Anglo-Saxon (Peter Solomon).

Inter-disciplinary and comparative research has its problems, though. One of these consists in finding a common language – searching for concepts that make sense to economists, political scientists, sociologists, philosophers and legal scholars. Ideally, these concepts have an equivalent meaning in different institutional contexts, that is, in different countries. At first sight, most social scientists are familiar with concepts such as state, government, bureaucracy, democracy and power (economists appear less interested in using the last concept[29] yet they actively refer to the first four). The task of achieving conceptual equivalence, however, represents a significant challenge because even the listed concepts have different meanings in Russian and in a number of European languages, including English.

What Thorstein Veblen said almost a century ago in differentiating the state as a commonwealth in English from the state as an all-encompassing entity in German remains true in present-day Russian, where the state 'is neither the territorial area, nor the population, nor the body of citizens or subjects, nor the aggregate wealth or traffic, nor the public administration, nor the government, nor the crown, nor the sovereign; yet in some sense it is all these matters, or rather all these organs of the state'.[30] Civil society appears therefore to be included in the state even in linguistic terms, which questions its position in other institutional and linguistic contexts as a separate entity. The overwhelming importance of the concept of state in Russian compared with 'partial' definitions appropriate in a 'complex', differentiated society (for example, the government, the public administration) also explains why one should be very careful while applying the conventional Western term of civil service to the Russian case. Civil service implies (i) a particular model of power relationships (the state as a provider of services to the population); (ii) a non-holistic perception of the state. Karl W. Ryavec correctly points out that 'the bureaucrats of Russia could not be "civil servants" but had to be "state servants" above all else'.[31] Similar problems arise in regard to the use of the term 'bureaucracy' because of its heavy connotations in European languages with the ideas of rationality and Weberian administration.

The meaning of the concept of power also varies from one language to another, even in the West. For instance, English, French and German highlight different attributes of power. German has two terms: power *to* (do something; *Kraft*) and power *over* (somebody; *Macht*), whereas the two other languages express the same idea with the help of rather awkward constructions.[32] French allows a fine differentiation between power as potential or capacity (*puissance*) and power as the act (*pouvoir*), which has important implications for the discussion of dispositional versus performance definitions of power.[33] All these differences mirror particularities of underlying models of power embedded in the institutional environment of a particular country.

The introduction of Russian into the analysis further complicates the picture. The term most commonly used in both ordinary language and scientific discussions, *vlast'*, refers to power in a pure form rather than to authority as a 'modest' and limited form of power.[34] This fact can be considered as indirect proof that the prevailing model of power relationships lies close to power in a pure form. The influence of this model goes far beyond the suppression of other terms by the word *vlast'*. As a linguistic study shows, the entire grammatical structure of Russian language was heavily influenced by the closeness of the prevalent model of power to power in a pure form. Several features of Russian grammar seem especially relevant. One is the spread of impersonal sentences without any clearly indicated subject: *mne ne spitsya* (literally, 'it does not sleep to me'), cf. 'I cannot get to sleep' (where the responsibility for failure lies with the individual): individuals controlled by power in a pure form have very limited opportunities for taking initiatives, hence they lose their capacity to be a subject. Other examples are the spread of passive forms relegating the subject to backstage: 'the door is open' cf. 'I opened the door'; the use of nouns to incorporate qualities defined in other languages by adjectives, so that a quality tends to overshadow a subject or an object which it characterizes: Russian *krasavets* (a noun meaning a male who displays beauty), cf. 'a handsome *man*', and so forth.[35] It is worth mentioning that these changes happened in the fifteenth–sixteenth centuries (when the centralized state was created under the auspices of the Grand Principality of Moscow), and can be considered indicative of the continuous reproduction of the prevailing model of power since then.

The inter-disciplinary and comparative approach to studying the triple-layer structure of administrative reform in post-socialist countries represents the kernel of the research agenda of the *AdmReformNet*, an international network of experts and scholars representing various disciplines in the social sciences, created with financial support from the Social Sciences and Humanities Research Council of Canada (SSHRC), the Faculty of Arts of Memorial University of Newfoundland, and the Centre for European, Russian and Eurasian Studies (CERES) at the University of Toronto.[36] The first meeting of the network members took place at Memorial University in St. John's, Newfoundland, in late August 2006. This collection contains essays written on the basis of papers presented during the workshop. Papers received extensive examination at the initial meeting (its schedule allowed devoting at least one to discussing each contribution), and subsequently went through a multi-stage process of internal and, in several cases, external peer-review. A website with a virtual reference library of sources on the three layers of administrative reform in comparative perspective was created after the workshop to enhance further co-operation and the extension of the network.[37] The design of the reference library permits uploading electronic versions of preprints and previously published texts, as well as retrieving ready-to-insert bibliographies in American Psychological Association format.

The essay by Valeri Ledyaev represents a rare attempt to connect the discussion of abstract philosophical categories such as domination, power and authority with practical issues of post-socialist reforms, namely the effectiveness of state management. In the proposed terms, Ledyaev links processes on the deepest level of the triple-layer analytical structure with those in the middle and at the upper layers. He also focuses on relationships between the ruling elite – the group vested in power – and the Russian population, and unveils the underlying model of domination which has several elements of power in a pure form.

Oxana Gaman-Golutvina focuses more specifically on the middle-level analysis. Her contribution highlights the key contradiction of catch-up modernization between, on one hand, the need for a more active involvement of the state in political, economic and social processes and, on the other hand, the actual form of this involvement in the Russian case. She also explores limits of transferring practices of New Public Management from one institutional context, namely Anglo-Saxon countries, to the other, namely Civil (Continental) Law countries and a number of developing countries. In the proposed terms, the introduction of a particular policy calls for changes or adjustments, or both, at the deeper layers of the state administration.

Rumen Gechev brings his practical expertise of working within one of the post-socialist governments to the analysis. He emphasizes the role of external constraints and pressures exerted by the European Union in the adoption and implementation of environmental policies (Bulgaria was admitted to the EU as a full member on 1 January 2007). Again, changes in a particular policy (environmental) appeared impossible without reshaping processes at the deeper layers of the state apparatus, namely without enhancing its capacity for reconciling the interests of different groups and for finding a sustainable compromise. Needless to say, such capacity undermines some basic principles of power in a pure form.

Karine Clément explores probably the most challenging question of whether social movements embody a new model of power and can transform themselves into a lever to move administrative reform towards changes at the deeper layers of the state apparatus. In other words, do social movements potentially represent an alternative to external pressures in reshaping the institutional landscape in which a particular model of power is embedded? While attempting to answer this question, Clément uses her practical expertise gained through participant observation in a number of social movements and initiatives in Russia. However, social movements in Russia are at early stages in their development, and our knowledge about them appears too limited to give a definitive answer.

Richard Rose, William Mishler and Neil Munro ask another difficult question, namely why regularly held elections do not necessarily limit the discretion of individuals and groups invested with power. They develop the idea of multiple political equilibriums which suggests that the population can express – including through elections – support for a large range of political regimes, from democracy to autocracy in various forms. Resigned acceptance of the present regime – the longer it exists, the stronger the resigned acceptance, all other conditions being equal – thus reduces incentives for comprehensive administrative reform and lets power-holders keep the prevailing model of power intact.

Peter Solomon considers another potential constraint which to all appearances does not work properly in the Russian case, namely the law. Russian state servants have significant room for manoeuvre in interpreting and changing laws in the process of implementing them. Solomon urges the reader not to confuse the practices of 'delegated legislation' in Anglo-Saxon countries with the discretionary powers of Russian state servants, as they face fewer constraints in the application of rules. The fact that Western and Russian practices (delegated legislation and *ramochnye zakony*) are only apparently similar illustrates how concepts change meaning in consequence of the institutional context, and reminds us about the standard caveat discussed above in regard to all comparative research.

The essay by Marc Berenson focuses on the opposing preliminary outcomes of two tax administration reforms, in Poland and in Russia. In the former case a more rational bureaucracy emerged thanks to the existence of several institutional and structural constraints (the current structure facilitates external control and enhances the separation and specialization of functions). In the latter case tax administration reform contributes to the reproduction of power in a pure form and does not prevent the use of taxes as a lever to impose will on businesses and the general population. Target-driven versus compliance-driven tax systems outlined by Berenson represent more specific attributes of two forms of power – one 'pure', the other 'modest' and instrumental.

My own study, entitled 'Existing and Potential Constraints Limiting State Servants' Opportunism: The Russian Case', describes various constraints and analyses their particular configuration in Russia as of 2005–6. It is argued that the lack of a significant number of constraints or their loose character makes hopes for spreading administrative reform below the surface (that is, below its upper layer) rather superficial. The Russian state service keeps reflecting (and reproducing) power in a pure form.

Natalia Pohorila's essay focuses on privatization as a factor contributing to legitimization / de-legitimization of the political regime. She usefully applies the distinction between normative and instrumental (pragmatic) types of acceptance of political regimes to the Ukrainian case. The latter type appears especially interesting because it highlights that one's perception of the political regime has a direct impact on the organization of his or her everyday economic activities, e.g. the willingness to start a private business. Pohorila argues that the type of acceptance varies across social groups.

The contribution written by Joachim Zweynert represents a first yet very insightful attempt to put the methodology of comparative historical and institutional studies to work. When comparing the experience of catch-up modernization and administrative reforms in the Germanies (he usefully differentiates the path of Prussia and that of the South-Western Germanies) and Russia in the eighteenth century, Zweynert emphasizes the role of external pressures in promoting reforms and making the government committed to them. The French Revolution of 1789 and the Napoleonic wars, according to him, had an especially important influence on the process of modernization in the South-Western Germanies. Progress on the road toward modernity was also facilitated by particular ideologies, or shared mental models, deeply embedded in religion.

Unfortunately the death of one of the founding network members, Yuri Levada, precluded the full development of the ideas that he brought to our discussions (the workshop was virtually the last scholarly event that he attended). Long before the creation of the network, he considered the idea that the institutional environment in Russia can be changed only as a result of outside pressures. The exploration of this hypothesis serves as a tribute to Yuri Levada's significant role in the development of both theoretical and empirical sociology in the Soviet Union.

The publication of this collection would be impossible without assistance in language editing by Theresa Heath of Memorial University of Newfoundland, and the co-operation of external reviewers, Professor Wladimir Andreff of Université de Paris-I–Panthéon-Sorbonne, Professor Marc Raeff of Columbia University and Professor Ovsey Shkaratan of the State University–The Higher School of Economics (Moscow). The contribution of Theresa Heath went beyond the scope of purely technical editing and helped to improve significantly the quality of texts written by non-native English speakers. The assistance of Ms Heath and the external reviewers is greatly appreciated by the contributors and the editor of the collection.

NOTES

1. A detailed outline of the 'small' society can be found in Anton Oleinik, *Organized Crime, Prison and Post-Soviet Societies* (Aldershot: Ashgate, 2003). In contrast to the first two elements of the constitution of real socialism, the centrally planned economy and the single party political system, there is no sustainable agreement among scholars concerning the conceptual description of its third element. However, compared with the concept of a 'closed' society or a totalitarian society, that of the 'small' society not only refers to a particular model of the state but also implies a specific type of power and dominance which, as it will be shown below, is especially relevant to the present research.
2. Wladimir Andreff, *La crise des économies socialistes: la rupture d'un système* (Grenoble: Presses Universitaires de Grenoble, 1993), p.11.
3. Douglass C. North, 'Institutions', *Journal of Economic Perspectives*, Vol.5, No.1 (Winter 1991), p.97.
4. Wladimir Andreff, *La mutation des économies postsocialistes: une analyse économique alternative* (Paris: l'Harmattan, 2003), pp.15–21.
5. Thorstein Veblen, *The Theory of the Leisure Class: An Economic Study of Institutions* (New York: The Modern Library, 1934 [1899]), p.191.
6. Max Weber, *Economy and Society: An Outline of Interpretative Sociology* (New York: Bedminster Press, 1968 [1922]), p.34.
7. 'Postanova Presidii Verkhovnoi Rady Ukrainy vid 16.10.1995 *Pro prodovzhennia stroku pidgotovky proektu Kontseptsii administrativnoi reformy*' (Resolution of the Presidium of the Parliament of Ukraine from 16.10.1995 on preparing the project of a programme of administrative reform); 'Ukaz Prezidenta Ukrainy vid 7.7.1997 No.620/97 *Pro derzhavny komisiyu z provedenniia v Ukraini administrativnoi reformy*' (Decree of the President of Ukraine from 7.7.1997 on the state commission responsible for carrying out administrative reform); 'Ukaz Prezidenta Ukrainy vid 14.4.2000 No.599/2000 *Pro Strategiyu reformuvannia sistemy derzhavnoi sluzhby v Ukraini*' (Decree of the President of Ukraine from 14.4.2000 on the strategy for reforming the state service in Ukraine).
8. 'Poruchenie Prezidenta Rossiiskoi Federatsii ot 15.8.2001 *O razrabotke Programmy reformirovaniya gosudarstvennoi sluzhby*' (Order of the President of the Russian Federation from 15.8.2001 concerning the preparation of a programme for reforming the state service); 'Ukaz Perzidenta Possiiskoi Federatsii ot 19.11.2002 No.1336 *O federal'noi programme 'Reformirovanie gosudarstvennoi sluzhby Rossiiskoi Federatsii (2003–2005)*' [Decree of the President of the Russian Federation from 19.11.2002 on the federal programme for reforming the state service of the Russian Federation (2003–2005)]; 'Ukaz Perzidenta

Possiiskoi Federatsii ot 23.7.2003 No.824 *O merah po provedeniyu administrativnoi reformy v 2003–2004 godakh'* (Decree of the President of the Russian Federation from 23.7.2003 on means of carrying out administrative reform in 2003–2004); 'Rasporyazhenie pravitel'stva Rossiiskoi Federatsii ot 25.10.2005 No.1789-p *O kontseptsii administrativnoi reformy v Rossiiskoi Federatsii v 2006–2008 godakh'*(Direction of the government of the Russian Federation from 25.10.2005 on the programme of administrative reform in the Russian Federation in 2006–2008).

9. Weber, *Economy and Society*, p.988.
10. 'Rasporyazhenie pravitel'stva Rossiiskoi Federatsii at 25.10.2005 No.1789-p', Annex.
11. Daniel Kaufmann, Aart Kraay and Massimo Mastruzzi, 'Governance Matters V: Aggregate and Individual Governance Indicators for 1996–2005', working paper (Washington, DC: The World Bank, 2006).
12. Natalia Panina, za redaktsiyeyu, *Ukrains'ke suspil'stvo 1994–2004: sotsiologichnyi monitoring* (Ukrainian society in 1994–2004: sociological monitoring) (Kiev: Zapovit, 2004), p.20; I am indebted to Dr Natalia Pohorila for this source.
13. Alexander Gerschenkron, 'Economic Backwardness in Historical Perspective', in Mark Granovetter and Richard Swedberg (eds.), *The Sociology of Economic Life* (Boulder, CO: Westview, 1992), p.122.
14. Since 1997 experts of the World Bank have prepared a number of programmes and documents directly related to the issues of administrative reform; some of them have subsequently transformed into decrees and laws: see Tsentr doslidzhen' administratyvnoi reformy, *Administratyvna reforma v Ukraini: zagal'ni zasady administratyvnoi reformy* (Administrative reform in Ukraine: general principles) (Kiev: Natsional'na Akademiya Derzhavnogo Upravlinnya, 2001), Part 1.
15. Karl W. Ryavec, *Russian Bureaucracy: Power and Pathology* (Lanham, MD: Rowman & Littlefield, 2003), p.37.
16. Bertrand Badie, *The Imported State: The Westernization of the Political Order* (Stanford, CA: Stanford University Press, 2000), p.97.
17. Steven Lukes, *Power: A Radical View* (Basingstoke and New York: Palgrave–Macmillan, 2005 [1974]).
18. Weber, *Economy and Society*, p.53.
19. Viktor Makarenko, *Russkaya vlast'* (Russian power) (Rostov-on-Don: Izdatel'stvo SKNTsVSh, 1998), p.60.
20. This law, a key element of neo-classical economics, states that for any good or service, the marginal utility of that good or service decreases as the quantity of the good increases, *ceteris paribus*. In other words, total utility increases more and more slowly as the quantity consumed increases.
21. Dennis Wrong, *Power: Its Forms, Bases and Uses* (New York: Harper Colophon Books, 1980), p.25.
22. Thomas Wartenberg, *The Forms of Power: From Domination to Transformation* (Philadelphia, PA: Temple University Press, 1990).
23. David Beetham, *The Legitimation of Power* (Atlantic Highlands, NJ: Humanities Press International, 1991), pp.16–20.
24. James Coleman, *Foundations of Social Theory* (Cambridge, MA and London: Belknap Press, 1990), p.152.
25. Lukes, *Power*, p.30; see also Herbert Simon, 'Notes on the Observation and Measurement of Political Power', *Journal of Politics*, Vol.15, No.4 (1953), p.503.
26. These techniques are discussed in greater detail in Valeri Ledyaev, 'Domination, Power and Authority in Russia: Basic Characteristics and Forms', and Anton Oleinik, 'Existing and Potential Constraints Limiting State Servants' Opportunism: The Russian Case', both in this collection.
27. Makarenko, *Russkaya vlast'*, p.99.
28. Beetham, *The Legitimation of Power*, p.28.

29. For an overview see Vyacheslav Dement'ev, 'Problema vlasti i ekonomicheskii analiz' (The Problem of Power and Economic Analysis), in Rustem Nureev (ed.), *Postsovetskii institutsionalizm: Vlast' i biznes* (Rostov-on-Don: Nauka, 2006), pp.77–98.

30. Thorstein Veblen, *Imperial Germany and Industrial Revolution* (New York: Viking, 1939 [1915]), p.161; see also Yuri Pivovarov, *Russkaya politicheskaya traditsiya i sovremennost'* (The Russian political tradition and the modern situation) (Moscow: INION RAN, 2006), p.17.

31. Ryavec, *Russian Bureaucracy*, p.53.

32. Wartenberg, *The Forms of Power*, p.24.

33. Pierre Hegy, 'Words of Power: The Power of Words', *Theory and Society*, Vol.1 (1974), pp.329–39; Wrong, *Power*, p.10.

34. Anton Oleinik, 'A Distrustful Economy: An Inquiry into Foundations of the Russian Market', *Journal of Economic Issues*, Vol.XXXIX, No.1 (2005), pp.63–4; see also Valeri Ledyaev, *Power: A Conceptual Analysis* (Commack, NY: Nova Science Publishers, 1997), p.95.

35. Igor' Kim and Yelena Osetrova (eds.), *Vlast' v russkoi yazykovoi i etnicheskoi kartine mira* (Power in the Russian Linguistic and Ethnic World-View) (Moskva: Znak, 2004), pp.95–109. The use of nouns to describe qualities deserves special emphasis taking into consideration the recently coined concept of 'sovereign democracy' [see Vladislav Surkov, 'Natsionalizatsiya budushchego: paragraphy pro suverennuyu demokratiyu' (Nationalization of the Future: Paragraphs on Sovereign Democracy), *Ekspert*, 2006, No.43, at <http://www.expert.ru/printissues/expert/2006/43/nacionalizaciya_buduschego>, accessed 15 Oct. 2007]. The adjective 'sovereign' has a 'twin' noun, in both Russian and English. The quality expressed by such a noun-adjective might overshadow its subject, namely the Russian people who can seemingly express their will through democracy.

36. SSHRC awarded an International Opportunity Fund – Development Grant (file No.861-2005-0001); Memorial University and CERES contributed to covering the organizational expenses and the costs of publishing of a book in Russian (by ROSSPEN – Russian Political Encyclopedia). All contributions are deeply appreciated.

37. <http://www.arts.mun.ca/admreformnet>. Technical expertise and assistance in developing the website by Allan Farrell, Arts Computing Centre, Faculty of Arts, Memorial University, is greatly appreciated.

Domination, Power and Authority in Russia: Basic Characteristics and Forms

VALERI LEDYAEV

Political regime and power in modern Russia are usually discussed and explained in terms of authoritarianism or 'delegative (guided, deformed, illiberal) democracy',[1] focusing on deviations of the Russian regime from normative models of democracy. In this essay I suggest another model of power and politics in Russia which is based on a set of terms and distinctions developed by scholars involved in a conceptual analysis of power and its forms.[2] Application of the 'vocabulary of power' ('domination', 'power', 'authority', 'control', 'force', 'coercion', 'manipulation', 'the rule of anticipated reactions', 'non-decision-making', 'effects of power', and so on) allows an investigation of the whole range of power relations and can help to create a framework for comparative studies of power.

The following analysis of political power in Russia is based on three sets of concepts: (1) domination, (2) configuration of power forms, and (3) effectiveness of power. These three conceptual tools can help to discuss three key problems in the analysis of power: (1) who has power (who dominates), (2) how the power is exercised, and (3) what the effects of power are.

Domination

The concept of domination describes continuing relationships between social agents where the power 'is systematically used by one agent to detriment of the other agent' and the dominated agent 'is specifically harmed through the relationship'.[3] Thus, two basic defining properties of domination as a specific use of power can be distinguished: (1) the continuing (or recurrent) character of power relations, and (2) the benefits to the dominating agents and losses sustained by the dominated. Domination rests on different bases determining its forms and manifestations. It can be based on force, numbers, military and technological superiority, class privileges, religious norms and traditions, economic power, cultural identity, knowledge, and so forth. In all cases of domination, the advantaged position of dominating groups allows them to control options open to other (dominated) agents, thereby influencing their motivational structure and forcing them to accept particular, unequal exchange patterns or an unfair social order, or both.[4]

In Western democracies domination is usually attributed to the business or capitalist class. William Domhoff argues that in the United States the owners and top-level managers in large income-producing properties are the over-whelmingly dominant power: 'Their corporations, banks, and agribusinesses come together as a *corporate community* that dominates the federal government in Washington'.[5] John Scott holds a similar view of domination in the UK: 'Britain is ruled by a capitalist class whose economic dominance is sustained by the operations of the state and whose members are disproportionately represented in the power elite which rules the state apparatus'.[6] In both explanations, state bureaucracy – the political elite – plays an important but secondary role which is limited by the priorities of the business class.

In Communist Russia and Soviet-type systems domination has been explained in different terms. It was characterized by the absence of private property and a business class (class of owners), a one-party political system and state ideology of Marxism-Leninism that predetermined the domination of party and state officials (the bureaucracy) in the decision-making process, a system of distribution of goods and services based on privilege, and ideological hegemony.[7]

Who dominates in modern Russia: the business class ('bourgeoisie') or the administrative class (bureaucracy, *nomenklatura*)? At first glance, relations of power in post-communist Russia correspond (or are similar) to the Western model of domination since the transition to democracy and a market economy destroyed the monopolistic communist patterns of government and gave rise to a powerful capitalist class able to dominate other social groups. This appears true of Yeltsin's regime, which has usually been explained as an oligarchy ('oligarchic authoritarianism'), although after Putin's reforms such explanations have become less popular among scholars.

The modern political regime in Russia is commonly described as 'bureaucratic authoritarianism', with an emphasis on the dominant position of state officials (bureaucracy, or the political class) in the policy-making process and the shaping of social institutions.

What are the arguments that support a view of the predominantly bureaucratic nature of domination in modern Russia? For some scholars this is quite natural since power (state, administrative, bureaucratic) has always played a major role in Russian society. They argue that bureaucratic domination has been reproduced throughout Russian history despite the circulation of political elites and revolutions;[8] Russia has always been a 'political' society in contrast to other European 'economic' societies.[9]

However, this explanation is too abstract; instead, we need to concentrate on various manifestations of power and answer several relevant questions: (1) who benefits? (2) who governs – who occupies important institutional positions? (3) who wins – who successfully initiates, modifies, or vetoes policy alternatives? (4) who shines – who has the reputation of being powerful? (5) who exercises control over ideas? and (6) who determines the political agenda?[10]

In my view, bureaucratic domination in Russia has its roots in the expansion of state – that is, administrative – control of society. No matter how Putin's policy to strengthen the so-called 'power vertical' is evaluated – as the only possible way to increase the effectiveness of state power, or as an attempt to preserve the system of bureaucratic domination – this policy strategically coincides with the corporate interests of the administrative class. Control over organizations and institutions (mass media, political and civic organizations, regional and local authorities) which were relatively autonomous in the 1990s; growing state interference in the economy (the increase in the number of large corporations where the state has become the biggest shareholder, pressures placed by state officials on private enterprises to make business 'socially responsible', and so on); and the active role of the state in shaping values and ideological priorities – all these trends lead to 'widened reproduction' of bureaucracy, despite the proclaimed measures to cut the state apparatus.

Bureaucratic domination has been largely predetermined by an inefficient legal system which supports office-holders' opportunism, inspires frequent changes in the formal and informal rules of the game and limits the possibilities of society to influence and control the process of government. Dissemination of informal practices and violation of law (see below) allows the bureaucracy to use state powers to advance its corporate interests, thereby exercising power over other groups. The administrative class in Russian society is not an instrument of law but a principal power-holder able to convert laws into self-serving power resources.

The inefficiency of laws is closely related to the high level of corruption in the state apparatus.[11] In this particular context, corruption reflects society's dependency on state officials and the existence of numerous obstacles to citizens in solving their economic, commercial, professional or other problems through legal means.

The high level of corruption is evidence of the distribution of public goods in favour of the administrative class. Stable income growth, benefits, pensions and other social and economic privileges enjoyed by state officials that substantially exceed the income growth and benefits of other 'budgetary' social groups is another indicator of their privileged position in Russian society. However, the most important source of well-being for a substantial portion of the administrative class lies in its business opportunities. Many state officials have their own businesses and can use state powers, informal connections, information and other public resources to support their enterprises. For some, their official position becomes just an instrument in their business career.

Bureaucratic domination in the ideological sphere is reflected in a particular set of values or ideas that have been intensively instilled into people's minds by the Russian power elite and become widely accepted by the population: 'great Power', 'strong state', 'order', 'stability', 'governability', 'traditional way of life', 'cultural originality', and so forth. By contrast, other values, such as 'freedom', 'democracy', 'modernization' and 'global community', are on the periphery of mass consciousness and elite preferences. An 'ideological turn-around' has been caused by a broad set of circumstances including the pragmatic orientations of the governing elite. In the 1990s the administrative class supported the ideology of economic liberalism with an emphasis on a 'minimal state' to justify privatization and the accumulation of capital; in the following decade it turned to a conservative ideology to defend the existing social order.[12] Thus, the ruling class cultivates values that reproduce and maintain the conditions of its domination.

Finally, domination by the administrative class has become possible since the decline of political influence by corporate business after the economic failure and default of 1998, and especially the attempts of the new political leadership to narrow political space and exclude from politics all actors with a significant potential for power. Business has never been properly organized politically[13] and could not effectively resist this attack. Up to 2003 ('the Yukos case')[14] those who tried to maintain their political autonomy and participate in public policy were prosecuted. Business surrendered and was forced to accept a new pattern of relationships with the federal authorities called 'equal distance' ('ravnoudalenie'): consultations with business do not touch upon certain matters: strategic political issues – there is a 'complete ban on politics'; national economic development – there exists a 'partial ban on economics'; natural monopolies – the corporate community participates only at the stage of implementation of decisions made by the political class; and federal electronic mass media.[15] In contrast to Yeltsin's rule, where the Russian state was 'captured' by corporate business ('state capture'), now a reverse process of 'business capture' is taking place:[16] 'state officials exercise informal control over particular business enterprises and use their resources for departmental or personal purposes'.[17]

The process of formalizing and institutionalizing relationships between the power elite and the business community also leads to a strengthening in the position of the former and limiting the autonomy of the latter. The 'regime of consultations' and growing status of business organizations, including the Russian Union of Industrialists and Entrepreneurs, the Chamber of Commerce and Industry, and Business Russia, provide new possibilities for businesspeople in relationships with the administrative elite. However, in the process these organizations become more dependent on Putin's administration, which 'certifies' the list of participants in the negotiation process. Thus,

> changes in the political status of interest groups take place: 'pressure groups' are transformed into 'influence groups'. Pluralism survives at the expense of the autonomy of its elements. Institutionalization of interest groups is accompanied by strengthening of their weaknesses and dependency on the state. The balance of power within the system excludes any possibilities for interest groups to impose their will on the authorities.[18]

In everyday relationships on the micro-level, the domination of bureaucracy over business is usually based on a discretionary application of law, while controlling agencies (environmental health service, fire department, tax police, and so on) are used to create and reinforce formal and informal barriers to business activity.[19] The administrative class is interested in sustaining this order of things from which it derives 'rent status'. Therefore, regular attempts (or their imitations) to reform the system of government cannot substantially decrease office-holders' opportunism and their 'business opportunities'.

Finally, the Russian business class is not popular within the society and cannot successfully appeal to public opinion. This negative perception of businesspeople has become widespread among different social groups, and the state authorities have an interest in promulgating a negative image of 'oligarchs' to divert responsibility for poor economic performance on to the business community.[20] As a result, Russian corporate business refused to oppose or publicly criticize the power elite and accepted the new format of relationships, 'business capture' and other innovations in modern Russian politics.

This conclusion raises a question about the relevance of the idea of 'structural (systemic) power of business'[21] to the Russian social context. It is possible to discover and assess the 'structural power of business' in empirical terms only in cases of overt conflict between business class priorities and politicians' intentions, public opinion or the preferences of other interest groups. A set of indirect indicators – such as generally favourable conditions for business, rapid growth of entrepreneurs' incomes, 'market' orientations of the 'red' (that is, communist) governors in Russia's regions – show that the 'structural power' of the Russian business class really matters in considerations of reform.

However, the effect of systemic business power seems lower in Russia than in developed capitalist countries: the constitutional protection of private enterprise is not effective and investment risks are still very high; the growth of state property undermines the role of private capital; the ruling elite has its own resources ('administrative resources') which become the most effective instrument in Russian electoral campaigns; voting behaviour does not necessarily reflect the government's economic performance. The administrative elite does not need strategic political union with the business class (or indeed any other social group): on the one hand, it is 'affiliated' with the extremely popular president, Vladimir Putin; on the other hand, economic growth and the high prices of natural resources allow the government to fulfil its commitments without extraordinary financial mechanisms. The 'structural power' of the business class has also been undermined by strong egalitarian values supported by the 'anti-oligarchic rhetoric' of the ruling class.[22]

So far I have been discussing the dominant position of the state bureaucracy in contrast to the business class, while in reality these groups are highly interwoven. Therefore, many scholars point to a 'merging' of administrative and business elites in modern Russian society.[23] Close relationships between business and bureaucracy go back to the late 1980s and early 1990s and are associated with the 'Komsomol economy', privatisation and 'loans-for-shares' auctions. Today 'administrative enterprise' is a common feature of the Russian economic system: politicians and state servants, including top officials, use state powers and resources for their own business interests. This makes formal positions in federal, regional and local governments and legislatures highly attractive to many businesspeople.[24]

Thus, a significant part of the Russian administrative class is also a part of the business stratum. This does not contradict the idea of bureaucratic domination, since membership of the administrative class is usually the key factor of the business success of 'bureaucratic capitalists' (but the opposite does not necessarily hold true). Moreover, the concentration of economic as well as political resources in the hands of the bureaucracy increases its power and influence, while the 'double identity' of office-holders-cum-businesspeople helps to establish a better dialogue (mostly informal) between the two groups. 'Bureaucratic business' thereby reflects the privileged position of a state bureaucracy that is able to reproduce conditions for a successful merging of administrative and commercial resources for its own sake. The initiative and strategic positions are in the hands of the administrative class, which is powerful enough to impose severe sanctions upon the business community if necessary.

Rapid growth of wealth and increasing numbers of millionaires in the business stratum (despite the principles of 'prohibition of politics' and 'equal distance') also do not refute the idea of bureaucratic domination. Unlike the corporate community's political influence (which can really threaten bureaucratic domination), the growth of corporate wealth as such does not contradict the interests of the Russian administrative class: there is no 'zero-sum game' here. The existing order can benefit business and other social groups, but they have no power to change it. Therefore, Keith Dowding prefers the term 'systematic luck' instead of 'power', emphasizing the difference between an actor's ability 'to bring about outcomes' (power) and 'get what he wants without having to act' (luck).[25] In contrast to luck, exercise of power assumes overcoming the subject's resistance and making changes in the situation. From this point of view, one can speak about the power or domination of the Russian administrative class and the luck of the corporate community, although in some cases the latter can exercise power by imposing its will on other – that is, lower-order – social groups. Business was powerful in the middle of the 1990s, but the situation has now changed.

Forms of Power

There are many classifications of forms of power. I distinguish between force, coercion, inducement, persuasion, manipulation and authority.[26] I also consider it important to characterize spheres and instances of 'the rule of anticipated reactions'[27] and specific cases of political power (decision-making and non-decision-making, value-shaping, and so on).

Legal Authority

In the normative ideal of liberal democracy the basic forms of political power are (or should be): (1) *legal authority*, in cases when power is ascribed to particular state structures and state office-holders, and (2) *persuasion*, in relations between equal agents or agencies not formally subjected to each other. Legal authority is 'a power relation in which the power-holder possesses an acknowledged *right to command* and the power subject an acknowledged *obligation to obey*'.[28] The individual or group that is subject to power accepts and follows legal norms, and this motivates submission to the power-holder. Legal authority performs a major role in a political system only if legal rules are firmly embedded in society; otherwise they would not allow office-holders to exercise their legal powers. In the latter instance, power-holders need to use other resources of power that will necessarily transform legal authority into another form of power, such as coercion.

Legal authority plays a limited role in the power structure of Russian society. This seems evident and quite natural. The predominance of informal practices in the operation of state power has been commonly recognized by scholars[29] and explained as a result of the 'authoritarian experience' and the absence of the rule of law in the history of the Russian state. Another popular explanation concerns the nature of the modern Russian state, which is supposedly 'weak' but is becoming stronger in conjunction with the construction of the 'power vertical'. However, strengthening the administrative capacities of the state cannot by itself guarantee adherence to or enforcement of the rule of law. On the contrary, a strong state, as Vladimir Gel'man points out, 'can also create obstacles which are very difficult to overcome, when administrative force is combined with low level of autonomy. In this case formal institutions become just instruments in the hands of government to encourage loyalty and punish for disloyalty'.[30] The limited effect of formal rules not only decreases the overall effectiveness of political power (see below) but substantially changes the nature of power in society by increasing the role of other forms of power. Finally, the predominance of informal practices obviously corresponds to the interests of the administrative class which is outside popular control. These and certain other factors, discussed below, undermine the effectiveness of legal authority in all its manifestations.[31]

Personal Authority

In contrast to legal authority, personal authority has always played a major role in Russian politics. In all kinds of political institutions including state, party and civic organizations, top leaders have a large amount of personal power (although it is not based on personal authority alone). Vladimir Putin's personal authority plays a key role in legitimizing the political regime and the policy-making process.

On the one hand, strong personal authority increases the effectiveness of state power, although this does not increase the authority of the state itself; on the other hand, it decreases the legal authority of state institutions since strong personal authority allows its bearers to change the rules of the game and violate laws and traditions without substantial loss in political image and reputation. Moreover, Putin's authority does not really depend on his efforts to establish what he hailed as 'dictatorship of the law'.[32] This makes him relatively autonomous in choosing power forms and resources.

Force and Coercion

Ineffective legal authority is usually compensated by force and coercion, both legal and illegal.[33] If the power-holder has no formal powers or the subject is not inclined to obey (no matter what the reasons to disobey), the threat of force or the direct application of force becomes the power-holder's most effective instrument. There are several reasons why force and coercion have become widespread in Russian politics and society. First, the application of force and especially coercion usually does not require a large supply of material resources since it relies on the relatively inexpensive communication of threats.[34] Second, since ancient times force and coercion have played a major role in the resolution of social conflicts in Russia. In the Soviet Union the spread of violence resulted from the distortion of patron–client relationships by the nomenklatura system: the traditional *contractual* character of patron–client relationships was destroyed, so force (or the threat of force) became a major source of power and dependence. Mikhail Afanas'ev describes this 'animal-like' pattern of social relations as 'the dominant archetype of social being and/or consciousness' in communist Russia. Military service, prisons and camps became powerful agents of socialization, supplanting community (*obshchina*), school, and university, and this promoted violent practices in Russian society.[35] The modern political regime in Russia encourages these practices by 'making people accustomed to military and violent means of conflict resolution'.[36]

Third, these practices are commonly accepted by a large part of the population which prefers 'simple' or 'plain' solutions, especially regarding 'strangers', perhaps referred to as 'aliens', 'oligarchs' or 'liberals'. People perceive legal positions as coercive resources; law is not a 'rule of the game' they have to follow and use in their interests, but an imperative and repressive prescription that they are afraid of. According to sociological data, a small minority of citizens (6 per cent in 2002) fulfil their responsibilities towards other people because they 'respect the laws'; others are motivated by fear – that is, by coercion. These people do not understand why they should defend and respect the rights of others while no one else does so. Thus they are inclined to violate the rights of other people in every possible situation.[37]

Fourth, the replacement of legal authority by coercion and other forms of power has been catalysed by the shortage of legal norms (laws) that clearly and unambiguously establish the hierarchy of different state agencies and structures. Experts point to the absence of clearly defined criteria of hierarchy and typology of 'political' and 'career' positions, the preservation of too many departmental rules and regulations (which in turn leads to preservation of the former Soviet style of government), and the psychological discomfort of many office-holders who know that their positions and powers can be easily changed.[38]

Particular manifestations of force and coercion in political practice are diverse and largely depend on the subject of power. In Russia a wide variety of coercive instruments are employed against political opposition, business groups, and regional and municipal elites. Arbitrary use of physical force or the threat of force by the 'rule-protecting' agencies (the public prosecutor's office, the police, the FSB security agency, the courts and others) and 'controlling' agencies (the tax police, ecological and fire departments, and so on) is aimed at creating a sense of fear, uncertainty and inconvenience; threats of dismissal, financial cuts, deprivation of tax privileges or political protection are regularly used when particular groups and organizations act contrary to the will of the powerful elite.[39] Coercion – the use of force – does not necessarily take overt forms. Usually the subjects act without open threats from the power-holder because they anticipate the latter's possible negative reactions. Self-censorship in the mass media, 'voluntary sponsorship' of social projects by businesspeople,[40] and a decline in political ambitions of corporate business after the 'Yukos case' are the most prominent examples of 'the rule of anticipated reactions' in Russian political life.[41]

Strengthening the political regime decreases the necessity of direct applications of force in politics. This is evidently taking place in modern Russia, where the number of overt conflicts between the authorities and actual or potential opposition, be they political rivals, corporate business or regional elites, has been decreasing. The dominant power position of the administrative elites in Russian society allows them not to react adequately to citizens' demands, and to limit the spectrum of issues on the political agenda by preventing opponents from bringing forward any issues that might in their resolution be seriously detrimental to the preferences of the elite. Following Bachrach and Baratz,[42] this kind of political power – 'the second face of power' or 'non-decision-making' – has become a subject of study.

Non-decision-making belongs to no particular form of power mentioned above. In my view, the effect of non-decision-making looks very similar to certain manifestations of force or coercion: in both cases power-holders limit the scope of subjects' capacities by formatting the political domain or field. Non-decision-making in modern Russian politics takes place in different areas: control of the mass media (where the political agenda is legitimized), certification of participants in the negotiation process, creating and reinforcing barriers (ideological, procedural and financial, for example) for political opponents, blocking initiatives aimed at limiting bureaucratic control in the economy,[43] levelling of wages, opening access for political parties to state TV, and so forth.

Inducement

In this case the source of a subject's submission is a reward that can be obtained from a power-holder for compliance with a command. Like coercion, inducement takes various forms in political practice. State power not only allows its holders to use negative sanctions in cases of non-compliance but also to motivate or encourage the subject to obey their commands. The state possesses economic resources and may use them to support particular groups and policies. Inducement can be both legal and illegal. In the latter case the subject employs state resources without appropriate state powers. Obviously, coercion and inducement have much in common. In many cases it is not easy to distinguish between them; negative and positive sanctions (coercion and inducement) are often turned into each other and may be used together ('stick and carrot').

In Russian political practice inducement (like coercion) is actively used to 'compensate' for ineffective legal authority, especially in cases where power-holders are unable, or not inclined, to employ instruments of force. Weakness of legal norms and arbitrary rule are two highly interrelated sources of the widespread use of inducement: people prefer not to fight for their legal rights and opportunities but to bargain ('make deals') with the authorities. This can be explained in terms of both coercion (the office-holder extracts a bribe from the subject) or inducement (the office-holder encourages the subject to act in a particular way by promising benefits, protection, or both (for example, tax relief, administrative support during an election campaign, and so on). Usually office-holders demand money, media resources, financial support for particular events and projects, and other services of that kind. The readiness of both the bureaucracy and general population to accept illegal 'services'[44] has similar roots to the dissemination of coercive power forms. 'Light' forms of corruption are in fact seen as legitimate in the eyes of the population, especially in particular regions.[45] From this point of view, inducement, more than other forms of power, is associated with moral degradation, cynicism, careerism and other attributes of a large part of the modern Russian bureaucracy.

In comparing the roles of coercion and inducement in Russian political practice, it may be argued that coercive mechanisms prevail. Inducement is a basic form of political power in countries with oligarchic rule where the economic resources of the rich give them unlimited influence in the making of key political decisions. Bureaucratic domination in Russia renders administrative (that is, coercive) resources of special importance, since such resources determine the whole set of opportunities open to the administrative class. Administrative resources are cumulative; they can lever other resources, including economic ones, and use them at a lower expense or cost than threats or force.

Manipulation and Persuasion [46]

After 1917, ideological power became a major instrument of political domination, used effectively by the governing communist elite. In the 1990s ideological pluralism and freedom of speech destroyed the ideological monopoly of the regime; however, the role of ideology (ideological debates and controversies) in modern Russia is still very important. Since 2000, the administrative elite's ideological domination has substantially increased with the monopolization of the most important resources of ideological power. Thus, television channels strictly follow the guidelines of state officials; several new ideological pro-grammes (such as 'Real politics') severely criticize alternatives to Putin's policy, while political opponents have no comparable chance of being heard by the population. Critics of the regime may present their views in some news-papers and internet sites. However, this does not compensate for their absence on television. During election campaigns informational support for the 'party of power' and its candidates oversteps all formal and moral restrictions. In this situ-ation the role of manipulation in the 'manipulation–persuasion' continuum is increasing: there is no objective or critical analysis of Putin's policy in TV pro-grammes; the authorities deliberately conceal information about the decision-making process and key political nominations; positive economic trends are clearly exaggerated.

It is not easy to evaluate whether the administrative elite really believes that its domination has been positive for Russian society. On the one hand, Putin's course largely corresponds to the mentality of the modern Russian bureaucracy; on the other hand, the administrative elite hardly believe that the appointment of provincial governors can help in anti-terrorist campaigns or that 'American imperialism' really threatens the sovereignty of the Russian state. Doubts about the sincerity of the governing elite[47] inevitably arise when it acts contrary to declared principles and values, such as 'dictator-ship of the law', 'democracy', or 'civil society'.

The Effectiveness of Power

The effectiveness of power, or the exercise of power, has two dimensions. The first refers to an actor's ability to achieve the submission or compliance of another actor: this refers to the effectiveness of the very power relationship. This can be evaluated by Dennis Wrong's criteria of intensity, extensity, com-prehensiveness.[48] The second dimension refers to an actor's ability to achieve a desired result: this is effectiveness of management. A subject's submission to a power-holder's will does not mean that the power-holder will necessarily attain his or her ultimate ends. Effective power relations – the stable ability of an actor to get people to do something they would not do otherwise – may be flawed by ineffective management since power-holders cannot always predict the consequences of the exercise of their power or cannot always use it in an appropriate direction. In turn, good managers (say, a governor or a member of the state elite) can do nothing if their power resources are weak or inadequate. Thus, quite often evaluations of power and management do not coincide.

In relationships with a political opposition, the power of the Russian gov-erning elite seems effective. It can successfully initiate strategic political decisions in the Duma, block any policy alternatives, use instruments of coercion to threaten an opposition and control flows of information. In recent years, the ruling elite passed a set of laws – including the introduction of a proportional voting system, prohibition of electoral blocs, closing access to elections by those parties whose members were accused of former 'extremism' – that substantially reduced the opposition's electoral possibilities. The courts, public prosecutors' offices, the police, the federal security service and other state agencies realize that the will of the administrative class can be used against their political opponents. President Putin's high personal authority now guarantees the stability of the regime, so the opposition's political opportunities are minimal.

In relations with other groups with large potential or actual power resources (corporate business and regional elites, for example) there is a similar tendency. The creation of federal districts, the nomination of governors, the declining role of the upper chamber of the Russian parliament, the increasing share of federal financing in regional budgets, and the arbitrary use of the state's controlling agencies in the regions – all these make regional authorities loyal to the federal administrative elite. The predominance of informal practices over formal institutional procedures substantially increases the federal elite's power, especially in those realms where formal subordination is absent. Although regional elites still have zones of autonomy, they cannot play an active role in strategic political decisions.

The administrative elites occupy a dominant position in relations with corporate business, especially since 2003. Business has accepted a new format of relations with the power authorities.

It is difficult to evaluate the effectiveness of power in relationships between the ruling class and the general populace. As mentioned above, the possibility to assess power arises only in cases when elites demonstrate their ability to initiate obviously unpopular decisions and block initiatives supported by a majority of the population. Another dimension of power in this particular relationship reveals itself in the ability of the elite to form political priorities and values necessary for the reproduction of the patterns of domination (Lukes's 'third dimension of power'[49]). Putin's high rating allows the administration to say that many Russian citizens either support the regime's policy or are largely indifferent to the policy-making process itself. In any case, the regime does not need to overcome large-scale resistance on the part of the population. The latter generally accepts policy aimed at increasing the role of the state in the economy, strengthening the 'power vertical' and bureaucratic control, and active involvement in world politics.

Taking into account the relatively low living standard of the population, it may be assumed that this has been a result of ideological domination by the administrative elite. The predominance of 'statist' and 'patriotic' rhetoric in both political discourse and everyday domestic conversations; the justification of informal and coercive mechanisms of power demonstrated by the power elite; poor reactions to undemocratic tendencies in modern Russian politics – all these things show that the preferences and values of the Russian power elite and the population largely coincide.

To what extent is this intersection a result of deliberate efforts by the governing elite – in other words, its ideological hegemony? The term 'Conservative turn' has evident structural roots, especially in political culture and traditions; the mistakes and failures of previous governments stimulated spontaneous rejection of the values of the Yeltsin era. However, it is also a result of effective ideological control. This becomes evident in the successful and very dynamic media campaigns aimed at creating new (that is, hitherto unknown) popular political leaders such as Putin and parties such as 'Yedinaya Rossiya',[50] and the effective propaganda in favour of the Russian government's international actions and of state policy in general.

So far I have been describing political power in terms of the possibilities of the ruling class to impose its political and ideological preferences in the decision-making process. However, the effectiveness of political power largely depends on political institutions and their ability to realize its basic functions. Since 2000 the Russian state has become much more effective and functional than it was in the 1990s; in other words, its power potential has substantially increased. Force and coercion, as mentioned above, are effectively used to overcome resistance, both actual and potential, on the part of the subjects of state power; alternative centres of political power, be they 'oligarchs', regional elites or mafia, have been neutralized; economic resources of the state are growing and the population supports the president. However, in many cases the state does not properly fulfil its functions (such as securing civil rights and liberties, collecting taxes, law enforcement, eradicating organized crime, and so on) because the power resources of at least some state agencies and office-holders are not sufficient; hence, the state often fails to carry out its own decisions and enforce its laws.[51] The majority of Russian citizens – 57.1 per cent – consider the state bureaucracy 'ineffective'.[52]

The power potential of various state structures differs. President Putin and his administration play a major role in the process of government in Russia, while legislatures, courts and governmental agencies and structures have limited autonomy. This balance of power between state institutions corresponds to the purposes of the ruling elite: centralization of power presupposes strengthening of the state hierarchy and unity of the governmental structures, with the president at the top, while separation of powers, 'checks and balances' and the relative autonomy of state institutions do not fit this model of power.

What are the outcomes of state power? Does it allow the administrative class to achieve its aims? These questions concern the effectiveness of government; they are not directly related to power, but their discussion is important for the analysis of the Russian political system.

Effectiveness of government is usually defined in terms of the state's capacity to provide people with a particular set of values. Michael McFaul assessed the Russian state against three criteria of state strength: internal cohesiveness, both ideological and institutional; the relative autonomy of the state from society; and the ability of the state to implement policy.[53] The first two criteria are largely related to power dimensions, and the third to both power and the governing capacity of the state.

Some evident manifestations of ineffectiveness of the Russian state, as argued above, largely refer to insufficient power resources. However, many other problems have been caused by ineffective government or management, or by the mistakes and failures of the governing officials in achieving public ends. These include (1) passing laws which nobody attempts to enforce (for example, banning the consumption of alcohol on the streets); (2) regular fluctuations in state policy caused by urgent issues; (3) populism in decision-making; (4) conservatism, unwillingness to change traditional (informal) forms of power; (5) inability to modernize the economy and the system of government, and so on.

The most evident negative consequence of state policy lies in the preservation of obsolete forms of government. The last decades have shown the inability of highly centralized political systems to take up the challenge of the third millennium. New patterns of social life enforce changes in the role of the state, transforming it from 'supreme governor' into 'manager'. Modern systems of government cannot effectively function without the co-operation of citizens and their associations. That is, the state does not refuse to be responsible for the development of society, but shares this responsibility (and thus power) with other social institutions.[54] Another evident direction of strengthening the state power lies in the sphere of laws and legal powers: the role of legal authority and institutional powers should be substantially increased.

However, reforming the state mechanism in this way will necessarily destroy the present system of power based on informal and coercive practices effectively used in the interests of the administrative class. As an instrument of bureaucratic domination over other social groups, the modern Russian state is quite effective: it is able to reproduce the monopoly power of the administrative class. But the state is ineffective in achieving public goals; attempts by the regime to strengthen the 'power vertical' do not actually make the state substantially better from this particular point of view. So there is an inherent contradiction or incongruence between strengthening the state as an instrument of domination and the state as the instrument of effective government for the benefit of the people. The future of the state largely depends on the way this contradiction is resolved.

Conclusion

To sum up, the administrative class is the dominant actor in contemporary Russian society. Existing social order and governmental policy reproduce the privileges and benefits of the state bureaucracy – the power to control political processes, set the agenda and make decisions. The position of the Russian administrative class corresponds to at least three (out of four) of Domhoff's criteria of power (domination): it occupies key institutional positions, successfully initiates particular political decisions (policy alternatives) and enjoys its privileged (beneficial) position. As far as the level of mobilization of corporate resources, class consciousness and 'control over ideas' are concerned, the Russian administrative class is hardly less coherent and organized than dominant classes in other countries, since its solidarity is strengthened not only by common interests and corporate consciousness but also by joint administrative functions requiring a high level of hierarchy, organization and collective action. Sociological data demonstrate that the administrative class becomes a 'caste'. Its representatives see their main task in 'preserving and increasing their power and protecting their interests' rather than the interests of society.[55]

The configuration of power forms corresponds to the bureaucratic nature of domination. Various forms of manipulation, coercion and force are commonly used instead of legal authority. This cannot be explained just by references to authoritarian political traditions or political culture (or a combination of the two): the administrative class wants to retain the possibility of arbitrary use of law to preserve the status quo. Attempts to build the 'power vertical' strengthen the coercive mechanisms of state power but its legal bases remain weak.

The predominance of informal mechanisms in political and governmental practices makes state power an effective instrument of bureaucratic domination. At the same time it decreases the effectiveness of the state in achieving public aims, protecting citizens and providing social values and services. In general, the Russian state under Putin is much more effective, coherent and powerful than under Yeltsin. However, it still cannot effectively perform its functions – either because the power resources of the state are insufficient, or because the configuration of resources impedes the rule of law and the modernization of the economy and government. Thus, *the modern system of power in Russia is simultaneously effective and ineffective.* It successfully reproduces *power over* which has not yet become *power to.*

NOTES

1. Kh. (Harley) Balzer, 'Upravlyaemyi plyuralizm. Formiruyushchiisya rezhim V. Putina' (Managed Pluralism: The Emerging Regime of V. Putin), *Obshchestvennye nauki i sovremennost'*, No.4 (2004), pp.46–59; Farid Zakaria, *The Future of Freedom: Illiberal Democracy at Home and Abroad* (New York: Norton, 2003); W. Merkel' (Wolfgang Merkel) and

A. Kruassan (Aurel S. Croissant), 'Formal'nye i neformal'nye instituty v defektnykh demokratiyakh' (Formal and Informal Institutions in Defective Democracies), *Politicheskie issledovaniya*, No.1 (2004), pp.6–17, and No.2 (2004), pp.20–30; Liliya Shevtsova, 'Rossiya – God 2006: Logika politicheskogo strakha' (Russia, Year 2006: The Logic of Political Fear), *Nezavisimaya gazeta*, 16 Dec. 2005.

2. Dennis Wrong, Stephen Lukes, Thomas Wartenberg, John Scott, Keith Dowding and others.

3. Thomas Wartenberg, *The Forms of Power: From Domination to Transformation* (Philadelphia, PA: Temple University Press, 1990).

4. For more detailed explanation of domination, see ibid., pp.115–39; John Scott, *Power* (Cambridge: Polity, 2001), pp.16–24, 71–91.

5. G. William Domhoff, *Who Rules America? Power and Politics in the Year 2000* (London: Mayfield, 1998), p.1.

6. John Scott, *Who Rules Britain?* (Cambridge: Polity, 1991), p.151.

7. Leslie Holmes, *Politics in the Communist World* (Oxford: Clarendon, 1986).

8. Yuri Pivovarov and Andrei Fursov, '"Russkaya sistema" kak popytka ponimaniya russkoi istorii' ('Russian System' as an Attempt to Understand Russian History), *Politicheskie issledovaniya*, No.4 (2001), pp.37–48; A. Akhiezer, *Rossiya: Kritika istoricheskogo opyta* (Russia: Criticism of Historical Experience) (Novosibirsk: Sibirskii Khronograf, 1997).

9. Oksana Gaman-Golutvina, *Politicheskie elity: Vekhi istoricheskoi evolyutsii* (Political Elites: Stages of Historical Evolution) (Moscow: ROSSPEN, 2006); Olga Kryshtanovskaya, *Anatomiya Rossiiskoi elity* (Anatomy of the Russian Elite) (Moscow: Zakharov, 2005).

10. Domhoff, *Who Rules America?*, pp.18–23; David Vogel, 'The Power of Business in America: A Re-appraisal', *British Journal of Political Science*, Vol.13, No.1 (1983), pp.19–43.

11. Valeri Grazhdan, 'Korruptsiya: Odoleyut li eё rossiyane?' (Corruption: Can Russians Overcome It?), *Vlast'*, No.12 (2004), pp.4–14; Georgi Satarov, 'Tranzit, demokratiya i korruptsiya: Regional'nye osobennosti v Rossii' (Transition, Democracy and Corruption: Regional Specifics in Russia), in Aleksandr Solov'ev (ed.), *Politicheskaya nauka v sovremennoi Rossii: Vremya poiska i kontury evolyutsii* (Moscow: ROSSPEN, 2004), pp.230–48.

12. Vadim Radaev, *Ekonomicheskaya sotsiologiya* (Moscow: GU-VSHE), pp.297–301; Vladimir Gel'man, 'Instutsional'noe stroitel'stvo i neformal'nye instituty v sovremennoi rossiiskoi politike' (Institutional Building and Informal Institutions in Modern Russian politics), *Politicheskie issledovaniya*, No.4 (2003), pp.6–25 (p.13).

13. Except in 1996 when the Russian corporate community supported Boris Yeltsin in his presidential campaign.

14. Mikhail Khodorkovskii, former head of the Yukos oil firm, and his business partner Platon Lebedev were found guilty and sentenced to eight years in prison. Many people believe that this case has a political context and that Khodorkovskii is being punished by the Kremlin for his political ambition.

15. Yanik Pappe, 'Otnosheniya federal'noi ekonomicheskoi elity i vlasti v Rossii v 2000–2004 godakh: Tormozhenie v tsentre i novaya strategiya v regionakh' (Relationships between the Federal Economic Elites and the Authorities in Russia in 2000–2004: Braking at the Centre and the New Strategy in the Regions), in Yakov Frukhtman (ed.), *Regional'naya elita v sovremennoi Rossii* (Moscow: Fond 'Liberal'naya Missiya', 2005), pp.77–92 (p.81).

16. Andrei Yakovlev, 'Evolutsya vzaimootnoshenii mezhdu vlast'yu i biznesom i dvizhushchie sily ekonomicheskogo razvitiya v Rossii. Do i posle "Dela Yukosa"' (Evolution of Relationships between the Power Elite and Business and the Driving Forces of Economic Development in Russia: Before and after the 'Yukos Case'), in Frukhtman (ed.), *Regional'naya elita v sovremennoi Rossii*, pp.12–36 (pp.13–18).

17. Pappe, 'Otnosheniya federal'noi ekonomicheskoi elity i vlasti', p.81.

18. Alexei Zudin, 'Vzaimootnosheniya krupnogo biznesa i vlasti pri V. Putine i ikh vliyanie na situatsiyu v rossiiskikh regionakh' (Relationships between Corporate Business and Power Authorities under V. Putin and its Impact on the Situation in Russia's Regions), in Frukhtman (ed.), *Regional'naya elita v sovremennoi Rossii*, pp.37–64 (pp.44–5).

19. Valeri Grazhdan, 'Antibyurokraticheskaya revolyutsiya: vozmozhna li ona?' (Is an Anti-bureaucratic Revolution Possible?), *Vlast'*, No.10 (2004), pp.42–52 (pp.48–9).

20. Zudin, 'Vzaimootnosheniya krupnogo biznesa i vlasti', pp.47–53.
21. 'Structural power of business' means the advantageous position of the business community in modern (capitalist) society based on structural and institutional features embedded in the social system (Claus Offe, Charles E. Lindblom, Stephen Elkin, Clarence N. Stone, John S. Dryzek).
22. Pappe, 'Otnosheniya federal'noi ekonomicheskoi elity i vlasti', p.81.
23. Valeri Achkasov, 'Rossiiskaya pravyashchaya elita i postroenie "effektivnogo, konkurento-sposobnogo gosudarstva"'(The Russian Ruling Elite and the Building of an 'Effective Competitive State'), in Alexander Duka (ed.), *Vlast' i elity v rossiiskoi transfornatsii* (Saint Petersburg: Intersotsis, 2005), pp.110–21 (pp.117–18); Tat'yana Vorozheikina, 'Gosudarstvo i obshchestvo v Rossii. Ischerpanie gosudarstvenno-tsentricheskoi matritsy' (State and Society in Russia: Exhausting the State-centred Matrix), in *Kuda idet Rossiya?* (Moscow: MVSHSEN, 2002), pp.34–42 (p.39).
24. More than 300 members of the lower chamber of the Russian parliament (the *Duma*) are somehow related to the business class (as owners of enterprises, managers delegated by corporate business, professional lobbyists, and so on); in the upper chamber, all the major large companies have their representatives; 13 governors are former top managers or owners of large corporations (Olga Kryshtanovskaya, 'Formirovanie regional'noi elity: printsipy i mekhanizmy' (The Formation of the Regional Elite: Principles and Mechanisms), *Sotsiologicheskie issledovaniya*, No.11 (2003), pp.3–13).
25. Keith Dowding, *Power* (Buckingham: Open University Press, 1996), p.71.
26. Valeri Ledyaev, *Power: A Conceptual Analysis* (Commack, NY: Nova Science, 1997), pp.183–99; Dennis Wrong, *Power: Its Forms, Bases, and Uses. With a New Introduction by the Author* (New Brunswick, NJ and London: Transaction, 2002), pp.21–64.
27. The term was introduced by Carl J. Friedrich to describe cases when the subject of power acts in accordance with a power-holder's will in fear of the repercussions for doing otherwise: Carl J. Friedrich, *Constitutional Government and Politics* (New York: Harper & Brothers, 1937), pp.16–18.
28. Wrong, *Power*, p.49.
29. Gel'man, 'Instutsional'noe stroitel'stvo i neformal'nye instituty', 2003; Mikhail Afanas'ev, 'Rossiiskaya Federatsiya: Slaboe gosudarstvo i "presidentskaya vertikal"'(The Russian Federation: Weak State and the 'Presidential Vertical'), in *Strana posle kommunizma*, Vol.I (Moscow: Institut Publichnoi Politiki, 2004), pp.175–206; Alla Chirikova, 'Regional'naya vlast': Formal'nye i neformalnye praktiki' (Regional Power: Formal and Informal Practices), in Aleksandr Duka and Viktor Mokhov (eds.), *Vlast', gosudarstvo i elity v sovremennom obshchestve* (Perm': Permskii Gosudarstvennii Tekhnicheskii Universitet, 2005), pp.185–206.
30. Gel'man, 'Instutsional'noe stroitel'stvo i neformal'nye instituty', p.10.
31. Bertrand de Jouvenel and Dennis Wrong have distinguished three different variable attributes of all power relations: *extensiveness* (number of power subjects), *comprehensiveness* (extent to which power-holders control the activities of power subjects), and *intensity* (range of effective options open to the power-holder within each and every area of the subject's conduct over which the former wields power): see Bertrand de Jouvenel, 'Authority: The Efficient Imperative', in Carl J. Friedrich (ed.), *Authority* (Cambridge, MA: Harvard University Press, 1958), pp.159–69 (p.160); Wrong, *Power*, pp.14–20.
32. Some scholars argue that Putin does not actually strive for the 'dictatorship of the law': see, for example, Afanas'ev, 'Rossiiskaya Federatsiya', p.204. On the contrary, the state often encourages shadow activity rather than deterring it: for instance, to compensate for fiscal losses stemming from shadow economic activity. Informal fiscal policy 'mitigates the effects of the problem [large-scale shadow activity] but impedes its resolution': see William Tompson, 'Putin's Challenge: The Politics of Structural Reform in Russia', *Europe–Asia Studies*, Vol.54, No.6 (2002), pp.933–57 (p.939).
33. Some scholars blur the distinction between 'legal authority' and 'legal power'. They argue that authority is exercised whenever an imperative is obeyed, including those cases where obedience is motivated by the fear of physical coercion: see David Easton, 'The Perception

of Authority and Political Change', in Friedrich (ed.), *Authority*, pp.170–96 (pp.180–82); Anthony H. Birch, *The Concepts and Theories of Modern Democracies*, 2nd edn (London: Routledge, 2001), p.32. In my view, it is reasonable to define them as distinct forms of power because subjects' motives for compliance are different. For the purposes of our study it is important to discover the balance between voluntary and involuntary acceptance of commands to understand the nature of power relationships in Russia: see Ledyaev, *Power*, pp.197–8).

34. Wrong, *Power*, p.47.

35. Mikhail Afanas'ev, *Klientelizm i rossiiskaya gosudarstvennost'* (Clientelism and Russian Statehood) (Moscow: MONF, 2000), pp.166–7.

36. Alexander Solov'ev, 'Institutsional'nye eksperimenty v prostranstve politicheskoi kultury: Realii rossiiskogo tranzita' (Institutional Experiments in the Area of Political Culture: The Reality of Russian Transition), in Solov'ev (ed.), *Politicheskaya nauka*, pp.313–37 (p.334).

37. Sergey Patrushev, 'Vlast' i narod v Rossii: Problema legitimizatsii institutsional'nikh izme-nenii' (Power and the People in Russia: The Problem of Legitimization of Institutional Changes), in Solov'ev (ed.), *Politicheskaya nauka*, pp.287–312 (p.302).

38. Mikhail Krasnov, 'Admistrativnaya Reforma (1991–2001): Pochemu sokhranyaetsya eë aktual'nost'?' (Administrative Reform (1991–2001): Why does it Retain its Currency?), in *Strana posle kommunizma*, Vol.I (Moscow: Institut Publichnoi Politiki, 2004), pp.84–115, (pp.85–91).

39. For example, during regional election campaigns the federal authorities dropped a hint that the 'wrong choice' would lead to budget cuts.

40. Here I mean only those cases of sponsorship where business was forced to demonstrate loyalty and willingness to support the authorities. However, the amount of business sponsorship in Russia is much higher than in Western countries: American corporations spend about 1 per cent of their profit on charity while Russian companies spend from 8 per cent (in the raw material sector) up to 24 per cent (in the industrial sector): see Lyubov' Polishchuk, 'Biznesmeny i filantropy' (Businessmen and Philanthropists), *Pro et Contra*, No.1 (2006), pp.59–73 (p.62).

41. One regional politician from Yaroslavl describes the situation in the Yaroslavl duma (regional legislature) in the following way: 'The Governor established total control in the Duma. He has various instruments to compel the deputies. *There is no need to quarrel and bring pressure to bear on the deputies*. Almost all the directors in the Duma have tax relief. They understand that it can be easily lost after "wrong" voting' (Chirikova, 'Regional'naya vlast'', p.210; emphasis added).

42. Peter Bachrach and Morton S. Baratz, 'Two Faces of Power', *American Political Science Review*, Vol.56, No.4 (1962), pp.947–52; Peter Bachrach and Morton S. Baratz, 'Decisions and Nondecisions: An Analytical Framework', *American Political Science Review*, Vol.57, No.3 (1963), pp.641–51.

43. For example, when a bill on reducing the number of economic activities subject to licensing requirements came before the government in March 2001, individual ministries and departments fought hard to preserve their own licensing powers: see Tompson, 'Putin's Challenge', p.943.

44. About 40 per cent of young people approved of making money 'by any means' including illegal ways; more than 60 per cent agreed that there are no 'unfair' ways of making money: Yuri Mazaev, 'Sotsial'nye otnosheniya korruptsii' (The Social Relationships of Corruption), in *Sotsiologiya korruptsii* conference papers (Moscow: INION-RAN, 2003), pp.42–5 (p.43). Yelena Shestopal argues that just 10 per cent of professional politicians are guided by communitarian motives: Yelena Shestopal, *Psikhologicheskii profil' rossiiskoi politiki* (The Psychological Profile of Russian Politics) (Moscow: ROSSPEN, 2000), p.365.

45. For example, in Dagestan region 'society is saturated with corruption'; people accept corrup-tion as a matter of fact; state power is associated primarily with just a set of privileges: Alla Bystrova, 'Korruptsiya kak element mekhanizma osushchestvleniya vlasti' (Corruption as an Element in Exercising Power), in Duka (ed.), *Vlast' i elity*, pp.186–200 (p.199).

46. Persuasive power is the ability of a power-holder to get a subject's submission by presenting rational arguments; in manipulation the source of a subject's submission to the power-holder lies in a power-holder's ability to exercise a covert influence on the subject that the latter is unaware of.

47. Sincerity is a feature of persuasion, while in manipulation the power-holder *deliberately* provides the subject with false information.

48. See Wrong, *Power.*

49. See Steven Lukes, *Power: A Radical View* (Basingstoke: Palgrave, 2005), pp.25–36.

50. These campaigns took place mainly in the Yeltsin period; today the manipulative capacity of the regime has been substantially increased.

51. In 2001 only 48 per cent of Putin's directives to several government departments had been fulfilled: see Grazhdan, 'Antibyurokraticheskaya revolyutsiya', p.45.

52. *Byurokratiya i vlast' v novoi Rossii* (Bureaucracy and Power in the New Russia) (Moscow: IS RAN, 2005), p.55.

53. Tompson, 'Putin's Challenge', p.936.

54. Vladimir Komarovskii, 'Administrativnaya reforma v Rossiiskoi Federatsii' (Administrative Reform in the Russian Federation), *Politicheskie issledovaniya*, No.4 (2005), pp.172–8 (pp.172–3; 177).

55. *Byurokratiya i vlast' v novoi Rossii*, p.95.

The Changing Role of the State and State Bureaucracy in the Context of Public Administration Reforms: Russian and Foreign Experience

OXANA GAMAN-GOLUTVINA

Introduction

Observation of Russian policy shows that after Vladimir Putin's election in 2000 as the second Russian president essential changes took place in the field of public administration. Previously, under Boris Yeltsin, the three most powerful political actors were the federal and regional bureaucracies and big business. Seven years of Putin's presidency testify that central executive power became the uncontested winner; it not only gained a victory over the 'right–left' opposition with a slashing score, but also secured undoubted advantage in respect of its 'junior partners' – the regional executive and business. This resulted from the formation of a mono-centric political regime, which could be defined as a *mono-archy* (in contrast to Robert Dahl's classic concept of polyarchy[1]) with the president at its core, and the state bureaucracy as the foundation of his power.

So, from the structural point of view, the configuration of Putin's inner elite differs significantly from Yeltsin's. Under Yeltsin, 'vertically integrated' elite clans, embracing federal and regional actors of various origins (entrepreneurs, law-makers, executives, political party functionaries, mass media, and so on) became the most influential political actors. The weakness of political institutions (such as political parties) determined that elite clans[2] (groups linking business and power) were the leading political actors while Yeltsin held office.[3] The divisions of clans, not the division of powers, was a peculiarity of the intra-elite disposition. At the federal level clans formed in the mid-1990s, and in the regions a little later. The difference between federal and regional groups was determined by the political priorities of bureaucracy within the bureaucracy–business link on the regional level and with business dominating at the centre.

By the beginning of the second term of Putin's presidency, bureaucracy[4] had turned into an influential political actor, not only at the regional but also at the federal and national levels.

Paradoxically, the strengthening of the federal bureaucracy does not automatically result in the meaningful strengthening of state authority;[5] rather, it quite often marks the rise of a political group affiliated with the state. This fact makes it necessary to differentiate *the role and function of the state* from that of the *state bureaucracy*. It is quite evident that these two phenomena may both coincide and differ. Changing the role of state management in the direction of greater efficiency was proclaimed by Putin to be one of the key tasks of his presidency. This objective became the main initiative of his administrative reform. We share the opinion of those experts who consider that unlike his predecessor, Boris Yeltsin, President Putin offered the project of administrative reform as something 'more than philippics. He has set in motion a concrete, large-scale planning process involving capable lawyers, social scientists, and government representatives that is intended to overhaul the state bureaucracy in its entirety'.[6] Indeed, the very attempt at civil service reform initiated by Putin is a huge step beyond Yel'tsin's meaningless promises, promptly forgotten, to cut the size of the state bureaucracy by 50 per cent.[7] However, for this author, the methodological approaches of the reform and its practical realization are not yet satisfactory. A review of the conceptual problems of the changing role of the state and state bureaucracy in the context of comparative analysis of public administration reforms in Russia and some other countries is presented below.

The essence of administrative reform (AR) in the Russian Federation is the comprehensive transformation of the system of public administrative bodies in order to make them more flexible and effective.[8] AR involves a *reform of the civil service* (touching upon a whole number of aspects related to the process of hiring civil servants, wages, the system of personnel training and promotion, and so on); *budgetary reform* (a transition from the budgetary principle of financing state ministries and departments to programme-targeted financing based on results); and a *transformation of the system of executive governmental bodies* (people most often have this aspect in mind when they speak of AR). In this essay, we mostly touch upon the conceptual aspects of civil service reform.

The following areas have been given priority in administrative reform: limiting the interference of the state in the economic activities of business, including ending excessive state regulation; eliminating the redundancy of functions and powers among federal executive bodies; developing a system of self-regulating economic associations; re-dividing the organizational functions relating to the regulation of economic activities, supervision and control, the management of public property, and the delivery of services by public sector organizations to citizens and legal entities; completing the process of the division of powers between executive bodies at the federal and regional levels; and optimizing the work of the territorial agencies of federal executive bodies.

So far, the main milestones in the implementation of reform have been a cutback in superfluous state functions (out of the 5,000 functions inspected, 20 per cent were declared to be redundant and another 30 per cent were said to require delimitation); the classification of central state agencies as law-making, law-enforcing and supervisory, resulting in a tripartite government structure (ministries, services, and agencies); a reduction in the number of ministries from 23 to 14; and the submission of the project 'Administrative Reform Federal Target Programme' by the ministry of economic development and commerce to the government of the Russian Federation in the autumn of 2004 (this programme was rejected after eight months of discussion and replaced by a *conception* of AR, which was approved in the autumn of 2005, and for which an implementation plan for the period 2006–8 was adopted and 500 million roubles of financing were allocated for 2006). At present, the main area of reform work is the development of standards and procedures for the delivery of public services.

Concepts of Administrative Reform

The struggle to implement AR in the Russian Federation corresponds to international ideas and practice of improving public administration. It is well known that a large number of comprehensive programmes for reforming public administration systems in different countries were put into practice from the mid-1980s to the late 1990s; they were conceptually based on the theory of New Public Management (NPM).[9] The key targets of public administration reform included lowering public expenditures; increasing the capacity of the state to develop and implement its policies; improving the quality of public services; and increasing the confidence of the private sector and society in the state. The key target of international public administration reform was bringing about a profound change in the *technologies of implementing* state functions in contemporary society and ensuring greater effectiveness, flexibility and transparency, and closer ties with citizens, who are the consumers of public services.

The essence of public administration reform in the spirit of NPM was ultimately the delegation of a series of functions that had previously been implemented by the state to commercial structures: the large-scale commercialization of public administration that presupposes the multiform extension of the basic principles of commercial activity to the sphere of public administration. Another essential aspect of NPM is the delegation of a series of functions that had previously been fulfilled by the state to independent civil organizations.

When public administration reforms were implemented in different countries, the national models of civil service were taken into account.[10] Public administration reform in the spirit of NPM was most successful in countries characterized by high traction. The latter refers to the combination of leverage and institutional malleability that can be used in the course of reform.[11] According to experts, high-traction countries include New Zealand, Australia, Great Britain, Canada, Finland and Hungary. The Russian Federation (along with Germany, Brazil, Poland and the Netherlands) is considered low-traction, which makes it difficult, according to experts, to implement public administration reforms.[12]

In most countries, a number of important results were achieved during the reforms: public sector employment was reduced, along with the aggregate wage bill; the administrative system became more transparent, flexible and efficient; and merit-based principles became more effectively and more widely applied in the promotion of civil servants.[13]

Nevertheless, when speaking of the results of public administration reform, the fact should not be overlooked that reforms in the spirit of NPM were also accompanied by a series of problems. In particular, public administration reform in Great Britain and the US brought to light the contradiction between the civil service, which is non-commercial by its very nature, and the attempt to reorganize it on a commercial basis. In Germany, reforms led to a growth in red tape and considerable cutbacks in the public sector labour force, accompanied by a reduction in the range of public services. Experts have also noted other problems, including the declining legitimacy of the civil service, an outflow of qualified personnel from the public sector, and an overall reduction in the prestige of the civil service. For this reason, a number of specialists (including World Bank experts), who prepared materials for the Russian Governmental Commission for Drawing Conclusions from the Experience of NPM Reforms, were reserved in their assessment of reform results in different countries, noting that most were ambiguous and fell short of the initial targets.

Administrative Reform in the Russian Federation

What are the results of efforts to implement AR in contemporary Russia? It is no secret that reform is progressing with difficulty; there have been four directors of reform in two years (Boris Aleshin, Dmitrii Kozak, Aleksandr Zhukov and Sergei Naryshkin). Reduction in the number of federal structures in the framework of AR has increased once again (to 83 as of the end of 2006). It has been recognized de facto that the measures for reducing the number of directors of federal structures are inexpedient: the prime minister of the federal government Mikhail Fradkov ordered that the number of deputy ministries be partially augmented once again, and the number of deputy prime ministers has also increased. The Presidential Commission on the Reform of State Administration – which was headed in April 2006 by Sergei Sobyanin, director of the presidential administration – has intensified its activities. Nevertheless, officials recognize in private that the results of AR are unsatisfactory. The administrative personnel remain inefficient, corrupt, non-transparent, poorly meeting modern managerial and accountability requirements. Two years after the beginning of its active phase, the reform was recognized as unsuccessful by virtually everyone involved. For example, Yaroslav Kuzminov, rector of the Higher School for Economics and member of the Governmental Commission for Implementing AR, who had been one of the partisans of the reform, noted, 'We have found ourselves in a situation in which the best and most logical thing we can do is to return to the former state of things . . . And, to tell the truth, it seems to me that we have reached a dead end'.[14]

The steps taken in the framework of administrative reform have not yet improved the situation; in fact, they have worsened it.[15] One should give credit to the validity of the forecast by Robert Brym and Vladimir Gimpelson, who three years earlier wrote: 'Few people in Russia or elsewhere believe that civil service reform will be anything other than a highly politicized process with a not wholly predictable outcome'.[16] The failure of reform is commonly attributed to insufficient funding and the absence of a single team for its implementation, as well as the lack of political willpower and agreement among the political elite. The pertinence of these factors is evident. Yet this list does not seem exhaustive to us. In our view, an important cause of failure was the fact that the application of the AR model to Russian conditions had not been conceptually worked out to a sufficient degree, and in particular the question of the role and functions of contemporary government had not been thought through. The letter rather than the spirit of NPM was implemented in Russian administrative reform. In essence, the attempt was made to apply a number of sound and rational principles in the absence of many key preconditions that evoke a need for this model.

The following may be said to be the principal parameters of the system of public administration in contemporary Russia:

- The modern administrative apparatus in the Russian Federation is fairly distant from the Weberian model of rational bureaucracy. This can be seen from the widespread patronage and the lack of openness and transparency; the unsatisfactory level of public sector discipline; and extremely high corruption.
- Despite the enduring myth about the excessive size of the bureaucracy in historical and contemporary Russia, the ratio of the public sector labour force to the total population in the Russian Federation today is lower than in the advanced countries.

Experts note that between 1994 and 1995 the number of people employed in the broader public administration sector grew by about 6 per cent. This was by far the largest annual gain between 1994 and the beginning of 2001. Between 1995 and 1 January 2001, the number of government officials grew by a further 10 per cent. Employment gains were distributed unevenly across Russia's regions. Moreover, the effect of these gains was to increase inter-regional variation in state employment. By the beginning of 2001, the number of state officials ranged from four per 1,000 population (in Ingushetia in the Caucasus) to 58 per 1,000 population (in the autonomous Evenki region in the Far North), with the national average standing at eight per 1,000. The 'density' of state officials in a region was sensitive to budget constraints. Where budget constraints softened because of increased transfers from federal to regional budgets, the concentration of civil servants grew. Where budget restrictions hardened, growth was slow and in some cases the density of state officials declined.[17]

According to Goskomstat (the state committee for statistics), aggregate public sector employment in state bodies at all levels grew by 10.9 per cent, from approximately a million in 1994 to 1.462 million in 2004.[18] During the same period, the country's population fell from some 148 million to about 143 million. Thus, the percentage ratio of the public sector labour force to the total Russian population grew from 0.7 per cent to 1 per cent. This figure is quite small in comparison with the standards of developed countries; such a low ratio is typical for developing countries. According to the World Bank, the percentage ratio of the public sector labour force to the total population is 1.5 per cent in Brazil, 1 per cent in Chile, 1.6 per cent in China, and 0.7 per cent in Poland. In developed countries, the state apparatus is a lot larger: 6.1 per cent in Germany, 6.8 per cent in the US, and 11.7 per cent in Sweden.

According to the World Bank survey it is immediately apparent that the rich countries of the OECD differ from the less affluent countries of Eastern Europe and the former Soviet Union in two ways. First, while the mean size of public administration for the 21 OECD countries is 10.0 per cent of the employed labour force, the mean for the 16 countries of Eastern Europe and the former Soviet Union is 3.9 per cent. In general, public administrations in OECD countries are proportionately two-and-a-half times bigger than public administrations in Eastern Europe and the former USSR.[19]

So, the size of Russia's public administration is 'surprising only from the point of view of established wisdom about its "vastness." In point of fact, at 1.2 per cent of the labor force, Russia's public administration ranks 36th out of 37 countries. Only Moldova at 0.8 per cent has a smaller public administration. Russia's state bureaucracy is problematic in many ways, but size itself is not one of them'.[20]

World Bank experts consider that reductions in public sector employment may turn out to be an ill-advised and unproductive measure in view of the relatively limited number of civil servants,[21] and considering the following conditions:

- During the post-Soviet period, corruption grew considerably instead of being overcome.
- The inadequate financing of the administrative apparatus is another major cause of its ineffectiveness.[22] Experts note the unsystematic nature of the financing of the state apparatus: the increase in wages has mostly affected the upper echelons – ministers and directors of ministerial departments and central agencies – while the salaries of the bulk of civil servants grew at most by a third, even though civil servants have salaries that are up to two-thirds less than people working in the private sector.
- The effectiveness of civil society institutions is low in Russia, making it difficult for private organizations to take over major state functions.[23]

Thus a whole series of key parameters – the size, efficiency and rationality of the administrative apparatus; its low level of funding and high level of corruption (which are interrelated); and the quality of civil society and its capacity and readiness to take over a series of state functions – determine the considerable differences between the initial conditions for the realization of AR in Russia and the circumstances that stimulated analogous reforms in the spirit of NPM in developed countries. This explains the necessity and expediency of undertaking a thorough-going interpretation of the essence of the NPM paradigm in order to make AR in Russia correspond to the *spirit* of NPM rather than its *form*. This is particularly true of the conceptual foundations of AR, such as the role and function of the state in present-day conditions.

Let us begin with state function. In essence, AR was launched in response to appeals to reduce the excessive number of state functions (unrealistic figures were put forward: 500, 600, 800 and even 5,000 functions that were supposedly performed by the contemporary Russian state, whereas their number ranges from 5–6 to 10–12 in the theory and practice of public administration). Clearly, the thesis about excessive state functions is based on a broad interpretation of the notion of state functions that equates *functions* and *types of work*. Nevertheless, in a number of key sectors, the size, powers and functions of the Russian state are considerably lower than those of industrially developed countries (this is, for example, the case in the domain of law enforcement and the battle against organized crime). The data cited above concerning the size of contemporary Russian bureaucracy are contrary to the neo-conservative expectations of Russian administrative reformers of a negative correlation between economic efficiency and bureaucratic size.[24]

This incorrectly posed problem is further aggravated by the failure to distinguish between the interests, powers and functions of the state and those of the bureaucracy. Nevertheless, this distinction is very important from both the conceptual and the practical standpoint. In particular, one of the problems of present-day Russia is the fact that the interests, functions and powers of the state are lower than in developed countries (including such decentralized countries as Great Britain and the US), whereas the interests, functions and powers of the administrative and political bureaucracy in contemporary Russia are hypertrophied. At the same time, the bureaucracy employs state levers for attaining its own private (or corporate) goals and targets at the expense of public ones. In this context, it is very important to draw a distinction between the corrupt and arbitrary practices of the bureaucracy and the active role of the state as a political and economic player. Whereas society is unable to function normally in the presence of a corrupt bureaucracy, it cannot develop effectively in the absence of an active role for the state. The abandonment by the state of its administrative functions may in practice lead to the growth of corruption, further degradation of public sector discipline, a decline in the political role of the higher bodies of government, and a reduction in the number of executed decisions. This shows that it is necessary to adjust the conception of administrative reform: *although the hypertrophied power and functions of the administrative and political bureaucracy must indeed be curtailed, the state should not abandon its prerogatives and functions in a hasty and heedless manner.* Nevertheless, the most important thing is that AR should not be interpreted as a goal in itself, as it is in actual fact a complex and multipurpose (yet not self-sufficient) instrument for reaching important goals, the most crucial of which is ensuring national competitiveness.

The key reason for the imprecise conceptualization of AR is the simplistic understanding of the role of the state in the modern world. The state is implicitly considered to be, at best, a conglomeration of establishments and organizations and, at worst, a repressive apparatus that intrinsically defies rational reform. However, the notorious conception of the state as a 'watch-dog' corresponds to the theory and practice of the historic past rather than the present. Such a one-dimensional understanding of the role of the state reduces its functions to ensuring foreign and domestic security and administrative governance. At the same time, the modern conception of the state, as well as contemporary political and administrative practice, assigns manifold powers and functions to the state. A key notion here is the division of *traditional* and *modern* state functions. The former include the assurance of foreign and domestic security and administrative and general political governance; examples of the latter are public policy in such domains as education, public health, social welfare, and fundamental research. The evolution of public institutions at the start of the twenty-first century has been marked by the redistribution of traditional and new functions in favour of the latter. This redistribution can also be considered as a stage in the complex evolution of the state in the previous century and is the result of economic motives rather than humanitarian considerations.

The logic of this argument is fairly simple. The integrative aim of public policy is to ensure national competitiveness. In this context it is worth mentioning that the concept of competitiveness includes more than economic criteria. So, in the foreword to the World Report on competitiveness (2006–7) it is recognized that out of nine criteria of competitiveness only four are economic; others to some extent have 'social dimensions'.[25]

The history of the success of the most rapidly developing countries (including such diverse countries as the United States and Singapore) shows that one of the leading technologies for ensuring national competitiveness is the establishment and effective functioning of the *knowledge-based economy*. The key condition, premise and instrument for creating such an economy is high-quality human potential, and the development of human potential falls exclusively to the state. An example of success in this area was the US policy for designing a new economy by investing in human potential. In this context, it is pertinent to mention the efforts of the Clinton administration, which spoke of the necessity of 'reinventing government' and attempted to review state functions. In addition to the establishment of electronic administration ('e-government') and the reduction in public sector employment and the aggregate wage bill, a key direction of public administration reform was measures designed to drive the new economy by developing human potential. In particular, experts have noted the increase in funds allocated to this purpose during recent years. The total expenditures relating in one way or another to social development amounted to 49.4 per cent of the US federal budget in 1990 and reached 62 per cent by the year 2000;[26] this tendency has been stable during recent decades: the share of expenditures on the development of human potential in the US grew from 4.3 per cent of gross domestic product (GDP) in 1940 to 13 per cent in 2005.[27] Moreover, a considerable number of the budget's social items are not subject to market corrections. The administration of George W. Bush not only increased military spending to 3.8 per cent of GDP but also increased public social expenditures in the framework of the policy of 'compassionate conservatism'. The growth of the percentage share of the US federal budget in GDP from 18.5 per cent in the mid-1990s to 20.3 per cent in 2004 – a growth that is, on the whole, untypical of traditional Republican policy – is partly due to the increase in the budget's civil programmes, which grew by 36 per cent.[28] Today Republicans do not argue with Democrats about what kind of government the US needs – big or small: they argue about what a big government should look like.[29] The Iraq war and a series of other unfavourable circumstances led the Bush administration to lower social spending, yet its budget share remains fairly high.

Such an approach makes modern public policy differ considerably from the standards of the past. Until the end of the nineteenth century, the state's share in GDP seldom exceeded 10 per cent. Over the 50 years preceding the First World War, social spending amounted to approximately 1.5 per cent. Things began to change gradually during the interwar period and much more quickly after the Second World War, when state budgets started to grow rapidly in virtually all Western countries. By 1960, public expenditure surpassed 30 per cent of GDP in the United Kingdom, France, Germany and Italy, and 27 per cent in the United States. Social transfers affect the large majority – from 50 to 90 per cent – of the population in developed countries. The average figure in the European Union is 73 per cent. It is telling that Third World countries have also increased the share of the state budget in GDP; although this share differs from that of developed countries, it is nevertheless higher than it was in developed countries in the early twentieth century.

This trend gained in momentum by 1990 when the state share in GDP reached 58 per cent in Sweden, 54 per cent in France, 47 per cent in Italy, 47 per cent in Germany, 33 per cent in Japan, and 33 per cent in the US. At the same time, social transfers accounted for 28 per cent of GDP in France, 25 per cent in Italy, 21 per cent in Germany and Sweden, and 15 per cent in the United Kingdom, the US and Japan. On average, public expenditure in Western countries grew from 27 to 48 per cent of GDP. Thus the growth of public expenditure in Western countries was due to the growth of *social* expenditure. An important reason for the increasing share of public expenditure in GDP was the new role of the state in the social sphere and the redistribution of income through the system of taxes and transfers. World public expenditure amounted to about 25 per cent of GDP, or \$7.8 trillion (7.8×10^{12}), in the year 2000. Over 90 per cent of this figure was attributed to developed countries, which contain about 15 per cent of the world's population. 'This leads us to conclude that the more developed the country, the stronger the state': in Organization for Economic Co-operation and Development (OECD) countries, it is the state (which accounts for 87 per cent of all social expenditure) that carries the bulk of the burden for financing the social sphere.[30]

These figures allow the conclusion that the relationship between different types of public functions has changed considerably. Today, only 20 per cent of the public budget is spent on traditional items (general public management, maintaining public order, and national defence). Furthermore, the higher the level of development, the smaller the share of expenditures on traditional functions (see Table 1). Developed countries spend only 11 per cent of state budgets on these items, while developing countries spend 24 per cent. At the same time, developed countries spend over 70 per cent of their budgets on modern functions, while developing countries spend only 56 per cent.[31] OECD countries spend at least 5 per cent of their GDP on public health and, as a rule, allocate over 4 per cent of their GDP to education. The average expenditure on education amounts to 4.8 per cent of GDP in countries with a high level of human development, 4.2 per cent in countries with a medium level, and 2.8 per cent in countries with a low level. In the US, education amounts to over 15 per cent of total public expenditures, and public health to approximately 20 per cent (respectively, 5.6 per cent and 6.2 per cent of GDP). In Norway, which has the highest Human Development Index (HDI) in the world, these figures amount to 6.8 per cent of GDP; in Sweden (second in terms of the HDI), they amount to 7.6 and 7.4 per cent, respectively.

In the contemporary world, state expenditure on modern functions amounts to 17.8 per cent of GDP and on traditional functions to 5.3 per cent. The ratio of these budget items is 3.4 : 1. These figures amount to 25.0 per cent and 3.9 per cent (a ratio of 6.4 : 1) in developed countries;

TABLE 1
STRUCTURE OF PUBLIC EXPENDITURES IN SELECTED COUNTRIES, 2004
(% OF GDP)

	Health care	Education	Defence	Social security (old-age pensions, etc.)	Interest related to public debt
Russia	3.3	3.8	3.9	5.8	4.1
Brazil	3.4	4.0	1.4	9.8	11.4
Canada	6.9	5.2	1.2	5.4	2.5
China	2.0	n.a.	1.9	2.7	2.4
France	7.7	5.6	2.5	13.4	0.2
Germany	8.7	4.8	1.4	12.1	2.7
India	1.2	4.1	2.3	n.a.	2.6
Italy	6.3	4.7	1.9	17.6	5.3
Japan	6.4	3.6	1.0	6.9	1.5
Mexico	2.9	5.3	0.4	7.8	6.8
United Kingdom	6.9	5.3	2.6	10.3	1.5
USA	6.8	5.7	4.0	7.5	1.8
OECD average	6.7	5.6	2.6	n.a.	n.a.
World	5.9	4.4	2.5	n.a.	n.a.

Source: World Development Indicators 2006, at <http://devdata.worldbank.org/wdi2006/>, quoted in S. Rogov, 'Sotsial'noe gosudarstvo: Rossijayi mirovoi opyt', paper presented at the conference 'Social Justice: A Modern Dimension' (Moscow, May 2006).

14.4 per cent and 6.1 per cent (a ratio of 2.4 : 1) in developing countries; and 22.1 per cent and 3.8 per cent (a ratio of 5.8 : 1) in transition countries.

If we consider the above-mentioned problems in a broader context, we see that stimulating the 'knowledge-based economy' corresponds to the modern understanding of effective economic development technologies. It is well known that the intellectualization of production plays a key role in modern economic growth: the intensity of research and development (R&D) determines the level of economic development. According to experts, the intellectualization of labour will become the most important factor in global competitiveness in the present century. In developed countries, 70–85 per cent of GDP growth is due to new knowledge that is embodied in technologies, equipment, personnel training and the organization of production. It is thus no coincidence that the share of expenditures on science and education in GDP is constantly growing in developed countries; today, it amounts to 3 per cent, and the state has a 35–40 per cent share in these expenditures.

The growing importance of the intellectualization of the economy has a particular significance in the case of Russia, as the introduction of new technologies, whose industrial application ensures economic growth, is an effective instrument for overcoming systemic economic crisis. This shows the urgent need for investments in human potential, which is the foundation of the knowledge-based economy. However, the opposite is taking place today in the Russian Federation. The share of traditional state functions amounts to 36.7 per cent of the federal budget in Russia – four times higher than in the developed world and 1.5 times higher than in developing countries; at the same time, social functions account for only 21.3 per cent.[32] Traditional functions account for 6 per cent of GDP, which exceeds the world average by almost 25 per cent, whereas social functions amount to only one-sixth. The ratio of expenditures on traditional and modern functions is 1.7 : 1. Although this ratio differs somewhat in the consolidated budget (1.2 : 1), the fact remains that such a structure is characteristic of nineteenth- rather than twentieth-century states.[33]

The priority area for cutbacks is the social sphere – public health, education, fundamental science, and social welfare. This is the context in which one should consider the reforms that began to be implemented in early 2004, aimed at large-scale commercialization of the social sphere and the actual reduction of its public financing. In essence, social reforms meant that the state was leaving the social sphere. This trend is related to reducing the share of the Russian federal budget in GDP. Federal expenditures accounted for 17.9 per cent of GDP in 2003, 16.2 per cent in 2004, 16.5 per cent in 2005, and 16 per cent in 2006.[34] The figures for the consolidated budget (including the budget of the territories) differ somewhat, accounting for some 30–32 per cent of GDP.[35] It should be borne in mind that these figures are lower than those of developed European countries: approximately 35–37 per cent in Great Britain, about 32 per cent in Germany, 41 per cent in Italy, 40–42 per cent in France, and 37–40 per cent in Sweden.[36]

Meanwhile, the favourable trend in energy prices makes it possible to use the resulting profits for the structural modernization of the economy, where preference would be given to high-tech industries and the transition to a 'knowledge-based economy'.

Of course, the implementation of national projects ('public health', 'public education', 'public housing', 'agriculture') corrects the course of public policy. Growth of social expenditures in the 2007 federal budget ranges from 38.1 per cent for education up to 72.1 per cent on the national 'public health' project. However, in analysing the budget, it is necessary to take account of its structure. The biggest item in the Russian consolidated budget for 2007, at 1.58 billion (thousand million) roubles, is 'surplus of budgetary resources'. Taking into account that this surplus is transferred to the stabilization fund, it is possible to conclude that significant resources are being used inefficiently. The second largest item of budget expenses is the national economy (1.28 billion roubles) – more than 60 per cent of which is financed through territorial budgets. The third and fourth items – education (1.23 billion) and public health services (0.87 billion) – are 76 per cent financed by territories. The priorities of the federal budget itself are expenditures on national defence (0.82 billion roubles) and national security and law enforcement activity (0.85 billion), which are financed by the federal government. Social policy (0.75 billion roubles), and housing and communal services (0.66 billion) continue the list of state budgetary priorities, and are financed mainly by the regions. Thus the absolute size of assignments from the federal budget on these purposes decreases respectively to 2.9 and 6.8 billion roubles. The last in size are allocations for culture (0.21 billion roubles) and protection of the environment (0.03 billion roubles), also financed mainly by the territories.[37]

How do these figures compare with the financing of modern state functions in advanced countries? It is known that expenditures on public health services should take between 5 per cent of GDP (the minimal permissible level recommended by the World Health Organization) and 10 per cent (the level of most developed countries). The efficient level of expenditure for science ranges from 1.5 to 3 per cent of GDP; for education – from 5 to 7 per cent. In the draft of the consolidated budget of Russia for 2007, expenses for education made up about 4 per cent of GDP, and for public health services about 2.8 per cent. If we summarize all assignments allocated in the consolidated budget for social needs (3,764 trillion roubles), their cumulative weight in GDP is 12 per cent. If we also add inter-budgetary transfers (one billion roubles), directed mainly in support of the social sphere and social programmes, the scale of social expenditures reaches 15.5 per cent of GDP. This is essentially less than the average level of financing for the state's social functions not only by the central governments of advanced countries (21.6 per cent), but also by those with economies in transition (18 per cent). Thus, the scope of financing on national projects more probably determines the correction of a situation, rather than its radical change.

Achievement in the Russian Federation of the mean world level of social sphere financing supposes an increase in GDP of about 5 per cent. This size corresponds approximately to the proficiency scale of the federal budget which is planned for the next year at a rate of 1.5 billion roubles, or 4.8 per cent of GDP. This volume of financing shows that national projects can indeed only correct the situation rather than change it radically; while improvement in the country's competitiveness demands another model for using the abundance of start-up funding.[38]

Conclusions

Does the argument presented above imply that one should abandon the ideas of AR in Russia? Certainly not. Moreover, the reform of the civil service and of the principles of its organization is an even more urgent problem in the

Russian Federation than in developed countries. Our argument, presented above, shows that AR must be implemented bearing in mind the specific nature of the reformed object in order to realize as much as possible the conceptual ideas of the AR as a means of ensuring the public administration's transparency, flexibility, responsiveness, and accountability to citizens.

In light of the above, we share the opinion of those experts[39] who consider that civil service reform in Russia should be based on the simultaneous implementation of two groups of tasks. The first involves efforts to implement the basic assumptions of the traditional (Weberian) model of the civil service, whose possibilities have not been exhausted. Experts have noted that a number of postulates of the Weberian theory of bureaucracy remain topical for Russia today: rationalism; the preference for formalized procedures over personalistic orientation to a patron; transparency, precision, and accountability to society; and the elimination of corruption. The second group of tasks presupposes the conformity of the administrative apparatus to classical criteria and the canon of rationality, and is based on the application of the experience of public administration reform in developed countries to the specifics of the contemporary stage of nation- and state-building in Russia and of the country's social, political, financial and economic condition.

NOTES

1. Robert Dahl, *Democracy and its Critics* (New Haven, CT and London: Yale University Press, 1989).
2. The concept of 'clan' is the most widely used in the literature on contemporary Russian elites. From a formal point of view this concept is not quite precise, since both relative and ethnic ties are not obligatory features of Russian elites. However, Russian clans have the same typical features, including secrecy, especially a particular corporate orientation, that constitute the core of clan relationships: see O. Gaman-Golutvina, *Politicheskie elity Rossii. Vekhi istoricheskoi evolyutsii* (Russia's political elites: landmarks of historical evolution) (Moscow: ROSSPEN, 2006), p.335.
3. T. Graham, 'New Russian Regime', *Nezavisimaya gazeta*, 23 Nov. 1995.
4. It is necessary to clarify the content of the terms 'civil service' and 'state bureaucracy'. The content of the terms both coincides and differs. As a rule the latter is broader than the former. By 'state bureaucracy' we mean those who realize 'a type of work consisting in the practical realization of state functions by the workers of the state apparatus, who occupy posts in state bodies and receive compensation from the state for their work': see A. Obolonskii (ed.), *Gosudarstvennaya sluzhba* (state service) (Moscow: Delo, 2000), p.10. The term 'civil servant' defines those members of the state bureaucracy who obtain a special rank (or status). In this context we mean the corps of the people who are professionally involved in the state management process, both those who make key decisions and those engaged in realizing them.
5. In this case the concept 'state' is used neither as a synonym for the totality of political institutions nor to refer to a machinery of repression, but as an instrument for achieving the common good.
6. Robert J. Brym and Vladimir Gimpelson, 'The Size, Composition, and Dynamics of the Russian State Bureaucracy in the 1990s', *Slavic Review*, Vol.63, No.1 (2004), pp.90–112 (p.112).
7. Ibid.

8. Note that the Russian word *effektivnyi* can be translated as both 'effective' and 'efficient'; in the present instance, the term 'effective' is more appropriate.

9. Barry Bozemann and Jeffrey D. Straussman, *Public Management Strategies: Guidelines for Managerial Effectiveness* (San Francisco, CA: Jossey-Bass, 1991); H. George Frederickson, 'Comparing the Reinventing Government with the New Public Administration', *Public Administration Review*, Vol.56, No.3 (1996), pp.263–70; H. George Frederickson, 'The Repositioning of American Public Administration', *PS: Political Science and Politics*, Vol.32, No.4 (1999), pp.701–11; Christopher Hood, *Beyond the Public Bureaucracy State? Public Administration in the 1990s*, inaugural lecture (London: Department of Government, London School of Economics and Political Science, 1990); Christopher Hood and Michael Jackson, *Administrative Argument* (Aldershot: Dartmouth, 1991); Organisation for Economic Co-operation and Development, *Managing Across Levels of Government* (Paris: OECD, 1997); David Osborne and Ted Gaebler, *Reinventing Government: How the Entrepreneurial Spirit is Transforming the Public Sector* (New York: Plume, 1992); B. Guy Peters, 'Models of Governance for the 1990s', in Donald F. Kettl and H. Brinton Milward (eds.), *The State of Public Management* (Baltimore, MD and London: Johns Hopkins University Press, 1996), pp.15–44; B. Guy Peters and Donald J. Savoie, 'Managing Incoherence: The Coordination and Empowerment Conundrum', *Public Administration Review*, Vol.56, No.3 (1996), pp.281–90; and others.

10. For example, European countries deploy several *models of civil service* and several *models of modernizing civil service*, which they use for optimizing their administrative systems. For further discussion, see M.K. Meiniger, 'Sravnitel'nyi analiz reform gossluzhby v strankakh ES' (Comparative analysis of state service reforms in EU countries), in *Reformy gosupravleniya* (Reforms of government) (Moscow: RAGS, 1999), p.47.

11. Nick Manning and Neil Parison, *International Public Administration Reform: Implications for the Russian Federation* (Washington, DC: World Bank, 2003), Ch.6.

12. Ibid., Ch.7.6.

13. Frederickson, 'The Repositioning of American Public Administration'; Bozeman and Straussman, *Public Management Strategies*; Lawrence R. Jones and Fred Thomson (eds.), *Public Management: Institutional Renewal for Twenty-First Century* (Stamford, CT: JAI Press, 1999); and others.

14. Ya. Kuzminov, 'Tupiki i perspektivy administrativnoi reformy' (Dead-ends and perspective of administrative reform), *Nezavisimaya gazeta*, 7 April 2006.

15. In this context it is worth mentioning the discussions on the issue that took place at the workshop 'Administrative reforms in post-Soviet countries' in St. John's in August 2006. Richard Rose considers that NPM may be assessed as an example of bureaucratization of ideology. It is possible to add that the opposite is also true: NPM in its Russian version may be assessed also as an example of ideological interpretation of *institutional transfers*, which in a broader context is one of the priority objects of our interest. The opinion of Anton Oleinik that NPM is a case of conservative modernization – an attempt to increase the efficiency of the state without changing the model of power relationships – is ambiguous. The validity of this assessment depends on the starting point of the evaluation. In comparison with Yeltsin's time, the AR model of power relationship in the spirit of NPM is really conservative modernization. Meanwhile, in comparison with the traditional (pre-Yeltsin) Russian model of power relationships, AR in accordance with NPM orientations is obviously non-conservative modernization, since it means a rejection of the former power model: NPM principles require changing the model of power relationships. As for the related question concerning the opportunity of administrative reform without changing the underpinning model of power relationships (Oleinik), it is possible to note that the answer depends on the scale of the planned reforms and their expected results. If you plan only cosmetic measures that are called to correct some aspects of the managerial system, you can do that without deep tectonic changes of the key elements of the whole management system. In the opposite case this is impossible.

16. Brym and Gimpelson, 'The Size, Composition, and Dynamics', p.112.

17. *Trud i zanyatost' v Rossii: Statisticheskii sbornik* (Labour and employment in Russia: a statistical collection) (Moscow: Goskomstat Rossii, 1996), p.2; Vladimir Gimpelson and Daniel

Treisman, 'Fiscal Games and Public Employment: A Theory with Evidence from Russia', *World Politics*, Vol.54, No.2 (2002), pp.145–83.

18. Brym and Gimpelson, 'The Size, Composition, and Dynamics', p.96.
19. Ibid., p.99. OECD: Organization of Economic Co-operation and Development.
20. Ibid., p.101.
21. Manning and Parison, *International Public Administration Reform*, Ch.8.5.2.
22. It should be said in passing that this resembles the situation that existed in the Russian Empire: a satisfactory level of wages for civil servants was attained only in the second half of the nineteenth century, despite all the efforts undertaken to this end during the sixteenth–nineteenth centuries. For further discussion, see Oksana Gaman-Golutvina, *Byurokratiya Rossiiskoi imperii: vekhi evolyutsii* (The bureaucracy of the Russian Empire: landmarks of evolution) (Moscow: RAGS, 1997).
23. Concerning the last two points I have to agree with Anton Oleinik's position expressed at the workshop in St. John's: comparing two major directions of AR – commercialization and the transfer of responsibilities to civil society – the willingness to move in the former direction is stronger than in the latter one.
24. Brym and Gimpelson, 'The Size, Composition, and Dynamics', p.100.
25. <http://www.weforum.org/pdf/Global_Competitiveness_Reports/Reports/gcr_2006/chapter_1_1.pdf>; see also: V. Inozemtsev, 'Prizrak konkurentosposobnosti' (The spectre of competitiveness), *Nezavisimaya gazeta*, 11 April 2007.
26. *Politicheskaya sistema SShA: aktual'nye izmereniya* (Political system of the USA: current soundings) (Moscow: Nauka, 2000), pp.133–4.
27. S. Rogov, 'Funktsii sovremennogo gosudarstva: vyzovy dlya Rossii' (Functions of contemporary government: challenges for Russia), Part I, *Svobodnaya mysl'*, No.7 (2005), pp.50–63 (p.53). This article is written on the basis of a large-scale comparative project conducted by research associates of the Institute of the US and Canada of the Russian Academy of Sciences.
28. Ibid., p.54.
29. Janet Hook, 'President Putting "Big" Back in Government', *Los Angeles Times*, 8 Feb. 2005, p.A1.
30. Rogov, 'Funktsii sovremennogo gosudarstva', pp.56–7, 58–9, 61–82.
31. Ibid., p.61.
32. Ibid., Part II, p.82.
33. Ibid., pp.82–3.
34. Ibid., pp.92–3.
35. *Rossiya i strany mira, 2002. Statisticheskii sbornik* (Russia and the countries of the world 2002: a statistical collection) (Moscow: Goskomstat Rossii, 2002), pp.78, 334.
36. Ibid., pp.78, 334.
37. Federal'nyi zakon 'O federal'nom budzhete na 2007 god' (Federal law 'On the federal budget for 2007'), Attachment 10, at <http://www1.minfin.ru>, accessed 27 July 2007; see also S. Glaz'yev, 'Nastional'nye proekty: illyuzii i real'nost' (National projects: illusions and reality), *Nezavisimaya gazeta*, 5 Feb. 2007.
38. Ibid.
39. V. Komarovskii and Ye. Morozova, 'Administrativnaya reforma v vospriyatii grazhdan' (Administrative reform in citizens' perception), *Vlast'*, No.6 (2006), p.35.

The Institutional Framework for Sustainable Development in Eastern Europe

Sustainable development has four inter-related dimensions: social, economic, environmental and institutional. These dimensions are only partly separate from one another. I define 'sustainable' development as that which is 'socially justified and environmentally sound'.[1] The creation of an appropriate institutional framework is a necessary condition for the fulfilment of the criteria for sustainable development. This is an essential premise for the development and implementation of different regulatory mechanisms, and norms and rules for the behaviour of businesses, consumers and social groups.

What is the core of the institutional dimension? It is the institutions and the system of laws, rules and norms that regulate sustainable development. In terms of level and scope, institutions can be categorized as (a) local, (b) national, (c) regional, (d) international and (e) global. They can also be governmental and non-governmental, business or consumer institutions.

Ideally, all institutions should work within a single system and in the same direction. In the modern world it is not acceptable to assert that one type of institution, for instance governmental, is more important than another, such as non-governmental, or that local institutions should be involved only in the implementation of the programmes of national institutions. In other words, different types of institutions perform specific functions that offer a unique contribution to sustainable development. For this reason the balance of interests between institutions should play a leading role. As pointed out by Mebratu and his collaborators and by Adkin, the politics of sustainable development needs to integrate this balance.[2] The second important step is the creation of a relevant administrative organization for the implementation of stated goals.

Specifics of Sustainable Development in the Transition Countries

The establishment of an institutional framework for sustainable development has its own specifics in the former socialist countries. The transition period poses significant obstacles for the achievement of social justice and environmentally sound growth, for a number of reasons. First, the formation of the main market institutions, including the transfer of ownership, requires substantial financial and human resources; consequently, government funds for social and environmental programmes are limited. Second, economic restructuring and the redistribution of national wealth deepen social polarization and increase unemployment; these processes push ecological problems to the bottom of priorities. Next, the transition slows down the process of improving ecological standards because of the need for survival of newly privatized enterprises and small and medium sized businesses. Fourth, democratic institutions and civil society are not yet fully established, and this inhibits the realization of policies for sustainable development. Fifth, pollution levels in Eastern Europe are substantially higher than those in Western Europe; indeed, the scope of environmental imbalance in the former socialist bloc is such that the new democracies cannot deal with this problem alone, and this supposes internationalization of the institutional framework for sustainable development and close co-operation with leading democracies. Finally, high levels of corruption – that oppose the private to the public interest – further impede the implementation of the criteria and goals of sustainable development.

The political elite, represented by the executive and legislative branches of power, has a decisive role in the creation of the institutional framework for sustainable development. This role is obvious in the making of new laws or the improvement of existing legislation, the supply of financial resources, the building of institutional capacity and, last but not least, management and control. I share Holmberg's view that in addition to the formation of new institutions, changes are necessary in the existing ones – in their objectives and mechanisms of functioning.[3]

Market regulations modify the market conditions, so that economic agents behave in a (supposedly) desired way. The so-called 'free market economy' can neither provide sustainability nor solve the problems of environmental disequilibrium or social polarization. However, not every type of market regulation leads to sustainable development; market regulation can ensure sustainability only if (1) it corresponds with the respective criteria (social justice and environmental soundness) and (2) it leads to achievement of particular pre-set aims.

The goals of sustainable development were accepted by a consensus within the General Assembly of the UN (Agenda 21) and were further specified during the UN meeting in Johannesburg in 2002.[4] The achievement of these goals is a complicated and delicate process, because some of them fully or partially contradict the political or economic interests of different countries. The intensity and scope of these contradictions depends on the particular conditions in a given country: the level of development of the legislative framework; the tools used by governmental and non-governmental institutions for monitoring and control, and so on; and, last but not least, the country's model of economic development. As Ayre and Callway aptly stressed, there is a tendency of deepening contradictions between institutions in the process of implementing sustainable development programmes.[5]

Clarification of the genesis, nature and versatility of interests, and the contradictions between these interests, is an indispensable condition for elucidating the need for institutionalization of the processes of sustainable development. The kind, scope and level of a state's standards, as well as the fines or taxes (that is, the stimuli) for their breach and observance bring forth different, often mutually incompatible, interests.

Take for instance the standards for nitrate levels per unit of farm production – vegetables, fruits, cereals, and so on. Experts have demonstrated that these nitrates are detrimental to people's health when their concentration exceeds accepted norms. All developed countries, and even many developing countries, have established norms for the maximum quantity of nitrates in food products. There are institutions that monitor adherence to the relevant standards. In so far as most of the countries in transition are full or associate members of the European Union, their ecological standards are close to those established in the Union. A number of programmes are being implemented for the synchronization of laws, including ecological legislation. So what is the reason for the discrepancy of interests at the national, regional and international levels?

In the above instance, the nitrate level depends on the quantity of fertilizers used. On the one hand, the use of fertilizers improves labour productivity, increases production volume per unit of land and consequently lowers the price of the product; thus, both producers and traders benefit because they achieve economies of scale. Buyers also enjoy a 'consumer surplus', because they get greater quantities of food for a unit of purchasing power. The state, too, benefits because it gains more revenues from taxes and incomes. On the other hand, the use of nitrate fertilizers has its negative effects. The consumption of food containing nitrates is risky to human health, and the higher the nitrate level, the greater the negative health effect. According to a recent study by Stoicheva and her associates, there are many instances of fruits and vegetables on the Bulgarian market with detected nitrate levels that many times exceed the established standards.[6] So far, fines and the termination of sellers' licences have not solved the problem, so that the economic stimuli for breaching the environmental and health standards prove stronger than the penalties.

Government bodies assigned to monitoring and control are unprepared for the scope of the violations. Often, employees of these bodies are involved in the corruption schemes, and increasing the penalties simply breeds further corrupt practices. It is obvious, therefore, that improvements are needed in the entire mechanism of monitoring and control. However, the establishment of a control institution is no guarantee of the effective execution of its functions. There are substantial reserves in the non-governmental organizations, such as the consumer unions, and at this stage their role is underestimated and they intervene sporadically.

Moreover, damage to health is not included in individual production expenditures nor is it present in the 'consumer surplus'. None the less, the effects are real – loss of human life, sick-leave from work and consequently losses in GDP, increased personal and state expenditures for health care. Furthermore, the extensive use of fertilizers changes the soil's structure and reduces, or even destroys, its fertility, creating a conflict of interest between landowners and tenant farmers. The latter's interest is to achieve maximum productivity for the time of the tenancy, whereas the owners strive to maintain fertility for longer periods of time.

State institutions have an obligation to make two types of expenditures. First come expenditures for the establishment, financing and management of specialized units for monitoring, control, prevention, research, and so forth. Second, in most countries the use of fertilizer is subject to government subsidies. And here we have a paradox – the government is spending in two incompatible directions: (1) increased use of fertilizers and (2) limiting the negative effects of their use. The larger scale of the subsidies requires larger expenditures for prevention and limitation of the negative effect.

Let us systemize the different economic, social and political interests and contradictions among different social groups. These interests were mirrored in the behaviour of politicians, particularly the mechanism of the search for solutions and their implementation. The subsidizing of agriculture, the use of fertilizers in particular, has been a matter of a bitter debate in recent decades. Notwithstanding the efforts of the World Trade Organization (WTO), these subsidies remain an important item in budget expenditures and, as a result, soil fertility and the quality of consumption continue to deteriorate.

This author shares the opinion of Sampson that the WTO should play a more active role in the elimination (or at least substantial down-sizing) of subsidies for activities that contradict the goals of sustainable development; in the introduction of more rigorous environmental standards in international trade; and in the encouragement of exporters who use environmentally friendly technologies.[7]

Region and Country Specifics

Political parties consider farmers an important segment of the population for broadening their electoral support. While less than 5 per cent of labour is employed in the agricultural sector in developed countries, this figure is much higher in many East European countries. Data from national statistics show that the proportion of workers employed in the agricultural sector is 9 per cent in Bulgaria, nearly 30 per cent in Romania, 25 per cent in Ukraine and 18.8 per cent in Poland.[8] Consequently, the pressure on government institutions for budgetary support of agriculture is substantial. These high levels of employment in the farming sector and the share of agriculture in GDP generate significant support for the agrarian parties in the countries in transition.

In most East European countries agrarian parties are or have been present in governing coalitions and the parliament: in Bulgaria, the Bulgarian Agrarian National Union, in Poland, the Polish People's Party, and in Romania, the Christian-Democratic National Peasants' Party (renamed the Christian-Democratic People's Party in 2005). In general, because of the economic structure and historical traditions, farmers and their political movements and parties play an important role in the political environment in the transition countries. Therefore, this serious electoral mass and its representatives in the parliament and the government constitute a significant barrier to radical decisions that would curb subsidies for the sake of environmental and social objectives.

Bearing in mind the difficulties in restricting farm subsidies even in the EU, the United States and Japan, it is unrealistic to expect better results from the countries in transition. As a matter of fact, in the first 10–15 years of transition, these countries had symbolic levels of subsidies because of other serious economic problems and limited budget resources. Since the beginning of the new century they have experienced positive economic growth and better economic conditions, and therefore can afford to increase the subsidies to agriculture.

Obviously, some softening of the contradictions between political, socio-economic and environmental interests supposes implementation of new approaches. Let us return to the example of farm subsidies for nitrate fertilizers. In general, these subsidies can be kept in place, but only if their structure is properly modified. Thus, instead of nitrate fertilizers, subsidies could be redirected to organic production. However, it is well known that organic production is environmentally friendly but unfortunately its productivity is substantially lower. This makes the product more expensive and generates less income owing to lower demand; also, the higher-priced product creates social problems.

The higher price makes organic products virtually inaccessible for the poor and hardly accessible for the middle class in Eastern Europe. Therefore the government could partially subsidize the price of organic products, thereby achieving three inter-related goals: (1) encouragement of environmentally friendly production and consumption; (2) reducing soil pollution and prolonging soil fertility; (3) diminishing the price difference between organic and non-organic products on the market.

Diminishing price differentials result from two factors: (1) raising the cost of production with nitrate fertilizers by eliminating the subsidies; and (2) budget financing of part of the production expenditures for organic products. This approach could help the countries in transition improve their competitiveness on the world market. Because of government policy and changing attitudes, the market niche for organic products is growing. The state could introduce export stimuli for organic exports, thereby facilitating the desired restructuring of its industry and markets.

Another institutional instrument is eco-tax reform, which would also change the behaviour of producers and consumers by affecting the price mechanisms. For instance, most Eastern European countries are restructuring their fiscal policies, one of the goals being environmentally sound production. The corporation tax in Bulgaria and Romania at present stands at 10–12 per cent, well below the EU average. This encourages both domestic and foreign reinvestments, accelerates technological and product renewal in accordance with higher eco-standards, stimulates employment, increases purchasing power, and limits poverty. 'Tax neutrality' is a basic principle of EU fiscal reform and it states that an increase of environmental taxes, broadening of the tax base, or both, must be accompanied with adequate decreases in other taxes, such as those on corporate profits, household incomes and social contributions.

The process of environmental tax harmonization is not an easy task even within the EU. As stated by the European Commission, there are still huge differences in the level of environmental taxes in the 'old' and 'new'

EU member states. For instance, excise duty rates on a tonne of unleaded petrol in Bulgaria, Romania and the Czech Republic are respectively €270, €327 and €400, while in developed economies they are much higher: €731 in the UK and €668 in the Netherlands.[9] Hastings and his collaborators correctly identified the difficulties faced by the countries in transition in fulfilment of the objectives of sustainable development.[10] Underdevelopment of environmental tax policy is one of the main problems that must be overcome in the next five to eight years.

In general, the contradiction between social and environmental objectives is particularly exacerbated in developing countries. In their analysis of countries in transition, Sachs and Stiglitz point out two major challenges: first, the burdensome environmental legacy; and, second, the long period (over four decades) of subsidies for heavy industries and the energy sector.[11] These subsidies led to inefficient use of natural resources and artificially lowered prices of the final industrial products.

Following the line of inter-industry relationships, the subsidized prices have led to poor efficiency in the whole economy. Furthermore, in the first five years of reforms these countries lost 10–15 per cent of their GDP (Czech Republic, Slovakia, Hungary and Poland), 20–30 per cent (Bulgaria and Romania) and even up to 65 per cent in Georgia.[12] These dramatic changes in the level and structure of national economies are reflected in reduced purchasing power of the population, unemployment, inadequate pension provision, and other difficulties. Consequently, governments have tended to focus on socio-economic problems at the expense of environmental issues. Thus, we can accept that developed countries enjoy more favourable conditions for the implementation of economically unpopular decisions that benefit the environmental equilibrium – decisions, that is, that promote long-term goals. The emphasis on the time period is necessary because in the long run many of the environmental and socio-economic objectives converge.

Private property is a mandatory condition for the establishment of the institutional framework of the contemporary market economy and democratic society. So, the transformation of state property in the former socialist countries is regarded as a step towards sustainable development. Privatization is in its final stage in the transition countries. Most of the institutions necessary for the proper functioning of the market economy are in place. At present, governments rely on two main levers to maintain the balance between ecological and socio-economic interests of society: budgetary policy and environmental legislation.

The strain on the budget in the transition countries is much heavier than that in developed countries. This is because budget revenue is insufficient and there exist a wide variety of issues – social, structural, organizational – that absorb significant resources. For countries such as Bulgaria, Ukraine and Hungary servicing the foreign debt engages substantial financial resources that otherwise could be used for environmental and social programmes. The World Bank estimates that for Hungary, Bulgaria and Poland this debt servicing is equal to 25–35 per cent of their export revenues.[13]

The countries in transition need considerable resources for the recovery of their environment. Despite the high GDP growth level of 4–5 per cent in Eastern Europe in recent years, it is unreasonable to expect that governments will significantly increase their spending on environmental programmes,[14] especially given the EU requirement for strict financial discipline and the maintenance of a low budget deficit. Hence the solution to environmental problems must be based mainly in the private sector. The state can utilize its limited budget resources not so much in direct financing of eco-programmes, but rather in attracting foreign and domestic investment (co-financing). Another indirect budget stimulus is tax exemption of environmentally sound investments. The results from the partial financing of producers and consumers of alternative energy sources such as solar and wind power are encouraging.

Another type of fiscal stimulus for households is co-financing by the state, perhaps combined with tax exemptions, for investments in the thermal insulation of houses. For instance, the EU, through the European Bank for Reconstruction and Development (EBRD) and the European Investment Bank (EIB), supplies Eastern European countries with free or low-cost funds for energy efficiency improvements. During the past 15 years EBRD, in partnership with Vivendi Environment Inc., invested more than €150 million in energy-saving projects in Hungary, Lithuania, Poland, Romania and the Slovak Republic, and expanded to other countries such as Bulgaria, Croatia, Bosnia and Herzegovina, and Russia.[15]

Many of the private commercial banks are participating in the same policy. So, apart from the positive public relations effect, these banks attract new customers, both private and corporate – namely producers of energy-efficient products and technologies. So far, the experience with these schemes in Eastern Europe shows that households save 20–30 per cent from the cost of a project. Both households and society benefit through better environmental parameters and better quality of life. Therefore, market mechanisms can quite successfully solve particular problems if the conditions in which these mechanisms function are modified. In accordance with Coase's theorem, 'the state should bestow property rights over rare resources to those economic subjects who are able to make more profits from using them than others'.[16]

The nearly two decades of transition in Eastern Europe have formed a trend of surmounting the lag, but the difference remains. Still, the former socialist countries consume three to seven times more energy per unit of GDP than developed countries do.[17] Keeping in mind the increasing costs of energy resources and the EU's policy of raising environmental standards, the need for reducing this difference becomes pressing.

The first years of transition were marked with high social costs, but also with some positive environmental effects. The comparative analysis of pollution data in Eastern Europe for the period 1990–2000 shows that most harmful emissions have been reduced, including greenhouse gases. This allows the transition countries to become net exporters of emission tradable permits (ETPs), regulated by the Kyoto Protocol: that is, to generate additional hard currency from lower pollution.

In practice, these 'surpluses' of ETPs are due to the dramatic drop in industrial production and agriculture, and are not the result of technological improvements or the introduction of a new institutional framework for development. With the advance of reforms and the establishment of an adequate base for development, expectations are that Eastern European countries will be able to come close to the levels of environmental growth in developed countries.

An Insider's View

My personal experience with legislative and executive power in Bulgaria informs my analysis of the genesis, nature and forms of conflicts of interest at different levels. Many of these contradictions can be solved, and others mitigated. This was the case when the Bulgarian government made an agreement with the Swiss government (1996) to implement the 'Debt for Ecology' project, worth 20 million Swiss francs.[18] This project converted foreign debt into investments for environmental protection. The mechanism for transformation of foreign debt into 'green' investments turned out to be a cornerstone for the converging interests of different ministries (environment, finance, social, economy).

This debt-swap operation illustrates Switzerland's programme for the support of environmental re-creation in Eastern Europe. From this perspective, new environmental policies by East European governments must be viewed as externally driven. In some cases, like the swap operation, the main external drive was the economic interest of the recipient. At the same time, EU pressure for legislative environmental reforms is a typical expression of externally driven power which suppresses the economic interests of different business groups, mainly in the heavy industry sector and transport which are the major polluters of the environment.

These newly established rules favour other business groups and society as a whole. For instance, induced higher environmental excise taxes on gasoline in the new EU member states stimulate new business with propane-butane and bio-diesel, and make profitable the production of electricity from renewable energy sources such wind, solar, hydro-power and so on. Therefore, if they are properly designed, externally induced reforms help to overcome resistance of some influential local groups and make possible the establishment of a new balance of interests at a different level.

In mid-1996 the Bulgarian government initiated unpopular but absolutely necessary steps towards economic restructuring. About 65 per cent of the state-owned enterprises were loss-making at the time because of outdated technologies, old-fashioned management, and inappropriate behaviour in competitive conditions. Most of these unprofitable companies were in the heavy industry sector (chemistry, metallurgy, machine-building, and so on), which meant unacceptably high toxic emissions. They caused a huge budget deficit and led to destabilization of the banking system. Regardless of these facts, the government's intentions for liquidation, privatization and restructuring were met with protests, the labour unions organized strikes, and the opposition parties argued against the government's programme, hoping to gain political dividends at the expense of the country's economic interests.

The main argument for the resistance to the structural reforms was 'the possible increase in unemployment' and 'the expected collapse of the national economy'. The fear that structural reforms would bring economic problems and social polarization generated strong opposition in the parliamentary group of the ruling coalition[19] – indeed, this disagreement within the ruling coalition was even stronger than the pressure from the opposition parties in the parliament.

There were some differences among the ministers themselves. It is well known that government members usually represent different wings or groups of their party or group of parties. From this perspective, the government mirrors the parliamentary and the parties' power structure. Furthermore, achieving a balance of 'intra-party' or 'intra-coalition' interests is a precondition for any possible balance of interests with the opposition or adequate counteraction against the opposition.

Achieving such intra-government balance of interest is not an easy task, especially when the government has to take hard decisions. In critical conditions, the balance of power and harmonization of interests among the governing institutions is more decisive than the power balance between the ruling party (or coalition of parties) and the opposition.

Power struggles within the ruling coalition itself and between the ruling parties and the opposition led to further delay of market reforms, to severe instability in the exchange market, and also to tremendous pressure on the national economy. The government was ready to implement the so-called 'currency board' at the beginning of 1997 but the lack of political support and the struggle for transfer of power made this impossible.[20] As a result, the currency board was implemented six months later, and this delay led to substantial economic losses, social disorder and a deterioration of living standards.

This is an ideal illustration of the mismatch between, on the one hand, externally driven power (International Monetary Fund, World Bank and the EU) and the government, and, on the other hand, the stronger power of certain influential 'grey business' circles and the opposition. Speculators, among them banks in liquidity crisis, had an interest in as high as possible a depreciation of the national currency, which consequently triggered an appreciation of their assets in hard currency. The opposition understood the advantage of the currency board for financial price stabilization, but it could keep them in opposition for at least another two years. So, they did everything they could to postpone its introduction until they obtained political power and converted it into economic leverage. In other words, the established model of power relationship in 1996 was a perfect source of instability.

Compared with the schedule of reforms in countries such as Hungary, the Czech Republic, Poland and Slovenia, the structural reforms in Bulgaria were delayed by nearly five years. No wonder those countries now enjoy a much higher standard of living and greater competitiveness than Bulgaria on the world market.

The good news is that in some conditions the power model can balance the interests of most influential interest groups. Externally driven reforms may create favourable conditions for internally motivated support from various governmental and non-governmental institutions. No doubt, the process of accession to full EU membership paves the road to consolidation and a certain balancing of interests among different social groups.

Toffler's 'third wave of shifting power' is applicable to the former socialist countries.[21] Now more people are interested in concrete results from a given policy model rather than in the ideological background of this model. Today, it is much easier for East European governments to implement unpopular policies if these are required for harmonization with EU practices. In this way, we witness how externally driven reforms may lead to externally 'transferred power support' which makes certain reforms more acceptable even if these look socially unjust, at least in the short run.

At present, most key objectives of the model of development in Bulgaria correspond to the UN's Agenda 21 and also to the EU's Lisbon strategy for sustainable development.[22] Such development supposes an adequate institutional framework and policy instruments which meet the criteria for sustainability. Such already established institutions in Eastern Europe are governmental and non-governmental agencies, laboratories and monitoring bodies. At the same time, 'old institutions' such as the ministries of the environment were accordingly empowered with adequate legislation, financial and human resources, and so on. The realization of the sustainable path of development supposes adequate institutional mechanisms for fulfilment of the relevant criteria and indicators.

Conclusion

The United Nations Economic Commission for Europe (UNECE) argues that the implementation of programmes for sustainable development demands devolution of the global process and widespread local activity. The motto 'think globally, act locally' is a yardstick in the formation of national policies for development. The last parliamentary elections in Bulgaria (25 June 2005) demonstrated that highlighting environmental issues in the candidates' programmes attracted additional voters. To keep its power in key regions of the country, the governing coalition initiated a number of environmental and social projects on the eve of the elections.

These types of projects depend on the support of various international institutions and foreign governments. Examples are many, including Lake Balaton (Hungary), the Baltic Sea Region (Estonia, Latvia, Lithuania, Poland, and the Russian cities St. Petersburg and Kaliningrad), Slovenia, and others. Denmark, for instance, is one of the most active EU members that initiates or participates in the so-called 'sector-integrated environmental programmes' in Eastern Europe. In Poland alone, programmes with Danish participation for the period 1990–2001 numbered 232, with $73 million coming from Denmark.

The Danish authorities administrating the sector programmes include the ministry of labour, the emergency management agency, the Danish energy agency, the Danish agency for trade and industry, the ministry of food, and the ministry of education. The Polish partners are the government and the non-governmental institute for sustainable development. These programmes underline the necessity and high effectiveness of the establishment of a relevant institutional network that implements particular projects.

The EU, along with the UN, the WTO and other specialized international institutions, contributes to changes in production and product standards, the use of economic stimuli in achieving these standards, and more active social policies for the eradication of poverty. The EU devotes significant budgetary resources to facilitating the adaptation process of newly accepted member states and associated states. Bulgaria, for instance, will receive some €12 billion of subsidies from Brussels in the period 2007–13. It is understandable that the utilization of this huge financial support depends on the appropriate capacity-building of all relevant institutions – in other words, on the efficiency of the institutional framework for sustainable development.

NOTES

1. Rumen Gechev, *Sustainable Development: Economic Aspects* (Indianapolis, IN: University of Indianapolis Press, 2005), p.18.
2. Desta Mebratu (ed.), *Sustainable Development Policy and Administration* (Delray Beach, FL: Saint Lucie, 2005); Laurie Adkin, *The Politics of Sustainable Development* (Montreal: Black Rose Books, 1998).
3. Johan Holmberg, *Making Development Sustainable: Redefining Institutions* (Washington, DC: Island, 1992).
4. Agenda 21, the 'Rio Declaration on Environment and Development', and the 'Statement of Principles for the Sustainable Management of Forests', were adopted by more than 178 governments at the United Nations Conference on Environment and Development (UNCED) held in Rio de Janerio, Brazil, 3–14 June 1992. Full text of Agenda 21 at <http://www.un.org/esa/sustdev/documents/agenda21/index.htm>, accessed 21 Nov. 2007.
5. Georgina Ayre and Rosalie Callway, *Governing for Sustainable Development: A Foundation for the Future* (London: Earthscan, 2005).
6. Dimitranka Stoicheva, Milena Kercheva and Venelina Koleva, 'Assessment of Nitrate Leaching under Vegetable Crops: A Case Study of Fluvisol in Southern Bulgaria', conference paper, No.170–4, presented to the 18th World Congress on Soil Science, Philadelphia, PA; available at <http://crops.confex.com/crops/wc2006/techprogram/P12255.htm>, accessed on 1 April 2007.
7. Gary Sampson, *The WTO and Sustainable Development* (Tokyo, Japan: United Nations University, 2005).
8. Bulgarian National Institute of Statistics, at <http://www.nsi.bg>, accessed 7 Jan. 2007; Central Statistical Office of Poland, at <http://www.stat.gov.pl/english/index.htm>, accessed 7 Jan. 2007; Statistics Ukraine, at <http://www.ukrstat.gov.ua>, accessed 5 Feb. 2007; Romanian National Institute of Statistics, at <http://www.insse.ro/index_eng.htm>, accessed 5 Feb. 2007.
9. European Commission, Tax Policy, Excise Duty Tables, REF. 1.023, at <http://ec.europa.eu/taxation_customs/resources/documents/taxation/excise_duties/energy_products/rates/excise_duties-part_II_energy_products-en.pdf>, accessed 17 March 2007.
10. Marilu Hastings (assistant), Jurgen Schmandt and Calvin Ward (eds.), *Sustainable Development: The Challenge of Transition* (Cambridge: Cambridge University Press, 2000).
11. Jeffrey Sachs, 'Economies in Transition: Some Aspects of Environmental Policy', Environment Discussion Papers, Harvard University (Boston, MA: HIID, 12 Jan. 1995), pp.3–14; Joseph Stiglitz, *Whither Socialism?*, Wicksell Lectures) (Cambridge, MA: MIT Press, 1996).
12. World Bank 2007, at <http://www.worldbank.org>, accessed 12 Dec. 2006.
13. World Bank, at <http://www.worldbank.org>, accessed 2 Feb. 2007.
14. European Commission, Eurostat 2007, at <http://epp.eurostat.ec.europa.eu>, accessed 9 Nov. 2006.
15. EBRD: 'Making Eastern Europe More Energy Efficient', at <http://www.ebrd.com/new/pressrel/2001/01oct221x.htm>, accessed 7 Jan. 2007.
16. For an overview see Anton Oleinik, 'Institutional Analysis of the State', in Anton Oleinik (ed.), *Institutional Economics of Russia's Transformation* (Burlington, VT: Ashgate, 2005), pp.246–7.
17. European Commission, Eurostat 2007, at <http://epp.eurostat.ec.europa.eu>, accessed 4 Dec. 2006.
18. United Nations Commission on Sustainable Development (CSD), at <http://www.un.org/esa/agenda21/natlinfo/countr/bulgaria/eco.htm>, accessed on 4 Oct. 2006.
19. The power struggle within the ruling coalition was caused by the conflict of economic interests among different groups of individuals. It was based on economic interests because political power opened opportunities for easier access to economic and financial resources. Certain groups had an interest in slowing the privatization process because they defended the interests of private business which used to buy cheap products from state-owned companies and resell them at much higher prices. As a result, the state was left with losses and profits

were seized by the newly established 'capitalists'. Other groups had opposite interests, namely to speed the privatization but under conditions favourable to themselves: in other words, privatization was seen as an opportunity to acquire assets at prices much lower than the market level. The Bulgarian government tried to neutralize, or at least to minimize, the pressure from these 'insiders' but it lost the battle, culminating in the resignation of the prime minister in December 1996.

20. The Currency Board is based on fixed exchange rate and the money supply is anchored to the hard currency reserves of the Central Bank. Under these conditions the monetary authorities do not have the right to exercise monetary policy.

21. Alvin Toffler, *Powershift: Knowledge, Wealth and Power at the Edge of the 21st Century* (New York: Bantam, 1991).

22. <http://ec.europa.eu/growthandjobs/key/index_en.htm>, accessed 27 April 2007.

New Social Movements in Russia: A Challenge to the Dominant Model of Power Relationships?

KARINE CLÉMENT

The reforms that began in post-Soviet countries in the early 1990s have caused a number of unexpected results in practically all spheres of society. In Russia, especially, the expressed aim of building democracy has turned into a strengthening of authoritarian power relationships, particularly visible at the top of the power system but also in the sphere of everyday life. As illustrated by most of the sociological polls, Russian society as a whole is characterized by weak citizenship, lack of trust in social relationships and a limited sense of belonging to a single society, not to mention civil society.[1] In this context, the building of democratic institutions is quite problematic, in so far as the norms and practices at the bottom of Russian society reflect the authoritarian and non-democratic norms and practices at the top. What might produce a change in traditional norms and practices? In this study we assume that the social movements[2] that have emerged during the past few years could bring new models of social relationships, norms and practices, potentially able to introduce change in the dominant model of power relationships.

We base our argument on the preliminary results of two research studies. The first is a project called 'The new emerging social movements in Russia', conducted by the Institute of 'Collective Action' (IKD, headed by the author) in collaboration with the Institute of Sociology of the Russian Academy of Sciences and the Maison des Sciences de l'Homme (Paris). The research proceeds by interviews with activists and rank-and-file participants of social movements in Russia. We have already transcribed up to 70 interviews which are complemented by other data from regular observation and daily monitoring of collective actions.[3] The material provided by this research will be compared with the primary data drawn from preliminary results of the Research Development Initiative 'Particularities of Power in the Post-Soviet Context: Theoretical Considerations and Empirical Studies of Bureaucracy' (Social Sciences and Humanities Research Council of Canada file No. 820-2005-0004), which is based on interviews with bureaucrats and experts.

Although Russian society can be considered as very fragmented and highly passive in the realm of social or collective action, the research on emerging social movements gives evidence of the possibility for collective action to occur and for certain people to become involved in collective action.[4] Why are they doing so, and what are their motivations and values? What is the nature of the relationships among activists, and between them and other social groups and institutions? Are they defining a new model of social relationships which, over time, could effect change in the dominant model of power relationships, largely imposed by the power elite and by bureaucracy? The answer is far from obvious, especially in light of the pregnancy of the dominant structure of power relationships that is supported and maintained by the participation of the whole society, which tends to reproduce the dominant model of power. At present we are unable to offer more than informed assumptions which we will work towards confirming at a later stage of our research.

The Co-participation of the Top and the Bottom of Society in Reproducing the Model of Imposed Power Relationships

The whole social structure of Russian society is marked by the pervasiveness of imposed power with a strong division between organs of power and society. As conceptualized by Anton Oleinik,[5] imposed power is based on the coercion, manipulation or co-optation of those who prove their loyalty. Moreover, this kind of power is not limited by any superior principle, and is an end in itself. It is a power 'over' which has nothing to do with the power 'to', and even less with the 'power together'. This essay does not aim to verify empirically this qualification of power relationships, but it does question the extent to which Russian citizens accept such a model.

First of all, it seems that most Russians do indeed see the dominant power as an imposed power. They are far from confident about the willingness or ability of power-holders to respect and implement the law, to listen to their demands and to guarantee equal respect for people's rights and interests. Interviews and empirical surveys show that ordinary people have very weak trust in formal political institutions such as the government or the Duma. Sociological polls show that Russians expressed high levels of distrust in all institutions except the president and the church.[6] Some research shows very clearly that Russian people want the law and other democratic values (fairness, impartiality, justice, honesty and so on) to be implemented, but do not rely on the official power – viewed as partial, corrupt, arbitrary – to do so.[7] So one could say that the Russian identity is enveloped by a disjunction between ideal values (which are expressed in the official discourses of state officials invested with power) and the reality of the power relationships, which is more comparable to the model of imposed power.

However, the paradox is that such a model of power relationships is accepted, if not seen as legitimate, by most of the people. There are no massive protest movements against illegitimate power. Even the holder of the highest power, President Vladimir Putin, enjoys very great popularity. But it should be noted that this popularity is linked to his person, and not to his policy, which is criticized in all dimensions except for the foreign one (according to polls conducted by the Levada Centre, 2003–6).[8] An interpretation may be that Putin symbolizes the recovery of the country's strength on the international scene; this fits the model of domination and subordination which structures power relationships in Russia.

From interviews with non-activist 'ordinary' people we can describe the more generalized scheme of relation to power, which is as follows:

> You do not trust it and do not see it as legitimate, but you cannot contest it, at least not openly, because the power is strong and has the ability to make arbitrary use of the law and violence; while you can hardly be protected by power, you can easily suffer its negative consequences. So the most rational choice and the most secure strategy is to procure the appearance of subordination and loyalty. Within this general framework you can either try to obtain advantages by building interpersonal relationships with some useful people in power, or you can retreat from the public sphere into your private micro-group. This is the general scheme that is reproducing at both macro- and micro-levels, at the bottom as well as the top of the society.

At the top we can base our argument on the data provided by interviews with bureaucrats. Interviews with experts and office holders show that bureaucrats exercise power with no attention to people's aspirations or demands. They ignore any kind of constraints which might limit their freedom to take unilateral decisions according to the interests of the clan to which they belong. The respondents say that pressure from below is non-existent or not taken into account:

> 'Today our Ministry encloses itself by a wall from the public.' (Head of a federal ministry department [*otdel*])
> 'Initiatives from below don't count for anything.' (Head of an executive power department in a Russian region)
> 'The population has no influence [on policy]; the main factor of influence is business.' (Head of a federal ministry department)

Most of the bureaucrats interviewed describe a situation where public opinion or social demands are manipulated in such a way that they match every kind of decision undertaken by the ruling class according to its own corporate interests. Activists and other citizens not under control are seen as provocateurs, and the only accepted kind of collective action is that which is set up and run by the bureaucracy. As for the law, it does not impose any constraints on the decision-making process. 'The laws are written by people, and it's always possible to send our people to write the laws', said one interviewee.

In their interpersonal relationships, bureaucrats seem to observe the rule (mentioned above) according to which the most important condition to secure one's position in the hierarchy is to demonstrate loyalty to the persons one is dependent on (business groups or power groups). This appears to be the only constraint; all other things are permitted, including breaking the law (provided this is not too overt). Another interesting point is that one can exercise power as one wishes so long as the appearances of democracy and loyalty to the higher power are respected; the form of behaviour counts more than its content. If these two principles (strong subordination and observance of appearances) are violated, punishment will follow, generally by being fired, from time to time by being subject to juridical or tax investigations, and less frequently by imprisonment.

The most striking feature of this model of power relationships based on the absence of control from below or formal constraints is that it is reproduced at the bottom, by ordinary people in their everyday lives. From our research among workers[9] we obtained evidence of widespread self-initiated practices designed to protect their own interests. Either they build some kind of client-style relationships with the boss or someone closer to power in the plant, or they retreat and try to do their job in such a way as to have the fewest possible contacts and problems with the hierarchy (by observing the appearance of loyalty, for example). Formal rules, institutions or rights, such as trade unions or justice, are mostly not trusted: they are seen as arbitrary tools used by power-holders.

The same can be observed in other spheres of everyday life. As many sociologists have pointed out, the most widespread strategy used by ordinary people to survive or improve their living standard is to appeal to micro-networks of informal interpersonal relationships providing reciprocal help.[10] Those networks constitute some kind of *cliques*, as A. Khlopin called them,[11] which means that the individual belongs to a limited micro-group where there is strong trust based on experienced interpersonal face-to-face relationships. But it should be noted, first, that this kind of relationship is limited to a micro-group or a micro-network of reciprocal help, and can rarely be opened to other groups and even less to society as a whole; second, that these micro-groups are not free from imposed power relationships. In most cases there are heads of groups or networks linked with people who have higher power and can arbitrarily make use of this position to control the group and impose rules so that group members are committed to loyalty.

While trust and helping behaviour exists in interpersonal relationships, it is problematic in considering the society as a whole. The micro-groups or cliques are tightly closed and quite unable to open themselves to other groups. They are also structured by very informal rules, mostly imposed by the head or heads of the groups, which are not easily translated to general rules or social norms. And, finally, these groups are not citizens' groups, since they are dealing with the private problems of individuals belonging to the groups rather than appealing to formal political institutions or even bypassing them. And they prevent people from getting involved in public life in general.

As mentioned above, collective actions are very infrequent, and, apart from the traditional act of voting (to demonstrate apparent respect for formal democracy), Russian citizens largely do not participate in public life. The Social Capital Survey[12] established that in Russia four-fifths to nine-tenths do not belong to a single voluntary association. This figure might appear to be comparable to other areas in the world (as indicated, for example, by the European Social Survey[13]), but we have to take into account that a large proportion of Russian NGOs exist only formally and do not engage in any real activity apart from collecting funds, so that these figures are obviously exaggerated. In the case of protest actions, official statistics (which underestimate these kinds of collective actions) and even polls indicate an unreal number of strikes and other kinds of protest actions (demonstrations or meetings). To use Hirschman's terms, 'Exit' and 'Loyalty' are predominant in a system that prevents people from having 'Voice'.[14]

All these observations provide a picture of a very stable and socially rooted system of imposed power relationships which fit and supplement each other at micro- and macro-levels, at the top and the bottom. So we have to question the capacity of such a system to change, or to be challenged. Obviously the system matches the interests of the people invested with power, so that changes, if they are at all possible, can be brought about only by constraints coming from outside (pressures at the international level) or by reactions from within, from people who are inside the system, but are suffering from it to a greater extent than they gain by participating in it.

How Can Social Protest Occur in Such Unfavourable Structural Conditions?

Taking into consideration the impact of imposed power on processes in diverse spheres of everyday life and in all groups of the society, the likelihood that some groups will challenge the dominant power model is very low. While acknowledging the strength of the whole political structure, however, we do not admit that there is no possibility whatsoever for challenging it. We are not trying to argue that structural and institutional frameworks, and the informal power relationships of today's Russian society, are not determining features of citizens' everyday lives. But the recent increase in social protest demonstrates that some grassroots social initiatives are emerging and beginning to build networks that could potentially challenge the dominant model of power relationships. In order to test the assumption, we will, on the one hand, first analyse the conditions for social protest to occur and then question the demands of social activists and their representation of ideal power and will, on the other hand, pay attention to the power relationships structuring the activist networks themselves.

New social movements have emerged in Russia since the first massive upheavals against the reform of the social benefits system at the beginning of 2005. Tens of thousands of people, mostly pensioners but also young leftist, trade union and human rights activists and so on, took to the streets of almost every town, in some cases for days, to protest against a law that threatened social security rights. This first wave continued for several months and forced the government to accept a compromise. After the end of 2005, protest actions flared up against the new housing code and the current so-called 'communal' (housing) reform. Besides these main social movements, other thematic networks are appearing, such as the movement of car drivers for safe roads or in favour of the protection of Lake Baikal, and hundreds of grassroots local initiatives are being undertaken by so-called 'initiative groups' of people at the micro-level of their household, neighbourhood or town.[15]

What are the main motivations and factors influencing involvement in collective action? The situation varies very much by region, but is not necessarily linked to objective regional characteristics; protest movements are strong in depressed and developing regions, as well as under more or less 'autocratic' regional power styles, so there are other explanations for collective action. At this stage of the research on social movements, it seems that the key role is played by the individual who initiates collective action. Regardless of the scale of the leadership (whether of the household or the region), the most important factor (see below) is that the person is recognized as having authority and being reliable. Many new leaders who had no experience in politics or public affairs have emerged in the wave of recent protest movements. They are characterized by a relatively high educational level, wide contact networks, social dynamism (many of them have interrupted ascendant professional careers to participate in protest movements), a sense of initiative, competence in public interventions, and organizational know-how. The role of leaders is one of the main points in trying to explain how social protest can occur under such unfavourable institutional constraints: they are able to resist the influence of imposed power thanks to a very strong personality.

Who are these leaders? Where are they from? Here we need to base our explanation on biographical research which is still in process, but let us give some examples. While following one of the first demonstrations against 'monetization of the welfare benefits' as a journalist, Andrei, aged 35 at the time, within a few months became the most respected leader of the citizens' action co-ordinating council, created in February 2005 in the city of Izhevsk. He was already active on a cultural level (he founded a students' theatre company) and an intellectual one (he confesses a great admiration for Immanuel Wallerstein) but in his youth he was scarcely interested in politics. Before devoting himself to the protest movement of his city, he had a relatively high standard of living as a journalist and specialist in 'public relations' for professional politicians. His participation in the movement, then his growing militant commitment, led him to discover another world but also reduced his income by more than half. Within two years, between two courses at the university, where he teaches history, and two articles in an oppositional newspaper in quasi-bankruptcy, he runs from one meeting to another, from one gathering to another, organizes the inhabitants in defence committees, and his telephone never stops ringing. In short, from a young intellectual with a career on an upward trajectory, he became the 'spoilsport' of the local authorities and the principal referent for thousands of people wishing to defend their rights.

Lena, aged 40, an economist, a board member of the association of the joint owners of her building, is a militant of the movement of the citizens' initiatives from Saint Petersburg. She managed a small Internet firm and was not at all worried about politics (she never voted). At the beginning of 2005, she was forced to close her firm because of the so-called 'State arbitrary' (in Russian, *gosudarstvennyi bespredel* – disregard for formal rules). Subsequently she has worked at home, and began to pay attention to the problems of her building, and started to study the new housing code and to seek information and contacts related to housing problems. Having experienced the administrative and legislative barriers to the self-management of the building and having met practised activists, she became increasingly committed to collective action. One year after her firm went bankrupt, she was elected to head the 'Our Building' local association of housing owners.

Sergei, aged about 60, a bus driver laid off in 2005, is one of the most active figures of the local bus workers' trade union in the city of Perm. From a family of workers without education, he tried all kinds of jobs and travelled all over the country before settling in Perm. He undertakes self-instruction and reads extensively. Very curiously, he developed a passion for the occult. To safeguard their employment, he took the initiative to mobilize his fellow workers against the municipal authorities' decision to privatize local public transport. Then, after having taken part in the demonstrations against the 'monetization of welfare benefits', he joined the co-ordination council of the protest actions of the city of Perm.

Nastya, Tat'yana, Igor', Vasya, Yevgenii, Nina – there are hundreds devoted to the improbable task of collective mobilization and of learning citizens' rights and capacities; hundreds of highly individual biographies that do not conform to any pattern. Perhaps we can provisionally conclude – subject to the full analysis of our biographical interviews – that leaders are strong individuals who present themselves thanks to certain character traits (sensitivity to injustice, curiosity and intellectual openness, a critical mind, social dynamism), the interplay of circumstances, the result of certain meetings and the willingness to take outstanding personal risks.

Although the personality of leaders is a very important factor in mobilizing people for collective action, it does not explain everything. A second explanation, as far as rank-and-file social activists are concerned, is the existence of a concrete threat to individual welfare. It must be emphasized that the first motivation for people to engage in collective action is the defence of their direct and very concrete or pragmatic interests: not to be expelled from their home, not to pay excessive communal charges, to protect the square in front of the house, to get support for medication and so on. Local campaigns are mounted on specific practical issues, such as combating plans to build a block of flats or car park on a local recreation ground, to turn people out of workers' hostels, or police brutality, linked with the new stage of reforms initiated under Putin's government; following economic restructuring, reform of the social sphere is being undertaken. As a consequence, most people, living until now just above the poverty line, see their standard of living threatened, and are beginning to react and defend themselves. State policy is encroaching upon people's lives through social reform, making it more difficult for them to retreat into the private sphere or to solve problems through informal interpersonal relations.

Facing new threats, people usually react initially in the traditional manner, appealing to networks of interpersonal relationships. But in more and more cases these appear to be of no help because, first of all, most of the problems cannot be solved at an individual level. Second, social activists often say they first tried to solve the problem through the usual means of writing letters to official bureaucrats, obtaining a meeting with them, reaffirming their loyalty and belief that state officials will take care of their citizens. But they faced 'arbitrary' responses, unwillingness to help, 'indifference' and 'dupery', 'corruption' and 'mockery'. Only after these appeals proved to be useless, and in turn produced anger and denunciation of alleged unfairness and social injustice, did some people engage in collective public protest. Thus people are progressively losing their final illusions of paternalistic power which from time to time deigns to help its subjects in exchange for loyalty. Sometimes the road to disillusion is quite long if the social activists initially call for the help of the highest authority (Putin), but sooner or later they usually come to the conclusion that power-holders do not care about citizens' complaints and demands. This provides strong motivation for people to mobilize collectively. They form citizens' initiative groups, organize protest actions, and actively seek contacts with other initiative groups facing the same kind of problems.

What are the general demands and values defended by initiative groups and participants in movements? At the stage when people already have experience of concrete relationships with power and collective action, their claims gain in generality. The most popular slogans and values proclaimed by social activists are 'citizens' control' (that is, their own identification as citizens who have the right to control power) and 'fairness' (that is, the same law and same rights for everybody, regardless of their place in the power hierarchy). It is very important to notice that activist groups demand full and genuine citizenship rights. Of course, these values remain abstract and weak but they represent an obvious challenge to the dominant institutional framework.

A second important feature of social protest is the rise of self-organizing initiatives, independent of formal institutionalized political parties or power representatives. For example, around problems aroused by the housing reform, we can observe a growing mobilization of housing committees, neighbourhood associations and groups of community leaders, or simply residents who are more active than the average over the issue of management of buildings and lands. Even though information about the reform is lacking, networks of activists have undertaken to propagate it and, as a result, more and more people are beginning to wonder about the future of their building. Building and neighbourhood residents' meetings are proliferating, sometimes organized by activists in certain networks or by political parties, but most frequently by the residents themselves. The idea of organizing themselves and managing their own building, so that it is not placed under the control of a management association imposed by the city hall, is beginning to enter their minds. The trend involves only a minority of the population at present, but if this movement establishes itself we can expect to see progress in the self-organizing of the general population. So the main idea here is the sense of individual empowerment: people are learning in practice that they can organize and exercise power themselves.

A third important tendency from the perspective of challenging existing power relationships is the trend to build alliances and co-ordinate efforts. More and more local initiative groups and campaigns move to work together and build networks or co-ordinating councils. These co-ordinating committees are beginning to create structures and to establish links in order to exchange experience and information. Activists claim the need for solidarity and the necessity of union, which appear to be important values, at least in activists' discourses.

As a whole, with the threads of discontentment and the nests of opposition being very diverse, the movement is still relatively scattered. However, the beginnings of co-ordination can be seen, thanks to the operators of several networks. The biggest protests are those which begin spontaneously or which are co-organized by a coalition of diverse social and political groups. In this respect, the Soviets Co-ordination Union (SKS) is a very interesting example. It is a union of regional committees for co-ordinating the struggles developed out of the pensioners' movement two years ago, continuing by spreading to incorporate new cities and towns and new social groups. The most socially active cities – Izhevsk, Perm, Omsk, Novosibirsk, Vladivostok, Saint Petersburg, the Moscow suburbs, Samara, Tol'yatti and others – have seen the development of co-ordination between coalitions of this type through the SKS network. The appeal made by SKS on the theme of 'a month of protests for a social housing policy' (12 February–18 March 2006) adds strongly to the growing dynamism of the movement. Taking the example of Izhevsk (Udmurt Republic), the local soviet or council ('for co-ordination of citizen actions') brings together representatives of the pensioners' association, the RKRP (the Russian Communist Workers' Party), independent journalists, students, trade unionists, anarchists, liberal opposition movements, inhabitants of workers' housing, neighbourhood committees and so on. At the demonstration on 12 February 2006, more than 4,000 people assembled at their behest and blocked the traffic for several hours.

The movement is still far from organizing itself politically at a national level, and it is not obvious that it can even be referred to as a social movement as such. But this author would argue that there is potential for the growth and structuring of a social movement. The success of active and open co-ordination of grassroots initiatives, such as that of SKS, shows the possibilities for development. Moreover, in the literature on social movements we can find approaches that indicate a chance for social movements to occur even when the 'structure of political opportunities'[16] is far from favourable. The point is to observe or ask protestors themselves about their perceptions, demands and desires. Thus Charles Kurzman in his study of the Iranian Revolution[17] shows that perceptions matter more than some underlying 'reality' of political structure. He argues that, although the Iranian people considered the coercive power of the state to be intact right to the end, they perceived the opposition as having increasing its strength and opportunities, which gave way to the Iranian revolution. And Kurzman concluded that social movement theory has to reconsider the relationship between 'objective' and 'subjective' definitions of political opportunity:

> If opportunity is like a door, then social-movement theory generally examines cases in which people realize the door is open and walk on through. The Iranian Revolution may be a case in which people saw that the door was closed, but felt that the opposition was powerful enough to open it. ... It turns out that Iranians were able to open the door on their *own*.[18]

Of course, we cannot extrapolate any conclusion for Russia from this example, but we can at least recognize the probability for a massive social movement to occur and challenge the dominant power system, despite unfavourable political opportunities. And we can understand how important it is to pay attention to the perceptions, representations, values and demands carried by social activists, especially by leaders. At present, compared with the Iranian case, Russian activists have no perception of their ability to challenge the existing system, but they do have a growing feeling of their citizens' power. They do think that there is another way, and that they have passively endured an unfair power system long enough. Here are some activists' comments:

> It's quite difficult to do these things, to fight all the time against arbitrary and illegal actions of the local government and our hostel's owner, to learn the laws, to become aware that you have not only obligations, but also rights. But if you don't do this, you are not considered as a human being, so we do it, we are beginning to get a sense of the fact that we are bosses of our lives and have rights. And you get satisfaction from it, too, because you feel that you can do something in that life, that

you can do something for yourselves and for the others. (Woman from the movement for hostels for workers, July 2005)

I may be naive, but I didn't know that in our country such things could be possible, that the state could behave like this with their citizens, as if we were enemies. It's quite unusual for me to participate in such protest actions, but I think we have to do it, we have to make things change. Unfortunately in our country people support each other very little. If we didn't wait until a problem occurs to us and supported people facing trouble, if there were more solidarity between people to defend common positions, we could change many things, change this system. (Woman from the movement of 'deceived co-investors' who are fighting for flats they have paid for in advance, May 2006)

At the beginning we only sent letters to the local authorities in order to protest against the demolition of our homes, but they ignored our letters, our opinion. When bulldozers arrived, we had no other choice than to block them. We settled on permanent camp here. All the neighbours came to help. We know each other very well; we are living like in a little village here in the Moscow suburb. Only thanks to our radical action did the local authorities start to pay attention to us. It's really pleasant to see how many people come to support us from Moscow and even from other towns. I believe that thanks to that we'll force Moscow municipality to respect the law and the inhabitants' rights. (Female member of the initiative group of the inhabitants of Butovo town in the Moscow suburb, July 2006)

The fact that citizens' initiative groups and coalitions are mobilizing is already a signal of the possibility for challenging the dominant power system, but in order to estimate the reality of the challenge we have to analyse the power relationships structuring the activist networks themselves.

Power Relationships Within Activist Networks

The question that we shall try to answer is whether or not the emerging social movements are reproducing the dominant model of power relationships, and to what extent they are able to introduce a new model, founded on democratic norms and social trust. Given the emergent character of activist networks and their fragmentation, it is quite impossible to give a complete or final picture of the power model by which they operate. Nevertheless we can start to analyse some key trends.

The first aspect we can point to is the informal mode of building activist networks. Nearly all the new networks appearing during the past couple of years have no formal status or formally elected executive bodies. They mostly emerged from spontaneous upheaval and are based on informal agreements between key personalities who represent some initiative groups or formal organizations but who engage more fully in the co-ordination process. The duration of such a model of relationships depends on permanent agreements and negotiations between key personalities, so interpersonal conflicts have to be kept smooth. It is an expensive model in terms of personal involvement.

Second, networks are founded on weak ties. Collective decisions are mostly taken by consensus and imply the possibility for the groups or individuals who disagree with the decision of the majority not to implement it. The model matches the democratic ideals (fairness, equality and freedom) of participants in new movements. It is also very convenient at the beginning in order not to threaten new partners with strict obligations and to protect the autonomy of each partner. But in the long term it weakens networks, especially in the face of institutionalized bureaucratic organizations with strict discipline and subordination. Freedom from constraining ties can also weaken the position of people deprived of power, as pointed out by Pierre Bourdieu.[19]

Third, as networks are structured on the basis of ties between leaders, there is a tendency for leaders (who are those working intensively to mobilize resources) to concentrate on their own resources such as contacts, information, authority and so on. Even if leaders tend to redistribute resources (as most of them are trying to do), there is a disproportion in this process. Although this disparity is recognized and legitimated by leaders' human and personal investment, for us it raises the question of the possible democratization of the process of mobilizing resources.

However, the main question, according to our analysis, is of the possibility for activist networks to go beyond the clique-style social model. Such a possibility implies other kinds of relationships based, on the one hand, on something more general than interpersonal trust and, on the other hand, on something other than leaders' imposed power.

Sociological literature concerning trust is very rich and the theme evokes intense debates. On the basis of a rational and cognitive perception of trust, some sociologists contest the thesis according to which trust is necessary for democracy.[20] However, in the institutional context of such new democracies as Russia we can argue, following Piotr Sztompka,[21] that trust is a key condition not only for democratization but also for the re-composition of the society (*socium*).

What is trust other than our personal and practical knowledge of someone's reliability or trustworthiness based on common belonging to the same micro-group? According to Sztompka, trust implies confidence, but not certainty, that some person or institution will behave in an expected way. A trusting person decides to act in spite of uncertainty about the future or doubts about the reliability of others' promises. Sztompka writes: 'facing other people we often remain in the condition of uncertainty, bafflement, and surprise'.[22] This remark is especially important in Russia's uncertain institutional framework, where most of the rules and relationships are characterized by changing informal logic. So trust is a gamble; it requires a person 'to make bets',[23] but it is a necessary condition for involvement in action, even more so in collective action. The problem once again is that, although it may be true, as Eric Uslaner argues,[24] that generalized trust in others has deep roots in individual psychology and upbringing, structural conditions are nevertheless important in influencing trust. As for Russia, we cannot imagine that a general trust in existing institutions and in the conditions of the existing type of social relationships could be possible (or rational). What do we observe among new activist networks in Russia?

In our research, we do find trust to lie at the basis of involvement in collective actions. First of all it is interpersonal trust. Social activists often say they attended their first meeting or demonstration in the company of trustworthy persons of their acquaintance, or in response to an invitation by leaders who were trustworthy in their eyes. However, there are also many other kinds of trust. A key point to notice is that activists gain confidence in themselves by participating in collective activities. Many of them recognize that they have discovered that they can 'do things on their own', they can 'have influence' in an external context. And this confidence makes it easier for them to establish relationships with other people on the basis of trust – to open themselves to others. Interviews and surveys also show that there is a higher degree of trust in the framework of a network of collective action. There is a sense of being committed to each other, which is based on sharing the same values and defending common interests. Activists co-operate with one another and each expects others to do what they are supposed to do. This is true even if money is involved; it is not rare for activists to contribute personal resources for common action. As far as common identity is concerned, we find evidence of a growing sense of community bringing people together on the basis of a feeling of having been deceived (in Russian, *obmanuty*) by state power, having been treated unfairly. And this motivation – the struggle for fairness and equity – becomes a very strong one. Most of the leaders talk about their sense of having more responsibilities and obligations than rights towards the activists, which also reveals their eagerness to be considered trustworthy.

But trust becomes especially important and needs to gain in generality when the network is growing, enlarging to embrace new participants and establishing durability. At that stage we could define trust as an expectation that all network members will respect the same rules. It is a sense of a community of interests, rules and norms. This is far from evident because of the informal character of rules inside activist networks, and even more because of the uncertain and unfair character of the general social rules of Russian society such as they are realistically perceived by the majority of the population. A good criterion to identify the existence of such trust (as engagement in a co-ordinating structure of durable collective action) is the extent to which people from the initial group or groups are keen to open themselves to new participants and to discuss with them the rules of their interaction, eventually to adapt and change the rules in order to satisfy everybody. It involves risks: you do not know the new entrants very well; you have no common experience of interaction. What does our study show in this respect? It seems that initiative groups and pre-existing networks act in different ways in facing the need to enlarge.

It is worth noting that some trends are already becoming visible although the survey has been undertaken only for the past two years. In 2006, when I first wrote about new social movements in Russia,[25] networks and co-ordinating structures were at the fledgling stage and were very weakly differentiated; problems of internal regulation and enlargement were not very visible. A year later, we observe the conflicts arising within and between groups and organizations. This evolution is quite understandable, given the continued development of activist networks. On the eve of several regional and national elections they became an object of competition between some leaders and some organizations – the primary stage of institutionalized political parties.

Demarcation lines follow two criteria: conditions of enlargement and regulation of power relationships. They give way to internal and external conflicts. As far as enlargement is concerned, conflict pits network leaders against one another and divides regional or thematic co-ordinating structures. To exaggerate demarcation as being understandable, we can say that those leaders who are attached to their leader status (they usually have formal titles such as 'president' or 'chairperson') are far less eager to invite new participants, seeing them as a threat to their status. And if they do accept new entrants, for example under other members' influence, they refuse to change anything in the way the co-ordination structure is functioning.

In contrast, more open-minded leaders are working to recruit new members and to enlarge the network to new groups. One of them declared an attempt to 'play the role of a social integrator' through building networks. And they do try to change the rules in order to make networks more attractive to new entrants. In most cases their strategy can be explained by their strong authority among the target groups and also among the initial group's members. They have a good reputation in larger segments of the population and have more social capital than leaders defending their position inside the initial group. Their authority is linked less to formal status, and more to personal qualities, good reputation and an approved way of acting.

In the same way, open-minded and monopolistic leaders differ where power relationships are concerned and the question of control is at stake. The more open ones defend democratic positions in the sense that they express the need to make people full citizens, to activate them or, to use a stronger term, to empower them. They used such phrases as 'we work in order to waken the population', 'we help people only if they help themselves first', 'we try to help people in self-organizing'. And observation of their activist practices shows that they do indeed try to act in such a way, helping to build initiative groups, organizing micro-collective actions, building links between different groups, founding new thematic movements and so on. As a result they really succeed in instilling confidence into rank-and-file activists, which is a key point for the building of a new model of power relationships.

Leaders of the second kind present logical arguments for controlling and managing their organization or network. They say they represent the organization, have to take care of its durability and are waiting for loyalty and respect from members because of their leadership. This attitude is closer to the model of hierarchical power than to that of collective empowerment. Even closer is the attitude of other political organizations trying to take control of new activist networks. Competition is intensifying around new networks and many political parties such as the RKRP, the Yabloko Party (headed by Grigorii Yavlinskii), or the OGF (United Citizen Front), a political organization founded by the former chess champion Garry Kasparov. They act by introducing divisions into existing networks, offering services and help to some leaders or key activists, and publicizing and agitating on behalf of their organization. The main objective in these cases is recruitment of new members at the expense of new activist networks, rather than the growing mobilization of the whole population. These organizations have abundant resources of many kinds – material, political, administrative, informational – and this poses a threat to less resource-rich activist networks. They are also more formally and bureaucratically organized, which means they can count on discipline and propose that their members rely on the party or the leader rather than on themselves and self-organization, which can be attractive to many new participants not very keen to engage in an everyday struggle. So this scheme tends to reproduce the dominant model of power relationships – relying on passive loyalty to an empowered leader, and delegation of power in exchange for service provision. It is worth noting that in some cases these political organizations have settled an alliance with some network leaders for whom the defence of status is at stake.

We have not mentioned other parties closer to institutionalized power such as the Communist Party of the Russian Federation or the governing party United Russia because they have totally embraced the dominant model of imposed power and deal with citizens' initiatives only if they can entirely control them. It should be noted that state power is now struggling with these initiatives in order to deprive them of autonomy, as was very clearly illustrated by the state officials' reaction to the second Social Forum in Saint Petersburg on the eve of the G-8 summit in July 2006. The government first consented to provide the right for activists of social movements to organize their forum in the Kirov stadium so that it could appear to be democratic. In reality it can be considered the most massive repression operation undertaken in post-Soviet Russia. Hundreds of activists were arbitrarily controlled by the police, thrown out of the trains, and jailed on false pretexts; some of them were beaten. Such repressive activities demonstrate one side of the 'official' policy towards these movements. The other side is the attempt to orchestrate them; the governor of the Saint Petersburg region came to visit the forum, the president proposed holding a meeting with the forum's organizers, and the media were told that the government was pleased to help 'anti-globalists'. This is important to note because it confirms the thesis that state power is not at all interested in the emergence of autonomous citizens' initiatives. So the new social movements could represent a potential challenge for the maintenance of imposed power.

Conditions for the Emergence of 'Democratic'-style Leaders

Our examination of the importance of leaders and the way in which they exert their leadership highlights further complexities of power that prompt us to extend the analysis. If the social and political context favours 'informal arrangements', egoistic behaviour or subordination to imposed power, not only does the emergence of social movements appear problematic – a socio-logical enigma which we partly examined above – but also the existence of leaders who defy this model of power relationships. It is thus necessary for us to try to understand where leaders come from, and what pushes them to act contrary to dominant norms. The question is: how do certain people, who obviously have a strong personality, engage in collective contestation (rather than, for example, in pursuing their individual professional careers) and take the responsibility of leadership while sharing their power, and how does their engagement pass the test of time?

The most effective method for this type of investigation is the biographical inquiry, which we have so far carried out with a very restricted number of leaders. In spite of the difficulty of this type of incursion into the private life of activists more eager to discuss their public life, it is necessary for us to continue this approach, as some theorists of social movements have attempted to do.[26]

On the basis of data available at this stage, we can already identify certain characteristics common to 'democratic-style' leaders:

1. They appeared or were confirmed in their capacity as leaders on a wave of mobilization, which means that they were recognized as leaders by 'the street', by a group engaged in collective action. The first source of their authority (or leadership) is thus the 'people', people not abstract and remote but people in action and close (their 'social base' to use political vocabulary). It should be noted that this proximity, the source of the specific authority acquired by local leaders, also causes difficulty for the emergence of a larger-scale movement since it thwarts the appearance of federal leaders.

2. The initiative group or activists' network is the principal source of their public recognition. While the leaders in question can also depend on other organizations of which they are members or leaders (political associations or parties), these do not provide the recognition or the authority that the broader militant networks confer. It has also to be noted that the public recognition of these leaders is usually not limited to the grassroots militant groups alone, but goes well beyond. If indeed they can participate in public debates or carry out negotiations on an equal basis with representatives of institutionalized power, they owe it especially to the authority that the militant networks confer to them (not to their formal status, personal contacts or material resources).

3. The leaders in question are made emotionally dependent on their social base by common struggle, successes celebrated collectively and failures endured in 'tightening the elbows'. In the interviews, the leaders lose themselves readily in long, detailed and romantic accounts of one or another episode of collective action that has marked them. Talking about such episodes, their eyes sparkle and emotion intensifies; feelings of joy, pleasure and pride are apparent. Lastly, the experience of collective capacity-making seems a source of self-assertion. It is a discovery made by the individual, but also for and with others – a self-assertion that does not occur through adopting dominant standards (to make money or to obtain institutional position) but, on the contrary, through challenging standards. The longer engagement lasts, the closer are the links between leaders and the basis of their legitimacy, and the less leaders are tempted to choose another line of action and conform to dominant norms. A rupture of the emotional bonds can even cause a serious personal crisis.

4. Leaders of this type profit from an increase in their social capital. They are recognized by more and more people, on a local scale initially, then on a regional one and, very slowly, in some federal networks. They are respected and trusted. In return, as interviews show, they insist on their

right to deserve respect, to be worthy of confidence, which thus implies as many obligations as rights.

From this we can identify the fundamental conditions authorizing us to see in the power exerted by these leaders the premises of an alternative model of power relationships. First of all, the source of their power is *organized people in action*, defending their rights and becoming aware of their ability to do something together and therefore being able, in principle, to control the leaders. However, power does not seem to be an end in itself: it is engagement in collective mobilization, rather than power in itself, that makes sense. It is the capacity to make something together which progressively becomes the driving force of their engagement. It is the opening perspective of emancipation from the dominant power model, the opening of the door of social transformations.

The Unsolved Question: Possibilities of Institutionalizing a New Model of Power Relationships

While the new social movements represent a potential challenge to the existent power system, it does not mean that they are able to achieve their goals and to implement a new model of power relationships. We have seen some features of such a model, based on collective empowerment and general trust in the framework of collective actions. But we also pointed out the strong impact of structural conditions which prevent this alternative model from being implemented and, above all, institutionalized in stable and durable norms, rules and regular practices. The new activist networks based on trust and empowerment are supported mostly by rare leaders with a very strong personality and commitment to the cause of governance by the citizenry.

To sum up our argument, we can say that people engaged in activist networks show increasing distrust in institutionalized official power and increasing trust in each other only on the basis of their participation in the same collective actions. It is not a generalized trust in everybody and anything under all circumstances, which would be quite dangerous in the Russian context. It is a specific trust in other activists sharing the same commitment. It is a trust in the framework of collective actions. But it is far more than interpersonal trust in micro-groups of reciprocal or client-like help, far more than cliques.

Inside the activist networks people also gain confidence in themselves, in their ability to act and to have an impact on their environment, which is a determinant in the potential to challenge the imposed power model. They begin to trust people they did not know before participating in collective actions. They are confronted with other specific demands and interests, learn to pay attention to them and find a way to associate them with more general claims. So they experience a process of rising up to make more general demands on issues of importance to the citizenry. Through discussions and debates on the key demands of the movement's agenda, participants are slowly becoming politicised, in the sense that they are dealing with some kind of public or common good.

The main problem, as we have noted several times, is the precariousness of the process which is occurring in the very unfavourable context of a dominant model of imposed power relationships. The emergence of another model mainly depends on the leaders' commitment, and we have seen that they are already facing pressures and competition. The strategy of opening and empowering is quite risky in regard to the hierarchical and authoritarian model of most other organizations. This weakness could be balanced if activist networks produced rules of their own and tried to formalize them; that is to say, if they begin a process of institutionalizing their own model of power relationships, at least in the framework of activist networks. The process is occurring in some regions and within some thematic networks through the adoption of regulations or statutes. But almost everywhere the process faces strong obstacles and leads to internal conflicts. So at this stage the question of the possible institutionalization of an alternative model of power relationships remains wide open.

NOTES

1. Since the middle of the 1990s sociological polls show a constant high level of distrust towards other people in the society (at the end of 2006 about 74 per cent of respondents thought that 'with people you have to be careful' and only 22 per cent that 'people can be trusted', whereas in 1991 the corresponding proportions were 41 and 36 per cent): see Civil Chamber of the Russian Federation, 'O sostoyanii grazhdanskogo obshchestva v rossiiskoi federatsii 2006 g.' (On Civil Society in the Russian Federation in 2006), available at <http://www.oprf.ru/files/doklad.pdf>, accessed 21 Nov. 2007.

2. By social movements we mean every kind of collective action provided by any kind of networks which have a certain regularity, are sustained by some co-ordinating or organizational bodies and advance some general claims about social and political issues. We have especially been paying attention to two mass movements: the movement of pensioners against the reform of the social benefits system, and the movement of 'housing activists' in connection with the so-called 'communal' reform.

3. The data provided by the monitoring of collective actions and their observation is both quantitative and qualitative. It includes weekly statistics of the number of collective actions and participation in them (arranged thematically according to the field of protest), observation reports on activists in action – in a meeting, conference, demonstration and so on (which can be matched with the activists' discourses), and self-reflection on experiences of participant observation by several sociologists who are at the same time activists (observer participants).

4. From summer 2002 to summer 2003 only 9 per cent of the respondents took part in any form of collective social actions, and from 1989 up to 2003 only 27 per cent. Figures are from FOM (Fond 'obshchestvennoe mnenie': Public Opinion Foundation), VTsIOM

(Vserossiiskii Tsentr Izucheniya Obshchestvennogo Mneniya: Russian Public Opinion Research Center), Levada Centre, cited by Vladimir Rimski, 'Tseli i motivy politicheskogo i obshchestvennogo uchastiya rossiiskikh grazhdan' (Purposes and Motivations for Russian Citizens' Political and Social Participation), Foundation INDEM (Information Science for Democracy), 2007, at <http://www.strategy-spb.ru/partner/files/rimskyi.pdf>, accessed 21 Nov. 2007. See also monthly press releases of the Levada Centre about the social and political situation in Russia, at <http://www.levada.ru/press.html>. However, in the past few years we can observe a growing number of participants in collective actions, especially in winter 2005. In January–February 2005 some 500,000 people participated in massive demonstrations across Russia for the defence of the social benefits system. It was the most massive social upheaval in the past decade. Afterwards, protest actions and other non-institutional forms of citizens' mobilization happened more frequently, but at a micro-level. Monitoring of collective action conducted by IKD shows an average of about 10,000 participants per week in collective actions from the beginning of 2006 to March 2007. The problem is that except for the 'pensioners' upheaval', sociological polls are not able to fix such a micro-sociological phenomenon as the growth of scattered collective actions on a lesser scale. Their data show a maximum of 1–3 per cent of the population being involved in protest actions. The only way to catch the trend is to choose activist networks as a preferential polling target. An attempt to do so can be found in Sergei Patrushev (ed.), 'Sotsial'nye seti doveriya, massovye dvizheniya i instituty politicheskogo predstavitel'stva: opyt 'starykh' i 'novykh' demokratii v usloviyakh globalizatsii' (Social Networks of Trust, Mass Movements and Institutions of Political Representation: Experience of 'Old' and 'New' Democracies), research paper (Moscow, Institute of Sociology, Russian Academy of Sciences, 2007).

5. See his introduction to the present collection, entitled 'Putting Administrative Reform in a Broader Context of Power'.

6. Levada Centre, 9 April 2007, 'Doverie institutam vlasti' (Trust in Power Institutions), at <http://www.levada.ru/pres/2007040901.html>, accessed 21 Nov. 2007.

7. Sergei Patrushev (ed.), *Institutsional'naya politologiya* (Institutional Political Science) (Moscow: Russian Academy of Sciences, 2006).

8. 13 Sept. 2006. 'Otnoshenie k presidentu V. Putinu' (The Relation to President V. Putin), in *Social'no-politicheskaya situatsiya v Rossii v avguste 2006 goda*, at <http://www. levada.ru/press/2006091302.html>, accessed 21 Nov. 2007.

9. Karine Clément, 'Formal'nye i neformal'nye pravila: kakov optimum?' (Formal and Informal Rules: What is the Optimum?), in Vladimir Yadov (ed.), *Stanovlenie trudovykh otnoshenii v postsovetskoi Rossii* (Moscow: Academicheskii Proekt, 2004), pp.135–92.

10. Richard Rose, 'What Does Social Capital Add to Individual Welfare? An Empirical Analysis of Russia', *Studies in Public Policy*, No.318 (Glasgow: University of Strathclyde, 1999).

11. Aleksandr Khlopin, 'Grazhdanskoe obshchestvo ili sotsium klik: rossiiskaya dilemma' (Civil Society or Cliques: Russian Dilemma), *Politiya*, No.3 (1997), pp.5–26.

12. Rose, 'What Does Social Capital Add to Individual Welfare?'

13. For information on the European Social Survey, see <http://www. europeansocialsurvey. org>, accessed 26 Oct. 2007.

14. Albert O. Hirschman, *Exit, Voice, and Loyalty: Responses to Decline in Firms, Organizations, and States* (Cambridge, MA: Harvard University Press, 1970).

15. For more factual information about these movements see Karine Clément, 'La contestation de gauche et les mouvements sociaux émergents' (Paris: CERI, 2006), at <http://www. ceri-sciencespo.com/archive/mai06/artkc.pdf>, accessed 27 Oct. 2007.

16. Doug McAdam, *Political Process and the Development of Black Insurgency. 1930–1970* (Chicago, IL: University of Chicago Press, 1982).

17. Charles Kurzman, 'Structural and Perceived Opportunity: The Iranian Revolution of 1979', in Jeff Goodwin and James M. Jasper (eds.), *The Social Movements Reader: Cases and Concepts* (Oxford: Blackwell, 2003), pp.38–48.

18. Ibid., p.112.

19. Pierre Bourdieu, 'Le capital social. Notes provisoires', *Actes de la recherche en sciences sociales*, Vol.31 (Jan. 1980), pp.2–3.

20. Russel Hardin, 'Conceptions and Explanations of Trust', in K.S. Cook (ed.), *Trust in Society* (New York: Russell Sage Foundation, 2001), pp.3–39.
21. Piotr Sztompka, *Trust: A Sociological Theory* (Cambridge: Cambridge University Press, 1999).
22. Ibid., p.22.
23. Ibid., p.69.
24. Eric M. Uslaner, 'Producing and Consuming Trust', *Political Science Quarterly*, Vol.115, No.4 (2000), pp.569–90.
25. Karine Clément, 'Poyavlenie novykh sotsial'nykh dvizhenii v Rossii' (The Emergence of New Social Movements in Russia), in Patrushev (ed.), *Institutsional'naya politologiya*, pp.229–64.
26. David Croteau, William Haynes and Charlotte Ryan (eds.), *Rhyming Hope and History: Activists, Academics and Social Movements* (Minneapolis, MN: University of Minnesota Press, 2005); Richard Flacks, 'Knowledge for What? Thoughts on the State of Social Movement Studies', in Goodwin and Jasper (eds.), *The Social Movements Reader*, pp.135–53.

Time Matters: Adapting to Transformation

RICHARD ROSE, WILLIAM MISHLER
and NEIL MUNRO

Time is the dimension in which ideas and institutions and beliefs evolve.
Douglass C. North[1]

The transformation of a political system is an event compressed into a short span of time: by comparison with the *longue durée* that led to democratization in Western Europe, the break-up of the Soviet Union occurred very abruptly. By contrast, adapting to the consequences of transformation can be a lengthy process. It takes time for subjects to learn about the strengths and weaknesses of the new regime and time to unlearn much that was taken for granted in the old regime. Yet it need not take generations. Former subjects of communist regimes in Central and Eastern Europe, including three former Soviet republics, have adapted to living under a democratic system of government within the European Union. Within a decade and a half after 1945 Germans socialized into Hitler's Third Reich had learned to adapt to the democratic institutions of the Federal Republic – and their parents had to learn even more quickly to adapt to the Nazi regime. We are now a similar length of time from the transformation of the Soviet system.

How and why have Russians adapted to political transformation? Unlike changes in political leadership in established democracies, changes in the Kremlin from Mikhail Gorbachev to Boris Yeltsin and Vladimir Putin have been part of a pervasive triple transformation of polity, economy and society. Even if a Russian chose to ignore news from Moscow, he or she could not ignore its consequences in many aspects of everyday life from working to shopping and viewing television. In the time that has passed since the Soviet Union disappeared, Russians have had to alter their behaviour or risk becoming marginalized in a post-transformation society.

In order to consolidate support for their authority, the leaders of a new regime, whether democratic or autocratic, want its subjects to adapt by giving support, or at least resigned acceptance, to the political system that they supply.[2] In any one year, variations may be accounted for by individual differences in social structure, economic circumstances or political attitudes, or by a combination of all three. However, an understanding of the dynamics of popular response to a new regime cannot be gained by testing rational choice or other theories of support for the regime at a single point in time, for both historical and national contexts matter.[3] Empirical evidence about public opinion is required for how popular attitudes develop during the critical early years from the launch of a new regime.

This study explains how support for the new Russian Federation regime has developed as Russians have learned to adapt to the consequences of transformation. It does so by drawing on a unique source of evidence, 14 nationwide New Russia Barometer (NRB) sample surveys conducted by the Centre for the Study of Public Policy from January 1992 to January 2005 with an average of just under 2,000 respondents (see Table 1). Because the New Russia Barometer repeats the same questions over more than a decade, it can test how Russians adapt their economic, political and social attitudes

TABLE 1
NEW RUSSIA BAROMETER SURVEYS SINCE 1992

	Date	Number of respondents	Context
I	1992 26 January–25 February	2,106	Start of Russian Federation
II	1993 26 June–22 July	1,975	Inflation high; no constitution
III	1994 15 March–9 April	3,535	After first Duma election
IV	1995 31 March–19 April	1,998	Relatively uneventful
V	1996a 12–31 January	2,426	Between elections
VI	1996b 25 July–2 August	1,599	After presidential election
VII	1998 6 March–13 April	2,002	Just before rouble devaluation
VIII	2000a 13–29 January	2,003	Between elections
IX	2000b 14–18 April	1,600	After Putin's first election
X	2001 17 June–3 July	2,000	Relatively uneventful
XI	2003a 12–26 June	1,601	End of Putin's first term
XII	2003b 12–22 December	1,601	After Duma election
XIII	2004 18–23 March	1,602	After Putin's re-election
XIV	2005 3–23 January	2,107	Relatively uneventful
	Total respondents	28,155	

and behaviour and how this in turn alters the support given to the new regime. Evidence of individual attitudes can test hypotheses that seek to explain individual responses as a reflection of positive incentives – households see their material circumstances as better or their new regime as granting them more freedom or are resigned to accept it as a lesser evil compared with other alternatives or simply because the longer the new regime remains in place the lower are expectations that it could be replaced and the more it is taken for granted as 'the only game in town'.[4] Analysis of the NRB data with multi-level hierarchical modelling statistics shows that time matters: the cumulative effect of the progress of the years leads Russians to adapt to the new regime whatever their political, economic or social characteristics.

The Changing Level of Support for the Present Regime

David Easton, who initially developed the concept of political support, defined it in very general terms as, 'A (the citizen) orienting himself favourably toward B (the regime)'.[5] This definition emphasizes that support is a state of mind. However, if it is to sustain the institutions of a regime, it must also lead to compliant behaviour. Individuals must learn new values and forms of behaviour if they are to support the new regime, and adaptation is likely to be more difficult if the new regime is not what people would like or requires a major shift or inversion of previous values and attitudes. Those who withhold support must adapt to being marginalized politically without attracting sanctions from the new regime. If a new regime is to survive, it requires subjects to comply with whatever it defines as basic political laws and avoid activities that it regards as challenges to its authority or punishes as crimes against the state.[6] In the absence of widespread popular support, a new regime is likely to invest substantial resources in political surveillance and intimidation of potential opponents and propaganda designed to create support or at least produce passive acceptance. In Soviet times, there were an estimated 12 million persons engaged in ideological work to boost support for the regime[7] as well as an elaborate internal security network.

Easton's definition of support is clinical rather than normative; there is no assumption that support can only be given to democratic regimes. The very detailed index of his 507-page study of political support lists only five references to democracy. This gives the term broad contemporary relevance, for many member states of the United Nations today have regimes that are autocratic rather than democratic. Not only does history offer many examples of undemocratic regimes achieving substantial support, but also contemporary surveys show a substantial measure of support for regimes in countries that are, at most, only partly democratic.[8]

Variable Support for the Regime – Within a Year and Across Time

To achieve a political equilibrium, the new regime must have a measure of popular support. This can be justified on a variety of grounds. People can positively value it; believe it is preferable as a lesser evil; or are resigned to accept it as the only government they can expect to have for the indefinite future. The level of political support at any given point of time is less important than how support is changing – and in what direction. In so far as a new regime has little or no reserve from habits of the past, losing support from one year to the next invites ambitious politicians to come forward with an alternative regime and mobilize support to replace the incumbent regime. As long as a new regime is gaining popular support, this discourages those who initially had doubts or preferred an alternative from endorsing regime change and can gradually lead to a steady-state equilibrium. Before either outcome is arrived at, support can fluctuate.

Since regimes can alter abruptly while the population does not, transformation raises questions about the extent to which public opinion changes when institutions change. If the values and beliefs of the public are fixed in youth and early adulthood, as theories of political culture and socialization postulate, a change of regimes will create a gap between what new rulers supply and what most subjects regard as normal and desirable. On the other hand, if elites create a new regime in accord with public opinion, then a high level of support can be promptly forthcoming. This has happened in East European countries, where a Moscow-imposed regime was replaced by a national

regime accountable to a national electorate. However, in Russia the collapse
of the Soviet Union was an unwelcome shock.

Current theories of democratization confuse support for democracy as an
ideal with support for current regimes, whether they are democratizing or not.
However, endorsement of the democratic ideal is not the same as the evaluation of a system of government as it actually is. Although very positive
about democracy as an ideal, the average Russian regards the new regime
as halfway between a democracy and a dictatorship.[9] Thus, the New Russia
Barometer takes a realist approach: it asks respondents to evaluate the
regime that political elites have actually supplied. People must accept or
reject it as it is – a package supplied by elite politicians. Like most political
packages, the institutions of a new regime are a mixture of attractive and unat-
tractive parts. Evaluating it is like voting in a referendum: a person can only
endorse or reject what is on offer, or abstain.

In established democracies the difference between a regime as a set of
durable institutions and the government of the day is not so easy to distinguish.
However, political transformation gives concrete significance to differences
between types of government, since it involves a very public change
between regimes. The New Russia Barometer measure makes use of this
fact. It first asks respondents to evaluate the pre-perestroika regime, which
was the regime that adults lived under longer, and then the present regime.

Q. Here is a scale for ranking how the political system works. The top,
+100, is the best, and the bottom, −100, is the worst. Where on this
scale would you put:

(a) The political system before perestroika?
(b) Our current system of governing?
(c) The system of governing we will have in five years?

The present regime is defined ostensively, that is, by pointing at what is there;
this avoids the use of a label that can be disputed, such as calling the system
democratic. Ostensive definition also avoids linking a system of government
to transient personalities, as is the case with American references to the
Bush administration or British references to the Blair government. The question avoids confusing institutions of the regime with its outputs, as happens if
people are asked about satisfaction with the performance of government,
which can be interpreted as referring to how well the government of the
day is managing the economy.

The NRB scale gives equal weight to negative and positive alternatives.
The scale is intentionally long to capture the intensity of respondents' feelings;
people can express 100 per cent approval or 100 per cent loathing. The scale
also captures important differences of degree between those who are

lukewarm or very enthusiastic in support for a regime. It also differentiates between those who are somewhat critical and those who are 100 per cent against the current regime. The mid-point for evaluating the regime, 0, is the psychological as well as the arithmetic mid-point. An individual can choose it if he or she has a neutral attitude or no opinion about the regime.

When the first New Russia Barometer went out in the field, the Russian Federation was four weeks old. While the old regime was gone, the new regime was a blank. The new regime started off with a big majority of Russians disliking it: 74 per cent gave it a rating between −1 and −100, 12 per cent had no opinion, and only 14 per cent showed positive support (see Figure 1). Statistically, this implied that the new regime's support could only rise from a low base. However, politically it implied that the new regime was vulnerable to collapse. Across the years, Russians have continuously been divided about support for the regime and aggregate support has fluctuated. By 2001 a plurality of Russians were positive about the new regime, and after the presidential election of 2004 a high point was reached when 65 per cent were positive. However, a year later support fell to 48 per cent.

FIGURE 1
TREND IN SUPPORT FOR NEW REGIME
Q. Here is a scale for ranking how our system of government works. The top, plus 100, is the best; the bottom, minus 100, the worst. Where on this scale would you put our current system of governing?

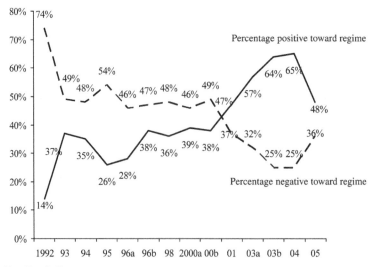

Source: New Russia Barometer surveys.

Since the NRB measure of support is a scale, the mean rating of the regime provides a second way of monitoring aggregate trends. With the passage of time, the central tendency of Russian public opinion has moved from being negative to neutral. In 1992 the mean rating of the regime was −38. It then began to rise, that is, to become less negative (Figure 2). Even though 64 per cent were positive about the regime in 2003, the tendency was to give it lukewarm endorsement: the average rating of the regime was only +14 on a scale that ran as high as +100. However, by 2005 the mean level of support had fallen back to 0, the exact mid-point of the scale.

While the mean rating of the regime tends to hover around the neutral mid-point, most Russians are not neutral. Russians voicing positive support tend to be counter-balanced by Russians who are negative about the regime. The extent to which Russians differ is summarized by the standard deviation, indicated by vertical bars in Figure 2. In every NRB survey there has been a wide dispersion of Russian opinion: the standard deviation has been as high as 55 points and never lower than 41 points. In the first NRB survey, when public opinion was most negative, two-thirds of Russians gave responses within the range −79 to +2. When the level of support was highest for the current regime in the twelfth NRB survey, two-thirds were between +61 and −34.

While Russians consistently differ about support for the new regime, there is no polarization between extreme supporters and extreme opponents. In the first NRB survey, when the greatest proportion of Russians were negative about the new regime, only 5 per cent gave it the worst possible

FIGURE 2

WIDE DISPERSION IN SUPPORT FOR NEW REGIME

Q. Here is a scale for ranking how our system of government works. The top, +100, is the best; the bottom, −100, the worst. Where on the scale would you put our present system?

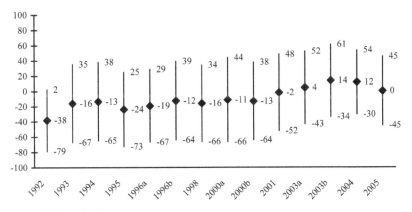

Source: New Russia Barometer surveys.

score of -100. In 2004, when support was highest, less than 1 per cent gave it the highest possible rating. The distribution of evaluations is bell-shaped; the largest proportion of Russians tend to be closer to the mean of the year than to the extreme ends of the scale. Thus, Russians are best described as tending to be moderately supportive or moderately negative about the regime.

Statements that Russians support or reject the new regime are misleading: in nine NRB surveys the median respondent has been neutral. There have only been two years in which an absolute majority of NRB respondents has been negative about the regime and three years in which a majority has been positive. However, neutral subjects are consistently the smallest of the three blocs of opinion.

A notable proportion of Russians have been floating supporters or opponents of the regime, sometimes endorsing it, sometimes being negative and sometimes voicing neutral opinions. For example, when the proportion of Russians with a positive attitude rose from 14 to 37 per cent between 1992 and 1993, this implied that a majority of those registering support had been neutral or negative the year before. The shift from 74 per cent negative about the regime in 1992 to 65 per cent positive in 2003 indicates that more than half those who had earlier been negative had subsequently switched their views. These calculations treat net and gross change as the same, assuming that every changer moves in the same direction. Panel studies that re-interview the same individuals several times find that a significant percentage of voters change their views.[10] This suggests that over the medium term a very large proportion of Russians float between supporting and being negative about the regime.

An important political implication of floating supporters is that people who are negative about the regime at one point in time are not necessarily implacable opponents of the regime: sometimes they favour it, sometimes they oppose it and sometimes they are neutral. The opposite is equally true of people who express support at a given time. Individuals who are intermittently positive and negative are more likely to show resigned acceptance of a regime rather than organize opposition to it. Thus, instead of generalizing about what all Russians think about their regime, we need to understand what makes Russians change their mind about it from time to time.

Multiple Equilibriums of Regime Support

A political equilibrium reflects a balance between the institutions supplied by the political elite and the support given in response by its citizens. As Peyton Young[11] emphasizes, 'Equilibrium can be understood only within a dynamic framework that explains how it comes about (if in fact it does)'. If changes offset each other by pushing with equal force in opposite directions, then a steady-state equilibrium is created. For example, an individual may be unhappy with the economic consequences of transformation but appreciate gains in freedom and in aggregate the dislike of a new regime by older Russians may be offset by support from the younger generation.

Steady-State and Dynamic Equilibriums

The dynamics of regime support involve shifting between periods of a steady-state equilibrium and periods in which that equilibrium is challenged, because the determinants of support change in ways that cause the level of support to deviate from what has been its average level.

A steady-state equilibrium is not static. The absence of movement is the result of a tension between a variety of forces pushing in opposite directions. For example, a thermostat maintains a room at a constant temperature by pushing up heat or air conditioning to offset a change in its ambient temperature. It is misleading to regard a long-established democracy as being stable, in the sense of unchanging. Young criticizes the tendency of neoclassical economics to concentrate exclusively on 'the way the world looks once the dust has settled'. He argues: 'We need to recognize that the dust never really does settle – it keeps moving about, buffeted by random currents of air. This persistent buffeting by random forces turns out to be an essential ingredient in describing how things look on average over long periods of time.'[12]

Sooner or later an abrupt and often unexpected challenge punctuates a steady-state equilibrium.[13] Dynamic challenges are those so strong that they cannot be met by routine responses that keep support fluctuating within its normal narrow boundary. To maintain support over a long period of time, governors must make changes that alter but do not disrupt core institutions of the regime. Governors can respond with measures intended to achieve a restoration of the regime as it was before, or reforms meant to alter the regime a little while retaining support; or the response can unintentionally lead to the disruption of the regime.

The greater the challenge to reform, the greater the risk of the disruption of a seemingly steady regime. The mobilization of tens of thousands of East Germans in demonstrations in early autumn 1989 is an example of a dynamic challenge going 'over the top' and leading to transformation. Likewise, Mikhail Gorbachev's structural reforms in the Soviet regime rapidly escalated into a struggle between advocates of alternative regimes and then the destruction of the Soviet Union.

A society cannot live forever in a state of transformation. The leaders of a new regime require some political support to be effective or else risk lawlessness verging on anarchy. If a new regime cannot collect taxes, it may print money, as Russia did in the early 1990s, but this created inflation, a new challenge to the regime. In an era of big government, subjects depend upon a new regime to continue providing such public services as water, rubbish collection, electricity, education, health care and public order.

The collapse of a regime is stark evidence that something was wrong with the way the country had been ruled. However, it does not mean that there is agreement about what was wrong. Even if there is agreement about faults of the old regime, this is insufficient to create a consensus in favour of what should replace it. Whereas the path of a steady-state regime tends to be predictable because it depends on what went before, transformation disrupts that path: the only certain prediction is that the future will not be the same as the past. To say that the leaders of a new regime choose either a democratic or an autocratic system grossly overstates their freedom of choice. Founders of a new regime cannot undo what went before. What is not in a legacy can also be a problem. Russia lacked the 'usable democratic past' that was an asset in building democracy in post-1945 Germany.[14] Because a new regime is in an unsteady state, governors must act in order to survive. However, they have little or no basis for anticipating what the consequences of their choices will be, singly or interacting with each other. An analysis of choices facing Russia's leaders in the early 1990s estimated that there were literally thousands of ways in which the institutions of a new regime could influence each other.[15] In such circumstances, leaders can only learn how to make the new regime survive by acting, observing feedback and learning from this process of trial and error.

Transformation undermines old beliefs about what can be taken for granted and forces people to think afresh about what government demands of them and whether to support it. The passage of time results in political re-learning, as experiences accumulate. Subjects learn from experience which expectations are met by the 'real existing regime' under which they now live, and which are not.[16] The longer a new regime persists, the more information subjects have about its political and economic performance. With the passage of time, the old regime and old ways of earning a living become more distant and less relevant. An individual who initially wanted the old regime to return can learn that this is unlikely to happen and become resigned to accept the new regime. Through feedback, attitudes and values supportive of the new system can gradually replace what had been learned before.

A new regime achieves an equilibrium of support when, as Juan Linz puts it, both governors and governed accept it as 'the only game in town'.[17] If this occurs, a new regime becomes path-dependent – but the path is not the same as before.

Hypotheses about the Dynamics of Change

While differences in public opinion are recognized in the great majority of social science theories, a variety of explanations are offered about why people differ. Culture and socialization theories stress the influence of youthful learning on the adoption of political attitudes. By contrast, institutional theories stress the primacy of the current performance of political and economic institutions. The two sets of theories can be reconciled in a lifetime-learning model of political attitudes, but they differ in the importance that they attribute to different categories of influence.

Culture and Socialization

> Hypothesis 1: Differences in regime support depend on what individuals learn from socialization into different roles in society.

Political culture theories postulate that, within a given society, socialization promotes homogeneous core values and Russians have often emphasized distinctive cultural values, citing historical experiences or even a Russian 'soul'.[18] However, Soviet society was divided in many ways, ranging from gender and age to education and material living standards. In the Russian Federation, a common history and political institutions have not produced a consensus in adapting to support the new regime or any single alternative. Moreover, re-socialization can be expected to vary according to early life experiences – for example, whether individuals received a higher or a minimal education. Better educated people ought to be better able to adapt to transformation than less well educated people.

At any given point in time, socialization experiences will differ substantially between generations. Older Russians have spent most of a long life giving positive or resigned support to the Soviet system. By contrast, younger adults were socialized when uncertainties about the old regime had become evident and the system that their elders had known all their lives could no longer be taken for granted. A critical question is the adaptability of Russian adults who have experienced a shift from one regime to another. In fact, adaptation has been occurring, albeit to a different degree, across all generations.[19] In 1998, when the Levada Centre first asked if people had adapted to the upheavals of the past decade, only 29 per cent had, and one-quarter hoped to do so in the near future. The largest bloc of Russians said they would never adapt. Russians underestimated their capacity for re-learning. By June 2006 an absolute majority, 61 per cent, reported that they had adapted to transformation and another fifth expected to do so in the near future.

Economics Matters

> Hypothesis 2: Differences in regime support depend on how individuals evaluate their household and national economic conditions.

Statements about the importance of economic conditions for politics raise the question: which economy? Is it the economy of the individual household or the national economy that is more important?[20] Standard micro-economic theories of behaviour assume that what counts is an individual's own economic circumstances as indicated by income measures. By contrast, macroeconomic theories emphasize collective concerns, such as inflation. Inflation is distinctive because enormous price increases tend to affect everyone in society similarly, whereas the benefits and costs of changes in the level of the Gross Domestic Product or unemployment have a differential effect on the population.[21] How these effects are evaluated depends not only on household circumstances but also on whether individuals favour a market or a non-market economy.

The costs of transformation, such as inflation and contraction of the economy, come before the benefits of economic growth and more consumer goods, implying that levels of support are not constant. If the key economic influence is the gradual and continuing growth of the national economy, this should lead to a gradual but steady increase in support. However, if the chief influence is the short-term cyclical fluctuation in economic growth rates, inflation and unemployment, this would cause support to fluctuate. In the course of time, calculations of costs and benefits tend to become ambivalent, since at one point many individuals are losing but at another they are beneficiaries from regime change.

Politics Matters

Hypothesis 3: Differences in regime support depend on individual values and the performance of political institutions.

Theories about the performance of institutions assume that individuals are always open to re-learning. Institutions can thus alter support whether they confer opportunities or obligations. Political performance can change more readily than institutions, for every government has policies that can go wrong unexpectedly, thus damaging the reputation of the party in power and, in a new regime, potentially reducing support for its institutions as well. Personalities at the top of government change, with implications for popular perception of government, for example the succession of Vladimir Putin to the presidency in place of Boris Yeltsin.

The evaluation of a given policy depends on individual values, and these vary: thus, Russians who favour democracy as an ideal are likely to evaluate 'get tough' measures of government differently from those who do not.[22] Political values also differentiate how citizens react to their new regime; the direction can reflect whether they are democratic, communist or nationalist. Individuals who value both freedom and order can none the less differ in the political priorities that they assign to the two. Because every subject of a new regime has lived under at least one other political system, this experience enables people to evaluate the current regime as better or worse than, or no different from, the old regime.

Testing Hypotheses Without Regard to Time

The conventional way to test hypotheses about popular support for a regime is to conduct a single survey and use Ordinary Least Squares (OLS) regression analysis to identify which of the above hypotheses is more strongly endorsed by the evidence. Doing so avoids simplistic stereotypes about all Russians thinking alike by determining what accounts for their differences. Pooling the results of all the New Russia Barometer surveys from 1992 to 2005, and weighting each year's set of respondents equally, avoids the risk of drawing inferences from a single survey (see Table 2) and helps clear the ground for a subsequent analysis in which time is taken into account.

The results not only confirm Hypothesis 2 – the economy matters – but also show that the element that matters most is the evaluation that Russians make of the current economic system (Beta: .55). A one-point change on

TABLE 2
SUPPORT FOR CURRENT REGIME: POOLED OLS REGRESSION

			Regime support variance explained: $R^2 = 44.4\%$	
	b	se	BETA	sig
Economy				
Pro current economic system	.53	.02	.55	.000
Household better off in past	−2.22	.68	−.06	.001
Satisfied household economy now	1.28	.97	.03	.183
Pro old economic system	.03	.03	.03	.236
Destitution	.15	.15	.02	.328
Number of consumer goods	−2.63	3.19	−.02	.410
Pro lots of goods in market	.37	.84	.01	.661
Politics				
More freedom now	5.73	1.09	.10	.000
Perception of corruption	−5.53	1.13	−.09	.000
Approves president	.49	.12	.07	.000
Democracy desired	.50	.32	.03	.117
Govt. fair, responsive	.73	.90	.02	.416
Trust political institutions	−.03	.11	−.004	.820
Pro old regime	.002	.02	.002	.940
Social structure				
Subjective status	1.18	.71	.04	.095
Education	−.75	.61	−.02	220
Age	−.06	.05	−.02	.242
Female	1.60	1.65	.02	.332
Ethnic Russian	−1.23	2.30	−.01	.592

Source: New Russia Barometer surveys; surveys pooled, 1992–2005.

the 201-point scale for evaluating the current economy alters the evaluation of the current political regime by half a point. Equally striking, the evaluation a person makes of their household's economic situation has little or no significance. Likewise, whether the family tends to be destitute or has lots of consumer goods does not influence support for the current regime. The importance of macro- as against micro-economic conditions is further underscored by the fact that the evaluation of the old economic system and a popular preference for an economy with lots of goods and high prices rather than a shortage economy also have a minor influence. In short, Russians judge the political system by how it manages the national economy rather than how it influences their own family's economic situation.[23]

Among the seven political indicators included in the OLS regression, three achieve statistical significance. The most important is the perception of being freer now than in Soviet times (Beta: .10). The impact is much less, however, than the rating of the national economic system. The second major political influence has been the perception of corruption (Beta:−.09). Approval of the president also increases support (Beta: .07). Neither trust in political institutions, which is very low, nor the desire for democracy registers a significant influence on support for the current regime (Table 2). Likewise, none of the five social structure influences entered in the pooled OLS regression achieves statistical significance.[24]

The above regression analysis gives a clear picture, but the dynamics of popular support can be inferred only by interpreting results in terms of if–then statements in the form 'if independent variable X changes by amount Y, then this will cause regime support to change by amount Z'. However, this assumes that all other conditions remain constant, whereas the passage of time justifies the opposite assumption: conditions influencing support for the regime do *not* remain constant.

The Influence of the Passage of Time

Time Matters

> Hypothesis 4: Differences in regime support depend on how long the new regime has been in place and when individuals make evaluations.

The passage of time produces political inertia, a moving force that can steadily affect support for the regime from one month to the next. At the start of a new regime, none of its subjects will have been socialized to support it. However, the longer it is in place the more pressure is put on adults to adapt, whether because of a regime's positive achievements or on the pragmatic grounds that it is better to join than to fight the system. The passage of time is also likely to lower popular expectations that regime change is possible and thus reduce support for alternatives. Socialization theories emphasize a different point, that the influences that have the strongest effect are those that come early in the process of transformation. If political benefits are perceived first, such as a gain in freedom, its effect will make subjects ready to bear subsequent economic costs. However, because economic costs of transformation come before mass benefits, according to the theory of populist myopia this sequence immediately places support for the new regime in jeopardy.[25]

Cumulatively, political inertia *creates* path dependence. Whatever happens early in the life of a new regime 'locks in' institutions and interests that fix a path that both elites and subjects then follow, because of the political costs of subsequently making major alterations.[26] The longer a new regime can survive, the more difficult it will be for advocates of alternative regimes to disrupt it and introduce an alternative regime. This then becomes an incentive for opponents of the regime to accept it.[27] Moreover, as long as the new regime retains the loyalty of the security services, those who are deemed its opponents can be subject to harassment, imprisonment or exile.

Because time is a characteristic common to all respondents within a survey, introducing the year of a survey as an independent variable in OLS regression is inadvisable, because it biases aggregate-level standard errors, thus inflating estimates of their significance. However, this can be done by turning to multi-level modelling (MLM), a statistical procedure that corrects the standard errors associated with higher-level variables. MLM is often used to control for the effect of geographical context when comparing respondents in different countries. It can equally be used to 'place' individual respondents at the particular month and year of an NRB survey and determine any interaction between the aggregate measure of time and individual-level variables.[28] By doing so it avoids the OLS regression assumption that relationships between independent variables and regime support are constant across time.

Hypothesis 4 postulates that time can have both direct and indirect influences on regime support. Hierarchical modelling makes it possible to test the extent to which the passage of time cumulatively increases support for the current regime or decreases support for alternatives.[29] At the individual level, attitudes toward the old regime may have a different impact on support when memories of the old regime were fresh in 1992 than a decade later, while measures of current performance may increase in influence over time as individuals gain experience of the new regime.

Passage of time increases support for the current regime

Taking into account the passage of time significantly improves our understanding of how popular support for the Russian regime has been changing since its launch in 1992. An MLM model that includes major influences identified in the OLS regression produces a very large pseudo-R^2 accounting for 42.7 per cent of the variance in support for the current regime. Moreover, it identifies both the direct and the indirect influence of the passage of time (see Table 3).

Political inertia has a major impact on regime support. Impact – the amount of change in the 201-point scale of support – is represented statistically by the Restricted Maximum Likelihood (RML) coefficient (b). The coefficient appears to produce a small change of 0.25 of a point in a month. In the course of 12 months, political inertia creates a three-point increase in support and, as the years pass, the cumulative impact becomes increasingly larger. By the beginning of 2005 it adds 40 points to mean support for the current regime (see Figure 3). Russians who were initially positive become more so, those neutral become positive, and the intensity of negative feelings toward the regime is reduced.

The passage of time has an indirect influence, too, changing the impact of some variables on regime support, as the initial b coefficient for individual-level effects is steadily modified by the b coefficient of a cross-level interaction term. The conjoint effect may reinforce the initial impact of an influence on support, or reduce or even reverse the direction of influence.

TABLE 3
SUPPORT FOR CURRENT REGIME: MULTI-LEVEL MODEL ADDING TIME

	Regime support variance explained: pseudo $R^2 = 42.7\%$		
	b	se	P
Individual level			
Economy			
Pro current economic system	.47	.02	.000
Economic system in five years	.10	.02	.000
Politics			
Democracy desired	1.7	.15	.000
More freedom now	2.6	.32	.000
Approves president	2.6	.32	.000
Perception of corruption	−1.6	.12	.000
Pro old regime	−.07	.02	.005
Aggregate level			
Passage of months	.25	.02	.000
Cross-level interactions			
Corruption x month	−.04	.00	.000
Democracy desired x month	−.01	.00	.001

Source: New Russia Barometer surveys. Only significant variables included in MLM to preserve degrees of freedom.

FIGURE 3
IMPACT OF POLITICAL INERTIA ON REGIME SUPPORT

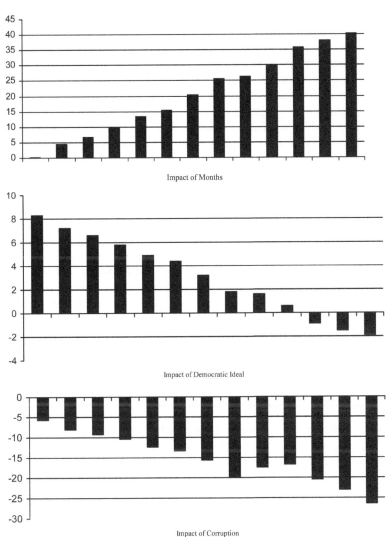

Source: New Russia Barometer surveys.

Corruption provides a striking example of the indirect importance of time. Since a large majority of Russians consistently see the regime as corrupt, its influence on regime support was statistically but not substantively significant in the pooled OLS regression analysis (Table 2). However, the multi-level model shows that with the passage of time corruption has increasingly influenced regime support, and its influence has been negative (Figure 3). As Russians have become more accustomed to their new regime, they have also become less tolerant of its corruption.[30] Whereas corruption reduced support for the current regime by only six points in 1992, it pushed regime support down by 26 points in 2005. Because the positive effect of the passage of time is independent of other influences, it is a countervailing force on economic and political influences that depress regime support.

The desirability of democracy and time interact in opposite directions. Over the period as a whole, Russians who view democracy as desirable have tended to be positive about the new regime. Initially, commitment to the ideal of democracy boosted support for the current regime by eight points net of all other influences. However, the MLM analysis shows that the longer Russians have experienced the performance of the present regime, the less inclined are those who value democracy to support it. The trend that started under President Yeltsin has continued under President Putin. Thus, by the 2003 NRB surveys, those committed to democratic ideals have been less likely to support the regime (Figure 3).

Although most significant influences on regime support are not affected by political inertia, their impact does alter if Russians change their views from one year to the next, thus altering the mean used to calculate the impact of an independent variable. Evaluations of the current economic system are the most important example, for not only is its impact on support great but also popular opinion of the national economy can go up or down from year to year. When the new economic system was at its worst, in 1992, this depressed regime support by 22 points net of all other influences. However, when economic evaluations improved in the following year, the negative impact was cut in half. Fluctuations have continued since; the impact of the economy became positive in 2004 but turned negative again in the following year (see Figure 4).

The influence of approval of the president on regime support reflects how popular the president is at a given point in time and not just who is president. It has gone up and down during the term of office of each president[31] (see Table 3 and Figure 4). During Boris Yeltsin's period in office, approval of the president boosted support for the regime by between eight and 11 points on the 201-point scale of regime support; during Vladimir Putin's time in office to date, his popularity in a given year has boosted regime support by 15 to 16 points.

The impact of freedom on regime support would fall if citizens began to take for granted gains since the end of the Soviet era; in addition, the greater role of the security services in the Putin administration could make Russians feel less secure. In practice, neither has happened. The appreciation of gains in freedom has been consistently high for more than a decade and its

FIGURE 4
IMPACT OF CHANGES IN INDEPENDENT VARIABLES ON REGIME SUPPORT

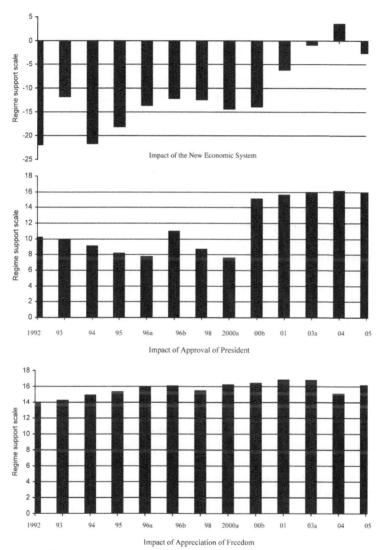

Source: New Russia Barometer Surveys.

impact on support for the current regime likewise has remained constant (Figure 4). Whatever the state of the economy or the behaviour of the Kremlin, the perceived gains in personal freedom have boosted support for the regime by 14 to 17 points.

Since regime support is the result of a multiplicity of pressures, the combined effect of steady and time-dependent influences is more important than that of a single influence. At the launch of the Russian Federation in 1992, support for the fledgling regime was extremely low and influences favouring the regime, such as an appreciation of freedom, were cancelled out by those that were negative, such as the evaluation of the national economy.

The development of a steady-state equilibrium of support has been primarily due to political inertia turning a new regime into a familiar fact of life. Between 1992 and 2005 the cumulative impact of political inertia increased support for the regime by 40 points while concurrently other significant influences have been pushing with more or less equal strength in opposite directions. Without the positive impact of inertia, support for the present regime in 2005 would have been about as low as it was in the early 1990s.

Whereas political inertia is a primary influence on support for the regime, the chief influences on the rejection of alternative regimes – democratic idealism, education and expectations of the suspension of parliament – are not affected, directly or indirectly, by the passage of time.[32] The steady rejection of alternative regimes by a majority of Russians is important in maintaining an equilibrium of support for the current regime. Their rejection provides a 'lesser evil' reason for accepting the existing system as the only one in town. However, projecting this conclusion into the future depends on all other conditions remaining equal or their combined impact cancelling out. This statement is a reminder that the political equilibrium of today could be disrupted in future if all other conditions do not remain equal.

Implications of Trajectories of Influence

Whether an equilibrium is democratic or autocratic, political leaders must watch out for challenges to the institutions that empower them. The question is not whether challenges to a regime will happen but when and how they will occur. A decade and a half after the launch of the Russian Federation, what *could* challenge the regime's equilibrium?

There can be no certainty that the impact of political inertia will remain the same indefinitely into the future, and there is a mathematical limit to its impact. Yet even if there is a gradual reduction in its impact before levelling off at a very high plateau,[33] its effect is likely to remain formidable. The continuing passage of time could indirectly give a continuing boost to regime support by reducing further the expectation of a change in regimes and thus increase resigned acceptance of the present regime – like it or not. The MLM analysis calculates that Russians more in favour of democracy as an ideal are now increasingly disapproving of the current regime. However, if this trend continues that does not mean that idealistic democrats will start demanding a change of regime, because idealistic Russian democrats are also much more likely to reject the alternative regimes on offer.

President Putin's repeated statements of the need to 'do something' about corruption show his awareness of this problem. However, the repetition of this exhortation calls attention to the obstacles to reducing corruption; thus, it would be unrealistic to assume that corruption will fall in the foreseeable future. Since corruption subtracted two points from regime support for every three points that political inertia added in 2005, it has a substantial potential to increase tension as its negative impact pushes against the positive impact of other influences. However, it is uncertain whether this negative pressure will increase in the future or whether Russians will become resigned to corruption as a continuing fact of life and its influence on their evaluation of the new regime will lessen.

Popular evaluation of the current economic system has a strong and variable influence on support. A major move up or down in popular evaluation of the economy can thus raise or lower regime support by upwards of ten points. Such movements are difficult to predict. Even if one assumes a lengthy period of economic growth and a greater diffusion of consumer goods in Russian households, trends that have been evident for half a dozen years or more, it does not follow that ordinary people will necessarily alter their evaluation of the system producing material benefits. It would be equally misleading to infer changes in individual attitudes from changes in aggregate economic statistics. Endorsement of the national economic system is *not* a simple reflection of growth in the Gross Domestic Product. After five years of economic boom, in 2005 only 41 per cent of Russians felt positively towards the system, 48 per cent were negative and 11 per cent neutral. On a 201-point scale analogous to that for support for the political regime, the mean score was −5.

The turnover of generations is steady: approximately one-fifth of the Russian population in 1991 has died; most were socialized politically in the time of Stalin. However, the total impact of generational turnover is often exaggerated. Four-fifths of the Russian adult population today consists of people for whom 'normal' politics was initially Soviet politics. It will not be until after 2020 that a majority of Russian adults will belong to post-Soviet generations and only after 2050 that almost all adults will do so. Furthermore, any extrapolation of generational trends is subject to the necessary qualification: all other conditions remaining constant. But this is not the case. Detailed cohort analysis shows that all age groups respond in the same way to changes in major political and economic influences on regime support.[34] The longer the span of time – and generational changes take many decades to register substantial effects – the more realistic it is to assume that the political and economic performance of the regime will *not* remain constant.

Journalists tend to treat each day's headline as an event that wipes people's minds clear of all they had previously learned. However, such a theory of 'instant re-socialization' implies that there will be as many changes in popular attitudes each year as there are major events and that each headline event will have its effect washed away by the next event. If this were the case, then the influence of any event would be transitory. Whether 'big bang' events have a major influence on the regime depends on the public's state of mind immediately before. In the case of the rouble crisis of 1998, Russians were extremely negative about both the economy and the regime in the NRB survey conducted in the spring of that year. Thus, the rouble crash served to confirm economic anxieties rather than being an event that redirected Russian opinion.

A rule-of-thumb test of a new regime reaching a steady-state equilibrium is that control of government changes hands twice without disruption.[35] The first turnover provides a public demonstration that the regime is different from the person or group that initially created it. A second succession reinforces this point. It also creates the expectation that subsequent successions will occur within the rules of the regime. Thus, the constitutional restriction of the president to two successive terms of office presents a challenge to Vladimir Putin to find a way to maintain not only his personal influence but also popular support for the regime that provides the base of his power.

Appendix

APPENDIX
CODING OF VARIABLES

	Range of codes	Mean	Standard deviation
Dependent variable			
Supports current regime	+100 best to −100 worst	−12.20	48.93
Political values & Performance			
Pro old regime	+100 best to −100 worst	23.77	54.21
Democracy desired	10 strongly favours democracy to 1 strongly favours dictatorship	7.23	2.57
Freedom now v.past Mean score for: religion, joining organizations, speech, political participation	5 much better now; 4 somewhat better now; 3 much the same; 2 somewhat worse now; 1 much worse now	3.74	.79
Govt. fair, responsive Mean score for: people can influence government, government fair	5 much better now; 4 somewhat better now; 3 much the same; 2 somewhat worse now; 1 much worse now	2.44	1.07

(Continued)

APPENDIX
CONTINUED

	Range of codes	Mean	Standard deviation
Trust in political institutions Mean score for: army, courts, police, Duma, parties	7 trust to 1 distrust	3.17	2.72
Approves President	10 approve to 1 disapprove	4.68	3.29
Corruption in government	4 almost all corrupt; 3 most corrupt; 2 less than half corrupt; 1 almost no corruption	3.23	.86
Economy			
Pro old economic system	+100 best to −100 worst	35.77	47.85
Pro current economic system	+100 best to −100 worst	−24.19	49.86
Satisfied household economy now	5 very good; 4 fairly good 3 neutral; 2 fairly unsatisfactory; 1 very unsatisfactory	2.27	1.06
Household better off in past	5 much better in past; 4 somewhat better in past; 3 much the same; 2 somewhat worse in past; 1 much worse in past	2.33	1.38
Destitution: Mean doing without: food, clothing, electricity	4 often; 3 sometimes 2 rarely; 1 never	2.34	1.82
Consumer goods: phone, car, colour TV, VCR	100 has all goods to 0 has none	47.68	31.59
Prefer lots of goods, high prices to controlled prices, shortages	4 strongly for lots of goods; 3 somewhat for goods; 2 somewhat prefers controls; 1 strongly prefers controls	2.53	.96
Social structure			
Age	Age in years	44.11	16.65
Gender	1 woman; 0 man	.55	.50
Subjective social status	5 highest to 1 lowest	2.00	1.43
Ethnic Russian	1 ethnic Russian; 0 other	.85	.36
Education	6 degree; 5 some university; 4 technical college; 3 academic secondary; 2 vocational; 1 less	2.91	1.44

NOTES

1. Douglass C. North, 'In Anticipation of the Marriage of Political and Economic Theory', in James E. Alt, M. Levi and E. Ostrom (eds.), *Competition and Cooperation* (New York: Russell Sage Foundation, 1999), pp.314–17 (p.316).
2. Richard Rose, 'Learning to Support New Regimes in Europe', *Journal of Democracy*, Vol.18, No.3 (2007), pp.111–25.
3. Joan Robinson, 'History versus Equilibrium', *Collected Economic Papers of Joan Robinson*, Vol.5 (Oxford: Oxford University Press, 1979), pp.48–58; Richard Rose, 'Political Behaviour in Time and Space', in Russell Dalton and Hans-Dieter Klingemann (eds.), *Oxford Handbook of Political Behaviour* (New York: Oxford University Press, 2007), pp.283–301.

4. Juan J. Linz, 'Transitions to Democracy', *The Washington Quarterly*, Vol.13, No.3 (1990), pp.143–64.
5. David Easton, *A Systems Analysis of Political Life* (New York: Wiley, 1965), pp.159ff.
6. Richard Rose, 'Dynamic Tendencies in the Authority of Regimes', *World Politics*, Vol.21, No.4 (1969), pp.612–28.
7. Vladimir Shlapentokh, *The Public and Private Life of the Soviet People* (New York: Oxford University Press, 1989), p.106.
8. Richard Rose and William Mishler, 'Comparing Regime Support in Non-Democratic and Democratic Countries', *Democratization*, Vol.9, No.2 (2002), pp.1–20.
9. Richard Rose, William Mishler and Neil Munro, *Russia Transformed: Developing Popular Support for a New Regime* (New York: Cambridge University Press, 2007), Figure 7.1.
10. Timothy J. Colton, *Transitional Citizens: Voters and What Influences Them in the New Russia* (Cambridge, MA: Harvard University Press, 2000), Ch.4.
11. H. Peyton Young, *Individual Strategy and Social Structure: An Evolutionary Theory of Institutions* (Princeton, NJ: Princeton University Press, 1998).
12. Ibid.
13. Frank R. Baumgartner and Bryan D. Jones, *Agendas and Instability in American Politics* (Chicago: University of Chicago Press, 1993), Ch.1.
14. Juan J. Linz and Alfred Stepan, *Problems of Democratic Transition and Consolidation: Southern Europe, South America and Post-Communist Europe* (Baltimore, MD: Johns Hopkins University Press, 1996), p.452.
15. Allen C. Lynch, *How Russia is Not Ruled* (New York: Cambridge University Press, 2005), p.173.
16. William Mishler and Richard Rose, 'Learning and Re-Learning Regime Support: The Dynamics of Post-Communist Regimes', *European Journal of Political Research*, Vol.41, No.1 (2002), pp.5–36.
17. Linz, 'Transitions to Democracy', p.156.
18. See, for example, Nikolai Berdyaev, *The Russian Idea* (New York: Macmillan, 1947); compare Peter J.S. Duncan, *Russian Messianism: Third Rome, Holy Revolution, Communism and After* (London: Routledge, 2000).
19. William Mishler and Richard Rose, 'Generation, Age and Time: Patterns of Political Learning during Russia's Transformation', *American Journal of Political Science*, Vol.51, No.4 (2007), pp.822–34.
20. Donald Kinder and D.R. Kiewiet, 'Sociotropic Politics: The American Case', *British Journal of Political Science*, Vol.11, No.2 (1981), pp.129–61.
21. Richard Rose, 'What Is the Demand for Price Stability in Post-Communist Countries?', *Problems of Post-Communism*, Vol.45, No.2 (1998), pp.43–50.
22. Ellen Carnaghan, 'Thinking about Democracy: Interviews with Russian Citizens', *Slavic Review*, Vol.60, No.2 (2001), pp.336–66.
23. For more details, see Rose *et al.*, *Russia Transformed*, Ch.8.
24. More than 40 different indicators from New Russia barometer surveys were initially tested for their potential influence in OLS regressions. The many found lacking in influence were discarded in order to focus on the most important results, including the theoretically significant null finding of social structure and household economic circumstances lacking influence on support for the present regime.
25. Susan C. Stokes (ed.), *Public Support for Market Reforms in New Democracies* (New York: Cambridge University Press, 2001), pp.9ff.
26. Paul Pierson, *Politics in Time: History, Institutions and Social Analysis* (Princeton, NJ: Princeton University Press, 2004), Ch.1.
27. See Rose *et al.*, *Russia Transformed*, Table 9.2.
28. Marco R. Steenbergen and Bradford S. Jones, 'Modelling Multilevel Data Structures', *American Journal of Political Science*, Vol.46, No.1 (2002), pp.218–37; Stephen W. Raudenbush, and Anthony S. Bryk, *Hierarchical Linear Modelling: Applications and Data Analysis Methods*, 2nd edn (Thousand Oaks, CA: Sage Publications, 2002).

29. Because the NRB surveys were conducted at different times of year, time is measured in months in order to ensure that it is an equal-interval measure for calculating its effect. Since NRB XIII did not have a full set of independent variables, it is omitted from the regression analyses; this does not affect the measurement of the passage of time.

30. To calculate the interaction effect of the passage of time, the monthly interaction coefficient must be multiplied by the number of months since the start of the Russian Federation and the product added to product of the coefficient for the independent variable and its mean value. In Table 3, the b coefficient for corruption (-1.64) measures its initial impact, when the mean level of perceived corruption was estimated at 3.50 on a four-point scale; the effect of corruption on support was thus $-1.64 \times 3.5 = -5.7$. In each subsequent month the interaction term of $-.04$ is added; thus, in month two it is -1.68 and so forth. Thus, even though in month 161 the level of perceived corruption was only slightly less, 3.28, the passage of time made the effect of corruption on support much larger, -26.5 points.

31. William Mishler and John P. Willerton, 'The Dynamics of Presidential Popularity in Post-Communist Russia', *Journal of Politics*, Vol.65, No.1 (2003), pp.111–31.

32. See Rose *et al.*, *Russia Transformed*, Table 9.2.

33. When and whether this will happen is the subject of a new CSPP research project on testing the durability of Russian regime support in response to the challenge of presidential term limits. The British ESRC is funding four additional NRB surveys in the period 2007–9. For up-to-date details, see <http://www.abdn.ac.uk/cspp>.

34. Mishler and Rose, 'Generation, Age and Time'.

35. Samuel P. Huntington, *The Third Wave: Democratization in the Late Twentieth Century* (Norman, OK: University of Oklahoma Press, 1991), pp.266ff.

Law in Public Administration: How Russia Differs

PETER H. SOLOMON, JR.

A core attribute of the concept 'law-based state' (*Rechtsstaat*; *pravovoe gosudarstvo*), as well as most versions of the 'rule of law', is the subordination of government officials to law (*pravo* or *jus*) in both the creation and the application of legal norms. At a minimum, officials must abide by the positive law or legislation (*zakony* or *leges*) of the state they serve, and according to some versions of the rule of law they face further constraints from natural law and human rights. The purpose of this subordination is to guard against arbitrary action or tyranny on the part of officials and to protect individual liberty.[1]

According to conventional wisdom, Russia (and most post-Soviet countries) have not had and still do not come close to this ideal. In the late Soviet period, according to Eugene Huskey, the USSR or Russia failed to observe the normal hierarchy of legal norms. That is, all too frequently regulations (or instructions) took precedence over legislation and might not conform with it. An observer of Hungarian bureaucracy in the same period asserted that East European communist governments had 'rule-creating' bureaucracies rather than 'rule-observing' ones, and that this characteristic made them not only powerful but also 'deviant'. Moreover, in post-Soviet Russia, at least, officials were thought both to make and to apply rules not in a universalistic way, but in the service of particular interests – their own, of their agencies, or of outside groups.[2]

These empirical generalizations contain more than a little truth, but understanding them requires both perspective and specification. To begin, this essay explores the baselines against which Russian realities are to be assessed. It will argue that public administration in modern democratic governments such as the United States and the United Kingdom does not meet the requirements of the law-based state. On the one hand, the prevalence of delegated legislation and the importance of regulations generated by officials renders invalid the traditional image of officials as appliers of laws. On the other hand, the travails of the implementation of most policies and laws, as well as the force of informal institutions and practices, give officials considerable power and often the capacity to shape policy apart from the law, despite efforts made to constrain them and hold them accountable. In short, the commonly assumed normative baseline for evaluating the actions of Russian officialdom is unrealistic.

The challenge remains to determine what it is that distinguishes the conduct of officials in Russia (and the post-Soviet space) from their counterparts elsewhere. This study goes on to present a series of illustrative examples from Russia (and Ukraine) of how officials in recent years have determined the meaning of laws and policies through the exercise of power (discretion) in the course of implementation. Finally, with these examples as background, the essay provides a general analysis of the behaviour of officials in Russia and a tentative explanation of how and why it seems to differ from that of officials in the West.

Legislation and Regulations in the Modern State

The traditional top-down view of democratic governance assumes that legislation sets both goals and the means for their achievement, leaving officials marginal discretion in developing operating documents and the actual process of implementation. Already in the late nineteenth century Arthur Venn Dicey, a major proselytiser for the rule of law in the United Kingdom, worried lest the administration of the welfare state should turn officials into legislators and leave them unaccountable to the courts (in part because of the latter's reluctance to guess the British parliament's intentions). For it was already clear that many agencies were created to effect a policy or programme and given rule-making powers for this purpose. They made discretionary decisions, and often combined legislative, executive and judicial functions in ways that offended the doctrine of separation of powers.[3]

During the twentieth century the phenomenon of 'delegated legislation' became widespread, for example in the United States in the design of the first regulatory commissions and again during the New Deal. The Congress of the United States passed laws that did not specify the crucial standards and operating procedures to be used in regulatory practices, but rather delegated their identification and development to particular agencies. Often, those agencies had the discretion to determine not only the content of relevant regulations but also the procedures by which they would be written and adopted. By the eve of the Second World War there was pressure to ensure that the production of crucial regulations by agencies of the executive branch or independent commissions was done in an open and fair way that enabled the voices of interested parties to be heard. This concern led to the Administrative Procedures Act of 1946, which not only set basic procedural standards for norm creation by agencies but also encouraged a new role for courts in assessing both the procedures used and ultimately the fairness of the results.[4]

This law and analogous ones in other countries made some difference, and arguably there is a place for more open procedures in the production of instructions by ministries and other agencies in the Russian Federation. At the same time, recent assessments of the relationship of laws to regulations in the West suggest that the latter are more important than ever. At the end of the twentieth century two specialists concluded that in the United Kingdom 'primary legislation has become a skeletal enabling framework conferring not just the functions of detailed implementation but the power to determine major policy questions on ministers'.[5] At the same time, the functions of government that are executed through secondary or tertiary rules grew exponentially. (Secondary rules are those generated by agencies with parliamentary authorization; tertiary rules are all the rest.[6])

Of course, it was possible that officials in the United Kingdom developed the various regulations in an open and fair manner and that their content normally reflected legislative intent. However, after a thorough examination of practice in the late 1980s and early 1990s, Robert Baldwin concluded that 'secondary legislation often lacks clear authorization, it is subject to weak systems of accountability and control, and the participatory rights of affected parties are often ill protected. These problems are all the more severe in relation to tertiary rules'.[7]

The British studies cited may present too uniform an image of delegated legislation. In contrast, a recent study of federal legislation in the USA by Epstein and O'Halloran suggests that there can be considerable variation in the amount of delegation across policy issues and in response to other factors. Thus, the Congress is least likely to leave details to officials when it can target benefits to particular constituencies, as is the case with distributive policies like taxation and social security. But policies that involve technical expertise or high levels of political risk often involve delegation, or what Huber and Shipan call 'deliberate discretion'. In their comparative study these authors associate the writing of detailed legislation with high levels of policy conflict and serious legislative capacity for drafting (not present in some countries). They found frequent delegation of rule-making to officials to be common in centralized or unitary states; in societies where there are high degrees of corporatism; and in civil law systems, where judges are less likely to review regulations.[8]

These studies make it clear that politicians or legislators often recognize when it is advantageous to leave the specification of operating details to officials. At the same time, interested parties, including industries subject to regulation and the officials charged with implementing regulation, typically prefer that legislative mandates remain vague, leaving the determination of crucial operational details to less visible negotiation, or what one observer calls 'bargaining in the shadow of the law'.[9]

In an admirable study reflecting broad and detailed knowledge of administrative practice in Britain and Israel, Margit Cohn adds to the traditional departures from legislative mandates a further set of practices that she calls 'fuzzy legality'. These include 'sweeping delegation', when legislation provides 'no true standards and operating instructions'; 'lop-sided mandates'; 'selective enforcement'; and the use of informal 'extra-statutory arrangements'. Furthermore, Cohn stresses that the regulators and the regulated alike prefer fuzzy legal arrangements precisely because they enhance their power or control over the situation.[10]

Even the rules that officials generate on the basis of delegated authority or fuzzy law face the subsequent challenge of execution, which, as we shall see, depends upon the interests and choices of the implementers. Sometimes, rules are not implemented much or at all; at other times they become objects of 'creative compliance', through which affected officials use legal means to avoid following the intent of a law without actually violating its content. In this situation, laws are not broken, but they are ineffective.[11]

The challenge in analysing public administration in developing or transitional countries is recognizing the extent to which observed phenomena are clones or cousins of counterparts in more developed countries, or instead special or unique. In the first post-Soviet decade the laws of the Russian

Federation were often not well written. To begin with, they frequently left key choices to administrators, and were described by Russian observers as *ramochnye zakony* (framework laws) or even as *skeletnye* (skeleton laws). Moreover, one law might contradict another, at the federal or regional level, or a presidential decree or government resolution, thereby enhancing the discretion of administrators and judges in their application. Certainly, regulations (*instruktsii*) remained of cardinal importance, as officials rarely applied laws directly.[12]

To what extent the regulations moved administrative practice away from legislative intent requires careful study. What is clear is that despite new requirements not all regulations were publicized; and that the process of making regulations was only partially transparent, despite efforts to improve rules on rule-making and strengthen screening of regulations by the ministry of justice.[13]

In short, for officials in Russia to have considerable rule-making power and discretion in the implementation of laws and rules was not unusual in the context of the modern state. To this regularity, however, one must add the dynamics of policy-making in Russia, informal practices, and even cultural dispositions in order to ascertain the distinctiveness of the Russian approach to law in public administration.

The Perspective of Officials: Policy Implementation and Informal Institutions

Operating with a legal paradigm, our inquiry has found that within established democracies government officials (as distinct from politicians) play a major role in determining what legislation comes to mean in practice. Two other paradigms or approaches – those of policy-making (from political science) and of informal institutions and practices (from anthropology and sociology) – reinforce this finding and give hints about factors that shape how officials perform in this role.

For at least a half century political scientists studying policy-making have identified *implementation* as a distinct phase of the process and as a phase that is inherently political. On the one hand, the officials and other actors charged with implementation activities, including rule-making, bring their own perspectives and interests to bear; on the other hand, other interested parties may seek to influence the officials involved in implementation.[14]

How easily and whether policies are implemented depends *inter alia* upon the number of separate actors involved in the process. When decisions must be implemented by many different officials within more than one administrative unit or hierarchy, the task becomes difficult. When the implementation of policies involves a federal system of government, where different levels of government have their own mandates and systems of accountability, the implementation of programmes becomes more complex. Both American and Russian experience illustrates this proposition, including a classic study of a federal programme in the United States. That study was called *Implementation. How Great Expectations in Washington are Dashed in Oakland; Or Why It's Amazing that Federal Programs Work at All.*[15]

The likelihood of difficulties in getting officials to co-operate in implementation – through inertia, lack of commitment, or opposition – increases with the novelty and scope of the policy. In particular, when a whole new direction or approach is involved – that is, an 'innovation' in policy – the policy process becomes more complex in all its phases. Some scholars picture an additional phase at the start, what is called 'agenda setting', a phase that comes before decision-making in both time and logic. Through or during agenda setting, traditional biases may be reinforced so that proposals for innovation are not considered, but sometimes new approaches and ideas become familiar and the demand for solutions to problems so acute that actors' thinking moves beyond the assumptions of the old paradigm. Agenda setting in this positive sense implies social learning. But even when this takes place, and the politics of the day lead to the adoption of innovations, implementation is far from automatic, for innovations are more likely to require that the officials implementing policy accept the new goals or approaches, not necessarily a precondition for adoption.

There is also the possibility that different groups, including officials, may support a particular policy innovation for different reasons, a fact that gains in importance during implementation. In a major study of the invention and rapid spread of probation and parole in the United States at the end of the nineteenth century, David Rothman shows that support for these alternatives to prison reflected an odd coalition. It included progressive-era reformers, convinced that the interests of rehabilitation required more than prison and prosecutors, and prison officials, who saw in these novelties potential management tools. For prosecutors probation represented a new basis for plea negotiation; for prison officials the prospect of parole represented an addition to the disciplinary arsenal that enabled them to keep order in the prison. In practice, neither parole nor probation met the expectations of reformers (in part because of under-funding), but both institutions were implemented as the officials had expected and in effect added to their *power*. In short, the political basis of the reforms included both the 'conscience' of reformers and the 'convenience' of officials, but in practice the latter loomed larger.[16]

The literature on policy-making and implementation declares loudly that the implementation of decisions often features conflict, especially if those decisions involve major changes in policy or the co-operation of many officials. It also assumes that those officials have their own perspectives, individual or agency-based, on the policies at hand, and that those perspectives will influence how they behave. The positions of officials may be based on many factors, not only inertia or self-interest but also their views of how best to accomplish the goals embodied in policy or even the appropriate hierarchy of values.[17]

How officials choose to react to new laws or policies that they are charged with implementing depends as well upon their connection to informal institutions and practices and the relationship of informal institutions to formal ones. Informal institutions include clientelistic networks, patronage systems and clans. They embrace the folkways and practices of people working in institutions (such as the US senate or police departments). They may serve to ensure that formal decisions and their implementation reflect the interests of powerful persons. Sometimes, informal institutions complement formal institutions and help them work well; at other times they compete with or serve as substitutes for formal institutions. Behind any set of informal institutions lie interests and power constellations that may be more important than those that support formal ones.[18]

Although informal institutions constitute an important part of the environment for government officials anywhere, they are especially prominent in the post-Soviet space. One reason is the Soviet legacy. The rigidity of the planned economy led already in the 1930s to the emergence of crucial informal institutions such as the *tolkach* (middleman) or *pripiski* (the de facto rules of accounting, entailing falsification). Later, with the emergence in the 1960s of a huge parallel economy, most of whose activities were technically illegal, further informal rules developed, for example about which officials needed to share in the profits. To a considerable degree, the private sector of the post-Soviet economy was based upon these rules, at least as a starting-point, including the principle that government agencies and officials had a right to a stake in profitable private enterprises.[19] Beyond inheritance, the post-Soviet economic transition, marked as it was by conflicts of laws and institutions that did not operate according to plan, led inexorably to a whole set of new informal practices, including an extensive system of *krysha* (private protection) and ways of hiding assets and employees so as to limit tax liability.[20] Electoral politics bred its own set of informal practices designed to enable powerful figures to manipulate the process. For a time, realities of economy and polity alike diverged so greatly from the formal institutions and laws that critics saw a 'virtual economy' and 'virtual politics' at play.[21]

In addition, the penetration of corruption into public administration often involved patterns so predictable as to constitute informal norms or institutions. Ethnographies of bribe giving and bribe taking can supply relevant details.[22] Often payments constitute a type of service fee to get an official to do what he or she normally would be required to do, or to do it promptly. Other payments, for example to obtain appointments (say, as teachers), came only on top of having the appropriate qualifications. But payments might also serve wholly inappropriate goals, such as getting a judge to rule in one's favour.[23]

In the Russian government, as in more established governments, the realization of laws is in the hands of officials, themselves responsible for necessary rule-making as well as the application of rules. Like their counterparts elsewhere, officials in Russia are influenced by their interests, including those concerning power, which are in turn shaped by both formal and informal institutions. What differs is the nature of those interests and perspectives, as well as the institutions and practices that shape them.

Before exploring the orientations of officials and their sources, it is useful to examine briefly some examples of the implementation of laws in post-Soviet Russia.

Stories of the Perverse Implementation of Laws

We present *four* stories of the implementation of laws in Russia of the late 1990s and early 2000s. The laws involved: providing judges with guns for self-defence; the management of judicial careers; privatizing land; and the rules for bankruptcy. In none of these cases did the realization of the law match its apparent intent. There are examples of selective non-compliance, and of compliance that took a distorted form – virtual or manipulated to a greater or lesser degree. The reasons for imperfect implementation of the laws range from inertia to the exercise of power through informal institutions; creative compliance for the good of the cause; and selfish manipulation of the law.

Guns for Judges

On 20 April 1995 a new 'Law on the Defence of Judges, Procurators, and Police Officials' authorized the police to issue judges service revolvers (handguns) whenever they felt threatened. The 1992 Law on the Status of Judges (Article 9) had already given judges the 'right' to have guns issued to them by the police, but without further legal authorization this right remained on paper. But by 1995 a sizeable number of judges were experiencing threats from the criminal world. In that year alone there were registered: 16 attempts on the life or health of judges or court employees; 36 work-related threats; 37 incidents of serious material losses by judges; 8 fatalities (including suicides); 15 cases of theft of case files from courthouses; and 93 instances of damage inflicted on courts through arson or theft.[24]

Although the law gave local police the discretion to assess the validity of a request for arms, further normative acts encouraged the police to be more cautious in handing out guns than the original law suggested. For example, a resolution of the council of ministers supplied an official 'procedure' for issuing weapons to persons deserving government protection. It emphasized that the weapons were to be issued only on a temporary basis and in connection with an 'authentic threat'.[25] The heads of the council of judges who had promoted the law thought that judges would be issued guns easily, as a matter of right. But already in the council of ministers' resolution the bias had shifted against this.

A further issue inhibited police officials in the regions in implementing the law, namely the failure of legislators to fund it. In the absence of special allocations, the ministry of internal affairs proved unwilling to provide for their subordinates to purchase guns for judges or other state officials needing protection, and there were no signs of regional or republican governments stepping into the void with supplementary funding.

The caution expressed by the government, and the ministry's concerns about financing, ensured that as of 4 April 1997 no judges had received the weapons needed to protect their safety![26] This situation prompted the council of judges to issue a strong complaint to the government, which resulted in the issuing in December of a new government decree directing the ministry of finance to provide extra funds to the ministry of internal affairs to pay for guns for judges, which would in turn become federal property. The government also confirmed a new (and more demanding) set of procedures for the issuing of guns to judges, replacing earlier rules at the governmental and ministerial levels.[27] While settling the outstanding legal issues, the decree of December 1997 did not result in the receipt of guns by most of the judges who needed them.

Flash forward to December 2005. The security of judges remained just as serious a problem as it had been a decade earlier. During the year there had been more than 200 incidents (*chrezvychainye proisshestviya*) involving judges or members of their families, including one murder of a judge and 17 physical attacks, despite the establishment of bailiff guards at most courthouses. It turned out that in the ten years since the original law was adopted only 6 per cent of judges had been given service weapons, despite the persistent efforts of the council of judges. The situation led the judicial department in 2005 to send a request to the government for a special allocation of funds to purchase guns for judges, and reportedly the government agreed. The judicial department also requested that the ministry of the interior (MVD) establish a special unit for the security of judges, their families and courthouses, but this does not seem to have happened.[28]

The provision of guns to judges in the 1995 law received scanty implementation in its first decade, in part because of the absence of budgetary support, and in part because of quiet resistance by the government and police officials alike, who used implementing regulations to impose strict conditions on the handing out of weapons. To what extent relevant officials actually objected to the substance of the law is unknown, but their selective non-compliance clearly minimized its impact.

Managing Judicial Careers

One of the major achievements of judicial reform in post-Soviet Russia is the establishment of security of tenure for federal judges. According to the law on the status of judges (1992), judges could be removed from office only for cause and only upon a decision of the appropriate Judicial Qualification Commission (JQC), initially made up only of other judges. 'Cause' ranged from serious matters, such as a pending criminal charge, breach of judicial ethics, or falsification of court documents, to vague peccadilloes such as producing red tape, labour discipline infractions, and violations of the norms of material or procedural law. Decisions of regional JQCs were subject to review by the Supreme Qualification Collegium and ultimately the Supreme Court of the Russian Federation itself.[29]

Chairs of regional and district courts were excluded from membership of the JQCs, but they still exercised undue influence on their work, even after the commissions' membership was expanded in 2002 to include representatives of the public (one-third) and a presidential representative. Perhaps it was inevitable that most of the requests for the removal of judges would come from the chairs of courts, and many of these requests were well founded. Naturally, chairs had the discretion to decide when to warn their subordinates, and when to enter into formal proceedings. At the same time, it became clear that chairs could use the dismissal procedure against judges whose main offence was 'political immaturity', as shown by giving too many acquittals or refusing to co-operate in a case with a powerful intervener. In recent years this fate befell at least two judges on the Moscow city court and one from a district court, as two chairs of the city court used pretexts against them. (The tactic boomeranged, as two of the three, with the help of the media, became dissidents after losing their posts.[30])

Judges aspiring to promotion to a higher court, or appointment as a court chair, used to face scrutiny not only by their peers and by the central authorities but also by regional politicians, persons whom they might easily offend in the course of conducting cases. The changes to the law on the status of judges of December 2001 removed the regional legislature from the screening process, but on the informal level regional politicians could still intervene against a judge who displeased them. As review of nominations by the president's staff became more intense under Putin than it had been under Yeltsin (producing more rejections of candidates), so the president's representatives (*polpredy*) in the federal district were asked to comment on candidates. To do their jobs effectively these *polpredy* usually had close working relations with the regional governors, who could use the *polpredy* to give their views on judicial candidates.[31] In regions marked by power struggles, rival players might press for favourite candidates with the governor or the *polpred*.

In contrast to the story of providing weapons to judges, where the law was implemented in a minimal way, the provisions of the law on the status of judges relating to judicial tenure and promotion were fully implemented and worked as expected more often than not. The problem was the operation of informal institutions, namely the large (and arguably excessive) power of chairs of courts and the relationship between governors and *polpredy*. The result was that in practice the law operated imperfectly, so that non-conformist judges were not effectively protected and could be both denied promotion and released from their posts.

Land Redistribution in Eastern Ukraine

A particularly revealing study of officials' undermining of a policy or law in the course of implementation has been provided by Jessica Allina-Pisano.[32] The legal instrument was a presidential decree (from Leonid Kuchma) designed once and for all to accomplish the transfer of land ownership away from collective farms to capitalist entities, especially private farms. The collectives were to be transformed into private leasing companies and were expected to give individual farmers the right to lease plots of land that were unified (that is, not separate physically) and suitable for agricultural production. While the decree gave the impression of a firm policy of privatization, it contained the seeds of its demise by calling for 'the preservation, as far as possible, of the integrity of use of the land and assets of former collective agricultural enterprises by private entities'.

In the Kharkiv region, at least, farm officials managed to speak in support of the decree and at the same time implement it in a way that ensured that little redistribution or real privatization of land occurred. The handing out of shares was not tied to particular geographical locations, and often the collective farms were allowed to re-register as private entities before they engaged in leasing contracts, not to speak of dividing land into plots. Moreover, lacking any funds to visit more remote farms, agricultural officials in the city avoided first-hand contact. When the dust settled in March 2000 after a four-month campaign to implement the decree, only 3 per cent of the land had actually been separated and distributed.

It seems that the agricultural officials engaged in a form of creative compliance, that is conforming with the letter of the law while using their discretion to disregard its spirit and ultimate goals. They did this, as Allina-Pisano insists, not for selfish reasons (such as rent-seeking) but out of a genuine belief that local conditions required the continuation of the entities formerly known as collective farms. Only large private farms, with the traditional forms of organization, and certainly not the small farms deserted at the end of the 1920s, could ensure the continued viability of post-Soviet Ukrainian agriculture in the Kharkiv region. For Allina-Pisano the behaviour of the agricultural officials constituted *sub rosa* resistance and their implementation of the law more virtual than real. Maybe so. At the same time, it represented a classic example of officials pursuing the approach they thought best (policy and law notwithstanding) 'for the good of the cause' (*dlya pol'zy dela*) – that is, the real cause of local prosperity rather than the false god of liberal ideology supported by foreign investors.

The Russian Bankruptcy Law of 1998

In contrast to the earlier bankruptcy law of 1992, which was tilted in favour of debtors and involved complicated disincentives to starting proceedings (including the need to calculate the firm's value), the Russian bankruptcy law of 1998 favoured creditors. To start a suit, a creditor had merely to demonstrate that a debt of about $15,000 had not been repaid for three months. The creditor could approach a court directly, without having made a recent attempt to collect the debt. In turn, the law empowered the court to appoint an external crisis manager or bankruptcy administrator, who would take over the firm and not allow the original owners either to pay the debt or to dispose of assets for this purpose. Crucially, there were no provisions to ensure that the court-appointed bankruptcy administrator would be neutral and law-abiding. In short, the provisions of the new law represented a disaster waiting to happen.[33]

In the difficult economic context of 1998, when many firms suffered from the economic crisis, the conditions were in place for raider firms to use the bankruptcy law as an instrument for achieving hostile takeovers of other firms. Law-makers did not intend this result, and in 2002 they changed the bankruptcy law once again to make this abuse of process more difficult (changing most of the favourable conditions listed above), but for a few years bankruptcy suits constituted one of the favoured methods of hostile takeover. And there were many of them (800–1,000 a year), because there were still a lot of valuable assets that belonged to vulnerable players.[34] Vadim Volkov has described the process by which a firm could accomplish a hostile takeover under this law. Typically, the raider did not actually hold a debt from the victim, so it needed to hire intelligence officials to learn what debts were outstanding and join in an alliance with another firm or financial institution that would take over the debt. Then, the raider could approach a court, usually an *arbitrazh* court, to initiate proceedings and obtain a court order, often with the use of inducements, to impose new external management (whose make-up would be determined by the raider). With the order in hand the raider would use a paramilitary contingent (perhaps from its own security service) to overpower the security people of the target enterprise and install itself and the new management. If the raider had sufficiently good connections with government, it might arrange for further pressure on the former owners through the launching of criminal prosecutions against them.[35]

There were obvious flaws in the bankruptcy law of 1998 that contributed to its misuse and abuse, including the low financial threshold, the difficulty in avoiding a suit through paying the debts, and the absence of guaranteed neutral administrators. But equally important to the abuse was a series of informal relationships and arrangements, including payoffs to judges, procurators and various officials of regional and local governments. As Bill Tompson put it, 'the problem was less to do with the letter of the law than with the environment in which it was administered'.[36] It was the informal unwritten rules of business practices in Russian regions whose intersection with flawed legislation produced such unfortunate scenarios.

These four stories illustrate selective non-compliance (guns), virtual or creative compliance (land), partial but manipulated compliance (judicial careers), and fully manipulated compliance (bankruptcy). Differences notwithstanding, none of the four laws (or policies) enjoyed simple or successful implementation. This commonality may derive in part from the connection of all of them to post-Soviet transition, and the controversial nature (if not also radicalism) of the required changes. At the same time, it is well known that a significant portion of laws, presidential decrees, and government resolutions do not get implemented. It would be useful to identify examples of successful implementation of laws and policies, and determine why relevant officials acted in an appropriate way.

The Behaviour of Officials

In any government the relationship of officials to a new law or policy is determined in part by their interests and orientations toward the law or policy, which could be altruistic or selfish, personal or collective (that is, the interests of their agencies). At the same time, their ultimate conduct may be influenced as well by two other factors: career-related incentives and cultural predispositions, which may provide a check on officials' inclinations.

Career-related incentives may, of course, be positive or negative. Positive ones would include rewards (praise, pay raises, promotion) for a professional approach to the implementation of laws or policies. Officials should be encouraged to engage in universalistic, law-based decision-making in both the formation of bureaucratic rules and the application of laws and rules and to use their discretion in principled rather than in particularistic ways. Such encouragement could be direct and explicit, or implicit in the system of recruitment, reward and promotion. Weber assumed that this kind of behaviour was encouraged by a public administration that shared certain structural features, including merit-based recruitment, merit-based progression on a career in government, good salaries, encouragement of and rewards for education and professional skills; and a clear delineation of roles and functions of particular offices. These features would make state administration into a civil service that displayed professionalism, had high prestige, retained most of its staff, *and* also was governed by laws.[37] Negative incentives might include the penalties for a markedly different kind of behaviour, for example designing or applying rules to favour patrons in clientelistic networks. They might also include direct accountability, such as serious screening of draft regulations within either the executive branch or the legislature (review of administrative rule-making and decisions by courts).

It would appear that the development of a professional civil service can supply incentives for less clientelistic and more law-oriented conduct, but the shift from a patrimonial bureaucracy (where patron–client relationships dominate) to an authentic civil service is hard to achieve. The lessons of Western history suggest that it requires strong societal demands for the curtailment of corruption and establishment of universalistic behaviour, and determined representation of these demands by politicians operating in a competitive environment.[38] Even these conditions may not prove sufficient. A recent comparative study of the reform of post-communist civil services in Eastern Europe concluded that de-politicization of personnel policy had not occurred even in Hungary and Poland, with the result that few higher civil servants pursued careers in public service. The officials used their discretion in blatantly political ways, and both delays in reform and the failure to implement legislation were commonplace, if not also endemic.[39]

As of 2006 Russia was also embarking on civil service reform, at least in the federal government (with experiments in some regions). Under the direction of the ministry of economic development and trade (MERT) serious efforts had begun to introduce competitions (*konkursy*) for posts in government and a system of open and competitive tenders for government contracts. Conflict of interest provisions had appeared in the civil service legislation, and a broader administrative reform promised anti-corruption measures.[40] However, in general the projected administrative reform (which involved many compromises and began with rocky implementation) focused on rationalization of the allocation of functions and responsibilities and the adoption of a business-based approach to operations (New Public Management: NPM), and it was not likely to help with the project of encouraging rule-based behaviour.[41] In Russia, as in much of the world, 'administrative reform' valued efficiency over quality of performance, and it threatened to divert resources from developing a professional civil service.[42]

Not only incentives but also cultural predispositions may help shape how officials deal with laws and regulations. Cultural predispositions might include an ethos of government service that places a high value upon legality. This could be part of a commitment to stewardship of the public interest, or what Heclo and Frederickson each call 'the spirit of public administration'.[43] Officials might also be influenced by the value placed on law by society and societal expectations about the impartiality and fairness of the conduct of officials.

An in-depth study (using questionnaires and focus groups) of 113 middle managers in Russia (half centre, half regions) conducted in 1998 found a contradictory picture of their relationship to law. On the one hand, most of them understood and even valued morally sound and legally appropriate responses to difficult situations and claimed to value justice. On the other hand, most were cynical about the real state of law in Russia, viewing it as arbitrary and a tool of rulers that provided few safeguards for middle-level administrators or for citizens. For this reason, at least some of these officials were ready to compromise with principles when the situation demanded it. And there was a sense that in Russia law did not meet the standards necessary to elicit respect and habitual compliance.[44]

Moreover, the attitude of society as a whole towards the laws in Russia also had a negative colouration, displaying considerable cynicism.[45] To be sure, the public increasingly turned to the courts to solve problems, perhaps in recognition that for conflicts lacking political salience courts usually provided fair results. This included suits against allegedly illegal actions on the part of government officials, where members of the public had remarkable success.[46] At the same time, belief in the corruptibility of law and judges, especially by political power, remained strong, reinforced periodically by high-profile cases like such as that of Mikhail Khodorkovsky, former head of the Yukos oil concern. While the public might hope for legality in government, it did not expect or demand it, and continued to deal with government officials on the basis of relevant informal practices, including payment for services.

All this is to say that, while Russian officials might have strong consciences and understand what was fair, they found little support for law-based behaviour either from a shared professional ethos or societal expectations. There was too little of the 'spirit of public administration'. Nor, in Kathryn Hendley's words, was a public 'demand for law' sufficiently developed to make a strong impact on the conduct of officials.[47]

At this time, with civil service reform at an early stage and attitudes towards law among officials and in society still ambivalent or mixed, officials in Russia did not face strong incentives to act within the law or the cultural baggage that would make them feel guilty when they failed to do so. In other words, the natural tendency to be guided by their own orientations and interests in implementing laws operated *without countervailing checks or balances*! At the same time, the nature of officials' interests might well differ from what was typical in modern democratic governments. Instead of merely identifying with the needs of constituencies or allies in political sub-systems, officials might be tied to clientelistic networks and act with the expectation of personal gain.

This situation is unlikely to change significantly in the short run. The implementation of civil service reform, whatever its ultimate effects on the legal grounding of officials' behaviour, represented a huge challenge amounting to an innovation in policy. Civil service reform may generate resistance on the part of some officials, because it threatens to reduce their discretion or power. Likewise, changes in how officials and citizens alike relate to the law (and the courts) in Russia required corresponding changes in practice, including transparency of court operations and their coverage in the media and a more open and consistent approach to administrative rule-making: that is, the process of producing government resolutions and ministerial directives.[48] Even better would be a visible retreat by the political authorities from their traditional approach to law as an instrument of rule and the courts as subject to manipulation when needed.

A fundamental change in the authorities' approach to law might require a shift away from the relationship between state and society that has characterized most of Russian history. In the Russian tradition the state, as an extension of the ruler, and its interests and goals (be they conservative or transformative), take precedence over the needs of society. With this, state officials impose their power on society, rather than deriving that power from it.[49] In a perverse way, the idea of the priority of the state may justify condescension and even irresponsible actions on the part of officials vis-à-vis members of the public. To what extent officials in twenty-first century Russia actually have this mentality is a matter of speculation, which requires empirical confirmation.

Conclusion

As in Western democratic governments, so in the Russian Federation, legislation is often confined to generalities and delegates to officials the task of creating operational rules. In writing and applying these rules, officials east and west have considerable discretion, which they often use to pursue their own interests or preferences, however defined.

But there are crucial differences: (1) legislators in Western democracies are more likely to include operational details in legislation if they see political advantage in doing so; (2) in contrast to their Western counterparts, officials in

Russia writing or applying regulations face few constraints on the pursuit of self-interest, either from career-related incentives or from cultural predispositions; (3) the actual interests of Russian officials relating to power and policy are more likely to derive from informal institutions such as clientelistic networks; and (4), as a result, officials in Russia are more likely to impede or distort the implementation of policies through such techniques as selective non-compliance, virtual or creative compliance, and partial or fully manipulated compliance, examples of which were provided in the case studies outlined above.

Civil service reform (but not efficiency-oriented administrative reform) may help provide incentives for officials in Russia to respect laws, as may initiatives designed to improve public understanding of and support for the law.[50] However, in the short run informal practices, through which players apply, interpret and manipulate rules both formal and informal in origin, will continue to define the real world of Russian public administration.

NOTES

1. Brian Z. Tamanaha, *On the Rule of Law: History, Politics, Theory* (Cambridge: Cambridge University Press, 2004), esp. pp.64–5; Roberto Unger, *Law in Modern Society* (New York: Free Press, 1976), pp.47–86.
2. Eugene Huskey, 'Government Rulemaking as a Brake on Perestroika', *Law and Social Inquiry*, Vol.15, No.3 (1990), pp.419–32; Kalman Kulcsar, 'Deviant Bureaucracies: Public Administration in Eastern Europe and in the Developing Countries', in Ali Farazmand (ed.), *Handbook of Comparative and Development Public Administration* (New York: Marcel Dekker, 1991), pp.587–600.
3. Tamanaha, *On the Rule of Law*; Richard Cosgrove, *The Rule of Law: Albert Venn Dicey, Victorian Jurist* (Chapel Hill, NC: University of Northern Carolina Press, 1980), Chs.4 and 5.
4. See Martin Shapiro, *Who Guards the Guardians?* (Athens, GA: University of Georgia Press, 1988).
5. J.D. Hayhurst and P. Wallington, as quoted in Robert Baldwin, *Rules and Government* (Oxford: Clarendon Press, 1995), p.59.
6. Tertiary rules include guidelines, circulars, practice statements, and administrative rules: see Baldwin, *Rules and Government*, Ch.4.
7. Ibid., pp.300–302.
8. David Epstein and Sharyn O'Halloran, *Delegating Powers: A Transaction Cost Politics Approach to Policy Making under Separate Powers* (Cambridge: Cambridge University Press, 1999); John D. Huber and Charles R. Shipan, *Deliberate Discretion? The Institutional Foundations of Bureaucratic Autonomy* (Cambridge: Cambridge University Press, 2002).
9. Gunther Teubner, quoted in Margit Cohn, 'Fuzzy Legality in Regulation: The Legislative Mandate Revisited', *Law and Policy*, Vol.23, No.4 (2001), pp.469–97 (p.488).
10. Cohn, 'Fuzzy Legality in Regulation', pp.469–97.
11. Doreen McBarnet, *Crime, Compliance and Control* (Burlington, VT: Ashgate, 2004), Chs.11–14; Baldwin, *Rules and Government*, pp.185–9.
12. 'Problemy podgotovki i prinyatiya zakonov v Rossiiskoi Federatsii' (Problems of Preparing and adopting laws in the Russian Federation, unpublished (28 April 1997); 'Sovremennoe sostoyanie Rossiiskogo zakonodatel'stva i ego sistematizatsiya', Kruglyi stol zhurnala' (The State of Russian Legislation and its Systematization: A Journal Roundtable),

Gosudarstvo i pravo, No.2 (1999), pp.23–31, and No.3, pp.2–37 (material prepared by L.A. Morozova).

13. 'Ob utverzhdenii pravil podgotovki normativnykh pravovykh aktov federal'nykh organov ispolnitel'noi vlasti i ikh gosudarstvennoi registratsii' (On Confirming the Rules of Preparing Normative Acts of Federal Executive Agencies and their Registration), Postanovlenie Pravitel'stva RF ot 13 avgusta 1997 g. N.1009, available at <http://www.procurator.ru/zakon/library/z1009.htm>, accessed 1 July 2006; 'Raz'yasneniya o primenenii Pravil podgotovki normativnykh pravovykh aktov respublikanskikh organov ispolnitel'noi vlasti, ikh gosudarstvennoi registratsii opublikovaniya' (Explanation of the Application of the Rules of Preparing Normative Legal Acts of Republican Executive Agencies and their Registration and Publication), utv. Prikazom Ministerstva iustitsii RF ot 24 oktyabrya 2002 N 01-01/19, available at <www.tatar.ru/?DNSID=clelc9f4c03135c164f08a7ffe07224f&note_id=2045>, accessed 1 July 2006. See also Yu. G. Arzamasov, 'Vedomstvennoe normotvorchestvo kak tip yuridicheskoi deyatel'nosti' (Departmental norm-creation as a type of juridical activity), *Gosudarstvo i pravo*, No.9 (2006), pp.11–17.

14. This picture assumes that policies are adopted through a single decision (the rational model), but more frequently policies evolve through a series of decisions, at the political and bureaucratic level (the incremental model). Sometimes, one decision guides the rest, but not always. On the conceptualization of policy-making and development, see Peter H. Solomon, Jr., 'The Policy Process in Canadian Criminal Justice', *Canadian Journal of Criminology*, Vol.23, No.1 (1981), pp.5–25.

15. Jeffrey L. Pressman and Aaron B. Wildavsky, *Implementation. How Great Expectations in Washington Are Dashed in Oakland; Or, Why It's Amazing that Federal Programs Work at All, This Being the Data of the Economic Development Administration as Told by Two Sympathetic Observers Who Seek to Build Morals on the Foundation of Ruined Hopes* (Berkeley, CA: University of California Press, 1973).

16. David J. Rothman, *Conscience and Convenience: The Asylum and its Alternatives in Progressive America* (Boston, MA: Little, Brown, 1980).

17. See, for example, Paul A. Sabatier and Daniel Mazmanian, 'The Conditions of Effective Implementation', *Policy Analysis*, Vol.5, No.4 (1979), pp.481–504.

18. Gretchen Helmke and Steven Levitsky, 'Informal Institutions and Comparative Politics: A Research Agenda', *Perspectives on Politics*, Vol.2, No.4 (2004), pp.725–40; Vladimir Gel'man, 'The Unrule of Law in the Making: The Politics of Informal Institution Building in Russia', *Europe–Asia Studies*, Vol.56, No.7 (2004), pp.1021–41; Anna Grzymala-Busse, 'Informal Institutions and the Post-Communist State', unpublished ms (2004).

19. Joseph Berliner, *Factory and Manager in the USSR* (Cambridge, MA: Harvard University Press, 1958, esp. Chs.11 and 12; Stephen Shenfield, 'The Struggle for Control of Statistics', in James B. Millar (ed.), *Cracks in the Monolith* (Armonk, NY: M.E. Sharpe, 1992), pp.89–120.

20. Alena Ledeneva, *Russia's Economy of Favours: Blat, Networking and Informal Exchange* (Cambridge: Cambridge University Press, 1998); Alena Ledeneva, *Unwritten Rules: How Russia Really Works* (London: Centre for European Reform, 2001).

21. Andrew Wilson, *Virtual Politics: Faking Democracy in the Post-Soviet World* (New Haven, CT and London: Yale University Press, 2005); Clifford Gaddy and Barry Ickes, *Russia's Virtual Economy* (Washington, DC: Brookings, 2002).

22. Caroline Humphrey, *The Unmaking of Soviet Life: Everyday Economies after Socialism* (Ithaca, NY: Cornell University Press, 2002), esp. Ch.6; Federico Varese, 'Pervasive Corruption', in Alena Ledeneva and Marina Kurkchiyan (eds.), *Economic Crime in Russia* (The Hague: Kluwer, 2000), pp.99–112.

23. As used by political scientists, the term 'informal institution' implies a high degree of consensus about how actors are supposed to conduct themselves, which is not always present and may be hard to determine empirically. This difficulty led the sociologist Alena Ledeneva in a path-breaking study of post-Soviet politics and business to choose instead the term 'informal practices', which she understands as embracing the shifting ways that players handle both formal rules and informal norms. As a lens for discovering and recording 'how Russia really

works', the concept 'informal practice' enables her to explore core aspects of administrative and political reality in the Russia of the 1990s, but for comparative purposes I would not wish to abandon the term 'informal institution' as a way of referring to well-established informal practices that in reality have a normative component (albeit informal in nature). See Helmke and Levitsky, 'Informal Institutions'; Alena V. Ledeneva, *How Russia Really Works: The Informal Practices that Shaped Post-Soviet Politics and Business* (Ithaca, NY and London: Cornell University Press, 2006), esp. Ch.1.

24. Federal'nyi Zakon RF ot 20 aprelia 1995 'O gosudarstvennoi zashchite sudei, dolzhnostnykh lits pravookhranitel'nykh i kontroliruyushchikh organov' (On state protection of judges and officials of law enforcement and control organs), *Rossiiskaya yustitsiya*, No.6 (1995), pp.58–62. The data on physical attacks on judges, thefts from courts, and arson at court buildings come from 'Analiticheskaya spravka po chrezvychainym proisshestviyam v organakh yustitsii i sudakh Rossiiskoi Federatsii za period s 1994 po 1998 g. vklyuchitel'no' (Analytical Memorandum on Extraordinary Events in the Justice Agencies and Courts of the Russian Federation 1994 to 1998), unpublished ms (Moscow, 1999).

25. 'O poryadke vydachi oruzhiya litsam, podlezhashchim gosudarstvennoi zashchite' (Procedure for the issue of arms to persons subject to state protection), Postanovlenia poravitel'stva RF ot 17 iyulya 1996 g., No.831, *Zakon*, No.1 (1988), pp.21–2. This issue of *Zakon* collects normative materials (including ministerial regulations) on the ownership, sale and record-keeping of guns in the hands of private and public persons.

26. 'Postanovlenie Soveta Sudei RF ot 4 aprelya 1997', *Rossiiskaya yustitsiya*, No.7 (1997), pp.9–10.

27. 'O poryadke vydachi organami vnutrennykh del Rossiiskoi Federatsii sluzhebnogo oruzhiya sud'yam (s izmeneniyami ot 3 fevralya 1999 g.)' (Procedures for the issue of service weapons to judges by the organs of internal affairs of the Russian Federation, with amendments of 3 February 1999), 'Postanovlenie Pravitel'stva RF ot 18 dekabrya 1997 g. N 1575', at <http://zakon.kuban.ru/orug/pp%601575.htm>, accessed 14 Nov. 2007.

28. '"Masshtaby rastut, zadachi uslozhnyayutsya". Beseda glavnogo redaktora zhurnala 'Sud'ya' Vladimira Verbitskogo s general'nym direktorom Sudebnogo departmenta pri Verkhovnom sude RF Aleksandrom Gusevem' ('The Scale Grows and the Tasks get More complicated': A Conversation between the Chief Editor of the Journal *Sud'ya* Vladimir Verbitskii and the General Director of the Judicial Department Aleksandr Gusev', *Sud'ya*, No.12 (2005); 'O praktike vypolnenii trebovanii Federal Zakona ot 20 aprelyia 1995 goda No.45–FZ "O gosudarstvennoi zashchite sudei…" Postanovlenie Soveta sudei RF 122 ot 29 aprelya 2004 g.', at <http://www.supcourt.ru/oss_detale.php?id=429>, accessed 21 Nov. 2007; 'O vypolnenii Postanovleniya Soveta sudei RF ot 29 aprelya 2004 g. No.122 po obsepecheniyu nadlezhashchei bezopasnosti sudei…', Postanovlenie Prezidiuma Soveta Sudei RF ot 28 iunya 2005 g. No.78, at <http://www.supcourt.ru/print_page.php?id=2679>, accessed 21 Nov. 2007.

29. Peter H. Solomon, Jr., and Todd S. Foglesong, *Courts and Transition in Russia* (Boulder, CO: Westview, 2000), pp.55–8.

30. See Peter H. Solomon, Jr., 'Informal Practices in Russian Justice: Probing the Limits of Post-Soviet Reform', in Ferdinand Feldbrugge (ed.), *Russia, Europe, and the Rule of Law* (Leiden and Boston, MA: Martinus Nijhoff, 2007), pp.79–92.

31. See Alexei Trochev and Peter H. Solomon, Jr., 'Courts and Federalism in Putin's Russia', in Peter Reddaway and Robert W. Orttung (eds.), *The Dynamics of Russian Politics: Putin's Reform of Federal–Regional Relations*, Vol.2 (London: Rowman & Littlefield, 2005), pp.91–122.

32. Jessica Allina-Pisano, 'Sub Rosa Resistance and the Politics of Economic Reform: Land Redistribution in Post-Soviet Ukraine', *World Politics*, Vol.56, No.4 (2004), pp.554–81.

33. William Tompson, 'Reforming Russian Bankruptcy Law', *International Company and Commercial Law Review (ICCLR)*, No.4 (2003), pp.154–62.

34. Vadim Volkov, 'The Selective Use of State Capacity in Russia's Economy: Property Disputes and Enterprise Takeovers, 1998–2002', in János Kornai *et al.* (eds.), *Creating Social Trust in Post-Socialist Transition* (London: Palgrave–Macmillan, 2004), pp.126–47.

35. Ibid.
36. Tompson, 'Reforming Russian Bankruptcy Law', p.154; see also Frederique Daban, 'Hope and Bitterness in the Reform of Russian Bankruptcy Law', in Denis J. Galligan and Marina Kurkchiyan (eds.), *Law and Informal Practices: The Post-Communist Experience* (Oxford: Oxford University Press, 2003), pp.135–50.
37. James Rauch and Peter B. Evans, 'Bureaucratic Structure and Bureaucratic Performance in Less Developed Countries', *Journal of Public Economics*, No.75 (2000), pp.49–71.
38. Ari Hoogenboom, *Outlawing the Spoils: A History of the Civil Service Reform Movement, 1865–1883* (Urbana, IL: University of Illinois Press, 1962); Anna Grzymala-Busse, 'Political Competition and the Politicization of the State in East Central Europe', *Comparative Political Studies*, Vol.36, No.10 (2003), pp.1123–47.
39. Jan-Hinrik Meyer-Sahling, 'Civil Service Reform in Post-Communist Europe: The Bumpy Road to Depoliticization', *West European Politics*, Vol.27, No.1 (2004), pp.71–103.
40. 'O konkurse na zameshchenie vakantnoi dolzhnosti gosudarstvennoi grazhdanskoi sluzhby Rossiiskoi Federatsii' (On Competition to Fill Vacancies in the Civil Service of the Russian Federation), Ukaz Prezidenta Rossiiskoi Federatsii ot 1 fevralya 2005, at <http://document.kremlin.ru/doc.asp?ID26352&PSC=1&PT=1&Page=1>, accessed 14 June 2005; 'O gosudarstvennoi grazhdanskoi sluzhbe RF' (On the Civil Service of the Russian Federation), Federal'nyi zakon RF ot 27 iyulya 2004 N79-FZ, at <http://www.rg.ru/printable/2004/07/31/gossluzhba-dok.html>, accessed 21 June 2005; 'Kontseptsiya administrativnoi reformy v RF v 2006–2008' (The Conception of Administrative Reform in the RF, 2007–2008), Rasporyazhenie Pravitel'stva RF ot 25 oktyabrya 2005 n 1789-r.', in *Sobranie zakonodatel'stva Rossiiskoi Federatsii 2005*, No.46 (14 Nov. 2006); 'Ob organizatsii raboty po realizatsii Kontseptsii administrativnoi reformy v RF v 2006–2008 i plana meropriyatii po provedeniyu administrativnoi reformy v RF v 2006–2008 v Minekonomrazvitiya Rossii i podvedomstvennykh federal'noi sluzhbe i federal'nykh agenstvakh' (On Organizing the Realization of the Conception of Administrative Reform in the RF 2007–2008 in the Ministry of Economic Development and Trade and Subordinate Federal Agencies), Prikaz Minekonomrazvitiya Rossii ot 22 fevralya 2006 g.', unpublished but available at <http://pda.kadast.ru/upload/www/files/prikaz 48 220206.pdf>, accessed 31 Oct. 2007. On earlier attempts to reform the civil service, see T.V. Zaitseva, *Reforma gosudarstvennoi sluzhby Rossii: Istoriya popytok reformirovaniya s 1992 po 2000 god* (Reform of the State Service in Russia: A History of Attempts at Reform, 1992 to 2000) (Moscow: Ves' mir, 2003).
41. Natalya Kostenko, 'Tupiki i perspektivy administrativnoi reformy' (Dead Ends and Perspectives of Administrative Reform), *Nezavisimaya gazeta*, 7 April 2006; see also O.V. Gaman-Golutvina, 'The Changing Role of the State in the Context of Public Administration Reform: Russian and Foreign Experience', in the present collection; and S.E. Naryshkina and T.Ya. Khabrieva, *Administrativnaya reforma v Rossii: Naucho-prakti-cheskoe posobie* (Administrative Reform in Russia: A Scientific–Practical Manual) (Moscow: Infra-M, 2006).
42. For a critique see Ezra N. Suleiman, *Dismantling Democratic States* (Princeton, NJ: Princeton University Press, 2003).
43. Hugh Heclo, 'The Spirit of Public Administration', *PS: Political Science and Politics* (Dec. 2002), pp.689–95; H. George Frederickson, *The Spirit of Public Administration* (San Francisco, CA: Jossey-Bass, 1997).
44. Debra Stewart, Norman A. Sprinthall and Jackie D. Kem, 'Moral Reasoning in the Context of Reform: A Study of Russian Officials', *Public Administration Review*, Vol.62, No.3 (2002), pp.282–97.
45. See, for example, R.S. Bainiyazov, 'Pravosoznanie i rossiiskii pravovoi mentalitet' (Legal Consciousness and the Russian Legal Mentality), *Pravovedenie*, No.2 (2000), pp.31–40; Marina Kurkchiyan, 'The Illegitimacy of Law in Post-Soviet Societies', in Galligan and Kurkchiyan (eds.), *Law and Informal Practices*, pp.25–47; Solomon and Foglesong, *Courts and Transition*, pp.82–4.

46. Peter H. Solomon, Jr., 'Judicial Power in Russia: Through the Prism of Administrative Justice', *Law and Society Review*, Vol.38, No.3 (2004), pp.549–82; and in Russian as 'Sudebnaya vlast' v Rossii: skvoz' prizmu administrativnoi yustitsii', *Konstitutsionnoe pravo: vostochnoevropeiskoe obozrenie*, No.3 (44) (2003), pp.108–24.

47. Kathryn Hendley, 'Rewriting the Rules of the Game in Russia: The Neglected Issue of Demand for Law', *East European Constitutional Review*, Vol.8, No.4 (1999), pp.89–95.

48. As of 2006 efforts were under way to make courts more transparent, including through the posting of their decisions on websites: see Vladislav Kulikov, 'Pravosudie v seti: Anton Ivanov predlozhil aribtrazhu pereiti v Internet' (Justice Connected: Anton Ivanov Suggested that Arbitrazh move to the Internet), *Rossiiskaya gazeta*, 25 May 2006; 'O vnesenii v Gosudarstvennuyu Dumu Federal'nogo Sobraniya RF proyekta federal'nogo zakona "Ob obespechenii prav grazhdan i organizatsii na informatsiyu o sudebnoi deyatelnosti sudov obshchei yurisdiktsii v RF'''(On the Introduction in the State Duma of the Draft Federal Law 'On Guaranteeing the Rights of Citizens and Organizations to Information on the Activity of Courts of General Jurisdiction in the RF'), Postanovlenie Plenuma Verkhovnogo Suda RF No. 6 ot 9 marta 2006 g. See also 'Kontseptsiya Federal'noi tselevoi programmy "Razvitie sudebnoi sistemy Rossii na 2007–2011 gody'''(The Conception of the Federal Targeted Programme 'The Development of the Court System of Russia for 2007–2011'), unpublished ms (2006).

49. The notion of imposed power comes from the writing of Anton Oleinik: see his introduction to this collection, 'Putting Administrative Reform in a Broader Context of Power'. On the relationship between state and society in Russian thought, see Nikolai M. Korkunov, *Russkoe gosudarstvennoe pravo* (Russian Public Law), 7th edn (Moscow: Tip Stasyulevich, 1908–9).

50. There are indications that the attitudes of middle-level officials, including those in some regions, have changed in recent years, at least in part because of civil service reform. Thus, a comparison of surveys of heads of administration conducted in 1997 and 2004 reveals a growth from 8.0 to 31.4 per cent in the proportion who believe that state officials defend the interests of citizens (as well as other interests). To be sure, in 2004 51.0 per cent still saw defence of the interests of their agency as a prime consideration, along with 58.1 per cent the interests of the state in general: see V.S. Komarovskii, 'Administrativnaya reforma v Rossiiskoi Federatsii' (Administrative Reform in the Russian Federation), *Polis*, No.4 (2005), pp.172–8.

Rationalizing or Empowering Bureaucrats? Tax Administration Reform in Poland and Russia

MARC P. BERENSON

Since the collapse of state socialism in Central and Eastern Europe in 1989 and of communist rule in the Soviet Union in 1991, the general tax collection trends in post-communist Poland and Russia have varied dramatically. The Polish tax system has been remarkable in its ability to raise tax revenue for the state without any major obstacles whereas tax collection has been more erratic in Russia. With respect to unpaid taxes, the total amount of year-end arrears averaged just 7.65 per cent of all taxes received by the Polish state for the years 1995–2003.[1] Meanwhile, in Russia, the total amount of year-end arrears averaged 29.39 per cent of all taxes received by the state for those years.[2]

Why has Poland been able to perform much better at ensuring tax compliance than Russia since the early 1990s? The answer is due in great part to a partial level of bureaucratic rationalism that exists within Poland's tax organs. Polish efforts at administrative reform within the tax service have focused on rationalizing the function and duties of tax officials in a Weberian sense. In contrast, Russia has designed a tax administration that is consistent with Anton Oleinik's concept of 'power in a pure form', or, more generally, 'power over'.[3] That is, Russia's tax bureaucracies lean towards securing their own power 'over' society through their tax collection mechanisms. The tax agencies thus seek 'power as an end in itself' rather than focus on rationalizing their function and roles in order to build a more constructive state–society relationship, built on trust and fairness that will better serve the state in the long run.

Efforts to reform the tax administrative system in both Poland and Russia, therefore, have different goals in mind – one Weberian rationalism and the other empowerment of the state over society. Polish reforms have sought to rationalize the tax bureaucracy by focusing on institutional design as well as by reducing the ability of bureaucrats to function with undue discretion. Meanwhile, in Russia, the implementation of reforms designed to make the tax administration more 'rational' in a Weberian sense often fails to shift the course of the state's goal of seeking power for itself, especially at the expense of society at large.

Rationalizing or Empowering Bureaucrats?

Rationalizing the State Bureaucracy: The Weberian Option

With respect to Max Weber's characteristics of bureaucracies, Michael Mann has stated that '*Bureaucratic offices* are organized within departments, each of which is centralized and embodies a functional division of labour; departments are integrated into a single overall administration, also embodying functional division of labour and centralized hierarchy'.[4] Mann also has identified autonomous state power as relating to enhanced territorial centralization, a concept central to state capacity.[5] In short, for Mann and for Weber, being able to implement certain tasks requires a state structure imbued with a certain amount of autonomy, so that fairly consistent rules are able to be applied without undue and incapacitating interference from outside groups.

The administrative reforms in the Polish tax system have sought to 'rationalize' the role of state bureaucrats as well as to limit the degree of discretion afforded to tax officials in order to constrain corruption. The structures and the human resources provided together with the use of historical reference points all combine to produce mixed bureaucratic rationalism on the part of the tax administration in Poland. It is the appropriate choice and application of past institutional models – a structural design infused with flexibility and constraints as well as the availability of personnel trained and capable – that enables the Polish tax system to function well in implementing its policy goals. That being so, the tax bureaucracy is more capable of building a healthier relationship with the public, enabling long-term goals to be accomplished.

Empowering the State Bureaucracy: The 'Power in a Pure Form' Option

In applying the nature of Oleinik's concept of 'power in a pure form' to Russia today, the descriptions of Valeri G. Ledyaev, who argues that Putin's regime is one of 'bureaucratic authoritarianism', and of Oxana V. Gaman-Golutvina, who finds that the bureaucracy today is even farther from the Weberian ideals than it was under the Soviet Union, are quite apt.[6] For Ledyaev, the application of the concept of the 'power vertical' through administrative and bureaucratic mechanisms enables the state to expand its control over society. Similarly, Gaman-Golutvina argues that the widespread patronage, lack of transparency and low levels of public sector discipline alongside extremely high levels of corruption have enabled Russia's administrative apparatus to operate as its own business group at the expense of society, particularly outside business sectors. The significant lack of 'Weberianness' in the bureaucracy, which has led to the rise of a bureaucratic authoritarian state, can be seen both in the state administrative organs as a whole and specifically in the tax agencies.

With respect to the tax administration, not only have the reforms in this sector not led to substantial improvements on the Weberian scale, the tax administration itself has become a primary tool of the *bureaucratic authoritarian state* – through its day-to-day contact with the public as well as through more specific and targeted political use of the tax bureaucracy. As will be shown below, in contrast to the processes in Poland, the administrative reforms in the Russian tax system have brought about the 'empowerment' of the state by increasing the state's ability to impose its control over society, while having failed to limit the degree of discretion afforded to tax officials.

Administrative Reform in the Context of the Tax Service: Towards Rationalization or Empowerment of the State

Poland's Tax Administration Structure

On the eve of the transition in 1989, Poland's administrative institutions carried with them the dual legacies of a more distant 'Weberian' bureaucratic past from the Second Republic (1918–39) and of a more recent, clientelist, strictly hierarchical bureaucratic past from the Polish People's Republic (1946–89). Some aspects of the Polish inter-war Weberian bureaucracy were preserved throughout the post-Second World War era, or at least began to reappear in the last decade of communist rule, while other aspects of the past were seized upon by Polish society and its leaders at the start of the transition.

The history of how Poland's tax administration was constructed mirrors the history of Poland itself – with alternating organizational structures that reach back to the inter-war period. The origins of some of today's tax agencies trace back to the beginning of the Second Republic, when the ministry of the treasury was formed in 1919 on an internal structure similar to the Austrian example and was staffed by bureaucrats from the former Austrian territory. Similar to today, tax chambers (*izby skarbowe*) and tax offices (*urzędy skarbowe*) were placed in charge of the collection of taxes, which included a personal income tax. After the Second World War, the tax offices and tax chambers returned until 1950, when they were disbanded,[7] and then, in 1983, they reappeared as subordinates to the ministry of finance.[8] That structure remained in place at the beginning of the transition until 1992, when the Sejm (the lower house of the Polish parliament) created the tax audit offices (*urzędy kontroli skarbowe*) and divided up the audit function.

Unlike countries such as Russia and Ukraine in the late 1990s and the early part of the present decade, the tax administration is not a separate entity, but is headed by the ministry of finance, an institution that has achieved a 'comparable level of autonomy' with respect to the parliament and government and whose powers in the budgeting process gives it 'far-reaching control over government policy'.[9] Throughout the 1990s, there were 355 tax offices across Poland, collecting more than 85 per cent of the income of the state's budget.[10] The tax offices in each province (*województwo*) are subordinate to a tax chamber. Tax chambers and tax audit offices both number one per province and are directly subordinate to the ministry of finance. Unlike in other parts of the former communist bloc, the tax offices in Poland do not depend upon the local government, by law or in practice, which provides the system with a degree of consolidation.

The actual collection of taxes appears to be a very routine procedure. Most taxpayers file a declaration and pay taxes such as the personal income tax by themselves. Perhaps, thanks to the ease of processing one's tax return, the tax office in one 1999 public opinion poll was viewed favourably by half of the respondents – the highest among public institutions in that survey.[11] (By contrast, in 2001, businessmen in Russia were asked to rate their attitude toward a variety of characters with whom they have to deal. Tax inspectors and tax policemen were given the least positive appraisals on the list, with the exception of a 'bandit'.[12])

In addition to registering and collecting taxes from all taxpayers, tax offices usually conduct audits of taxpayers (usually large firms) with significant liabilities. Appeals from the initial audits of both the tax offices and the tax control offices are made to the tax chambers. From there, a second appeal can be made to the Chief Administrative Court (NSA), which judges whether the tax chamber has infringed a law or ordinance. Hence, the tax offices and tax audit offices are known as offices of 'first instance', while the tax chambers are referred to as offices of 'second instance', a concept of Polish administrative law that dates back to the inter-war regime.[13]

Informal co-operation does exist between the heads of the tax chambers and the tax audit offices, but owing to the unique structural arrangement between the two organizations, some incongruence, lack of co-ordination, and lack of sharing of information on audited economic entities does arise – a phenomenon that Poland's Supreme Audit Chamber (*Najwyższa Izba Kontroli*, or NIK) has noted on several occasions.[14] The tax audit offices, which act as a form of tax police, are distinguished in that, unlike a regular tax office, the inspector functions as an organizational unit himself, empowered to make decisions on his own. Hence, employees of the tax chamber can have direct contact with individual tax audit office inspectors on cases, but they do not have direct contact with the entire tax audit office.

While the initial goal of separating out the tax audit offices was to draw more attention to large cases, at the end of 2001 plans appeared within the ministry of finance for dissolving the tax audit offices, placing the inspectors in the tax chambers and tax offices in such a fashion that the line of command is more direct and that competition between the different bodies is eliminated.[15] Thus, with the exception of the relationship between the tax audit office and the tax office, the tax administration does appear to have a clear, disciplined structure subordinate ultimately to the ministry of finance as well as some consistent practices for collecting tax revenue.

Russia's Tax Administration Structure

In March 1991, the State Tax Service of Russia (STS) was formed on the basis of the USSR's state tax service, then part of the ministry of finance.[16] (In the Soviet Union, taxes existed in a narrow sense, with turnover tax and enterprise payments tax the most common.) The STS, which became responsible for collecting all revenue for federal and regional budgets (except for customs duties), was separated from the ministry of finance later in 1991 as an independent agency. In December 1998, the STS was upgraded in status as the ministry of taxes and dues. In 2003, there were 82 directorates for the 89 regions of Russia, plus inter-regional inspection offices in the seven new federal districts (*okruga*), which control and supervise the directorates.[17]

Traditionally, Soviet institutions that were spread out across the vast country were accompanied by a strict, hierarchical system of control, usually led by the Communist Party. However, in the 1990s, relaxed relations between the regions and Moscow and the rise of locally elected leaders weakened intra-institutional control. Such was also the case with the tax administration. At a minimum, as a US Treasury official who had worked with the state tax administration for several years in the late 1990s observed, there existed very little communication across the immensely bureaucratic organization in which only one-third of one per cent of the employees worked at the centre.[18] At worst, dual subordination existed, whereby local tax officers served two masters: Moscow and the regional governments, which often supplied infrastructure facilities (such as housing and health-care services) as well as, in some cases, trying to finance local tax offices through regional budgets.[19] 'As a result', the IMF has written, '[local tax offices] exerted more effort in collecting taxes for local governments than for the national government, e.g., collecting first those taxes where the local take was highest; did not remit to the federal government all that it was owed; and provided more favourable tax treatment to locally based enterprises'.[20]

In the midst of the somewhat disorganized nature of governing institutions in Russia, a reform programme, the Tax Administration Modernization Project (TAMP), attempted to make at least a part of the tax system more bureaucratically rational. The TAMP programme, which was essentially geared towards the introduction of US-style audit-free filing of taxes in a country where all firms generally are audited once every two years, was initiated in 1994 with World Bank, IMF and US Treasury support in two regions of Russia, Nizhnii Novgorod and Volgograd, in addition to the capital. Among the outcomes achieved were a reduction in processing time, a reduced number of tax procedures performed by each inspector, a doubling of settled tax arrears in Volgograd oblast in 1999 in comparison with 1998, an increase in regional tax collection, an increase in the proportion of tax returns filed on time from 50 to 75 per cent between 1998 and 2000, and a 90 per cent fall in the arrears rate in Nizhny Novgorod and 170 per cent in Volgograd between 1998 and 2000.[21]

The project itself took five and a half years to implement, instead of the originally planned three and half years, because from 1996 to 1999 project supervision was suspended as the government wanted to cancel it. Furthermore, as evidence of Moscow's uncertainty about the reform project, one project regional directorate head was dismissed after a few years of dramatic increases in tax collection within his region because newer, even higher target levels set by the centre could not be met.[22] Such was the emphasis from above on target levels rather than on improving compliance through a more rational bureaucracy.

Nevertheless, despite some earlier reluctance on the part of the government, some of the principles of the pilot reform project (but not the audit-free filing aspects) began to be implemented across Russia in 2002 and a second phase of the TAMP was launched in 2003 aimed at modernizing data-processing centres in five federal okrugs and 12 to 16 regional tax administrations.[23]

The success of the TAMP programme in Volgograd and Nizhnii Novgorod illustrates that, given alternative training, a different structure and new incentives to allow for a work philosophy oriented towards 'customer service', Russian tax collectors can work much more effectively and efficiently. Hence, even in a country with a different history and culture, a change from a target-driven method to an audit-free, compliance-driven method yields much higher tax compliance. Thus, the degree of policy implementation need not vary by country because of cultural differences: policies to improve effectiveness can be applied across different states.

In recent years as well, four specialized inter-regional tax inspections have been established that focus on particular types of large-scale business activity (such as oil and banking).[24] Moreover, such specialization has taken place within Moscow, whereby the 45 or so tax inspection offices, each of which once concentrated on a particular geographical area of the city, now focus each on a particular type of business or personal income activity.[25] Specialization has not yet occurred within Poland, and it appears that Russia's recent reform efforts have been the result of available technical assistance as well as redoubled efforts by ministerial leadership to improve the efficiency of tax collection. Nevertheless, the greatest problem in Russia lies in the fact that the tax system is target-level-driven rather than compliance-driven (in contrast somewhat to Poland), which provides different incentives for tax inspectors.

After Mikhail Fradkov became prime minister in March 2004, a consolidation plan for all the Russian Federation's ministries began to be implemented, and the ministry of taxes and dues was eliminated and its functions transferred to a newly created federal committee for tax control, placed under the ministry of finance.

Indeed, the transfer of the tax functions to the Ministry of Finance was part of a revived attempt at administrative reform, which began under President Vladimir Putin back in 2001 and which proceeded at a relatively slow pace. The outward goal of the reforms is to reduce the number of ministries. However, the entire project actually appears to be part of Putin's plan for creating a tightly centralized state with the bureaucracies under greater control.

One year prior to Fradkov's consolidation efforts, in March 2003, Putin placed a few government agencies under the Federal Security Service (FSB – the successor organization to the Soviet-era KGB) and the defence ministry, ostensibly to streamline the government, but also to centralize control of the government.[26] Throughout the spring and summer of 2003, additional plans were announced to initiate administrative reform and to cut governmental functions as well as government bodies, but little progress was made beyond the forming of commissions.

Administrative reform efforts were restarted the following year with the arrival of Fradkov as the new prime minister in March 2004 and President Putin's re-election in the same month. In a series of decrees, Putin eliminated 13 ministries (including the ministry of taxes and dues, which was absorbed by the finance ministry), two state committees, one federal commission, four federal services and four federal agencies, and created five new ministries, five new federal services and one new federal agency on the basis of the old entities.[27] In commenting on the reforms, Olga Kryshtanovskaya stated that the total number of government departments had actually increased and that the system had become more complex.[28] A former State Duma deputy, Aleksandr Shokhin, also argued that the reforms were flawed, as oversight bodies were subordinated to the very ministries that they had been intended to oversee.[29]

Putin also significantly reduced the number of deputy ministers, but Moscow's *Kommersant-Daily* soon reported that many of them continued to oversee the same areas as they previously had, but with new job titles.[30] Meanwhile, a month after his re-election, Putin also decreed a pay raise of up to five times for top-level bureaucrats and ministers, as well as himself.[31] Government privileges and benefits-in-kind for bureaucrats and their families, however, were not touched at all (even while the government began an effort to cut social welfare benefits-in-kind for everyone else, to the bitter distaste of the populace).[32] In November 2005, Fradkov introduced another blueprint for administrative reform, a three-year action plan that sought to update the bureaucracy with standardization and regulation reforms and also to abolish or privatize one-third of some 25,000 state enterprises and organizations.[33]

Hence, while being part of the government's overall administrative reform plans to reduce the number of ministries, the March 2004 elimination of the ministry of taxes and dues was thought to be part of a move to consolidate tax policy within the Ministry of Finance so that there is a single voice on the issue.[34] Nevertheless, the transition has been said not to be smooth, as the International Tax and Investment Centre (ITIC), an independent non-profit foundation that provides tax and investment policy information to businesses and also trains key policy-makers in the former Soviet Union, has remarked repeatedly in its monthly bulletins that the process has been fraught with disorganization, slow integration, and 'continued uncertainty among many key staff positions'.[35] The process was also delayed because a new law was required to abolish the ministry of taxes and dues and to integrate it into the ministry of finance.[36] Even the World Bank has stated in its own reports that the slow reorganization has been a reason for the delays and lack of progress in the second phase of the TAMP.[37] Hence, while the process has been slow and somewhat chaotic (as well as late in comparison to the subordination of tax administrations to the finance ministries which took place much earlier in other countries such as Poland), the effort may be beneficial down the road, leading to better supervision of tax collection activities.

The Tax Police

In 1992, within the state tax service the Main Division of Tax Investigations (MDTI) was formed, which in 1993 was transformed into an independent governmental body, the Department of Tax Police, and in 1995 became the Russian Federal Tax Police Service. The tax police was created in response to the fact that tax inspectors were not allowed into some firms who were not paying taxes in 1992.[38] Hence, the initial 'need' for masks and guns when approaching taxpayers – accessories that were used less as time passed. The main duties of the tax police became the 'exposure, prevention and suppression of tax law violations and crimes'.[39] In 2003, Putin signed a decree disbanding the 40,000-strong force of tax police officers.[40] However, the tasks were merely transferred to the interior ministry, so that the federal tax police activities continued to live on even after the official 'demise' of the organization.[41]

The personnel for the federal tax police came from those who were sacked from the KGB, the Soviet army and other military organizations at the beginning of the 1990s.[42] The tax police had regional and sub-regional offices throughout Russia. While it had close contacts with the state tax service's regional directorates and local offices, it (and the interior ministry divisions that took over its activities in 2003) differed from the tax audit office structure in Poland in that it was an entirely separate government organization. The tax police was not accountable to the other tax administration bodies, and did not have its cases reviewed by them. Cases were either located by the tax police officers themselves or were referred to them by local tax offices, which would provide information on an individual basis rather than through open access to their files.[43] The ITIC has remarked that as tax auditors 'seem increasingly under pressure to find "problems" to report to their superiors', criminal investigations are automatically triggered as a result of the Russian tax code, thus providing continuous work for the 'tax police' (now, the ministry of the interior).[44]

Given the lack of transparency in the activities of both the federal tax police and the ministry of the interior, it is unclear to what extent co-operation between the two bodies and the state tax administration has been better or worse in Russia compared with the corresponding organizations in Poland. However, there may have been some disagreement as to exactly how much extra revenue the tax police brought in on its own. For example, from 1992 to 1994, according to one senior tax police officer, the tax police collected as much as the tax authorities collected when taxpayers willingly paid.[45] Meanwhile, a former deputy head of a regional tax directorate stated that the tax police tended to write down that they worked on cases that actually were carried out by the regular tax offices.[46]

The methods used by the tax police have been deemed questionable. A lot of what they did was political or paid persecution, according to one Moscow-based international lawyer.[47] The tax police are viewed by private businesses as using scare tactics. For example, according to another managing tax partner at one of the big four international accounting firms, immediately after a company receives a visit from the tax police, outside 'security firms' often approach the company offering 'help' in dealing with the tax police for a fee; such incidents were said not to happen with the regular tax authorities.[48] The tax police may also have worked on a quota system. An inspector could open up a case against a company at the end of one year, which he would then close at the beginning of the new year in order to meet his quota.[49]

As large companies began to comply more with paying taxes under Putin, such tactics have been deemed excessive for use in pursuing small and medium-sized firms. However, the tax police was judged to have been used successfully as a political weapon of sorts, as Vladimir Gusinskii and Boris Berezovskii's businesses, among others, were targets of their investigation in 2000. In addition, the fact that Putin might have wanted to bring more control and a more accountable structural design to the organization may have been his reason for disbanding it in 2003 and centralizing the activities in another ministry.

Reducing or Broadening the Scope of Tax Bureaucrats' Discretion

How the Polish and Russian states view their 'power' relationship with the public is best illustrated, perhaps, by the degree of discretion afforded to their tax bureaucrats. And, despite some recent reforms in Russia, the basis for the differences in the degree of discretion given to the tax officials in the two states is accounted for largely by the fact that the Polish tax system focuses to a greater extent on compliance while Russia's system is more target-driven. Whether a system is compliance- or target-driven provides different incentives for tax inspectors, which are illustrated best by explaining how the tax collection process operates in practice and by examining additional corruption constraints placed (or not placed) on the tax inspectors.

Collecting the New Taxes in Poland

In the early 1990s, several administrative reforms designed to have the bureaucrats interact more constructively with the public were introduced by the Polish tax administration in order to ensure that the newly adopted taxes would be implemented appropriately. First, training of heads and managers of selected divisions of the tax offices was conducted by the tax chambers in 1991, with tax office workers being trained in the first two months of 1992 prior to the rollout of the personal income tax that year.[50] Similar such training was conducted in 1992 and 1993 for the introduction of the value-added tax.[51]

Second, a tax information campaign co-ordination unit was formed in the ministry of finance, which oversaw activities that disseminated knowledge about the new taxes to the public.[52] In advance of the introduction of the new taxes, the tax chambers published brochures and conducted a mass media programme, including special tax broadcasts on radio and television. As part of their work, tax administration employees were interviewed. 'On the one side, society was interested', commented one tax chamber vice-director, who took part in such interviews; 'On the other side, we were interested that the tax laws were understood and worked'.[53]

Third, inside the tax offices and tax chambers 'information points' were established, staffed by employees who knew the laws. Today, many tax offices and tax chambers have their own websites, which enable taxpayers to write to their own tax office.[54] This ties into the fact that many employees within the tax administration when interviewed described taxpayers as 'clients', whom they assist. One large tax office even sends out a survey asking its 'clients' how the tax office treated them and how they could be better served.[55]

Fourth, the tax offices were instructed by the ministry of finance not to penalize taxpayers too harshly when these taxes were first being introduced.[56]

Finally, the numbers of those working in the tax offices increased with the introduction of the new taxes. Hence, all these Weberian-like reform programmes were geared towards ensuring that tax bureaucrats would help the taxpayer comply with the new tax legislation and making the transition smoother for both bureaucrat and taxpayer alike.

Collecting the New Taxes in Russia

In contrast to Poland, the work of the tax authorities in Russia has been more target-driven and less consumer-oriented – an emphasis that provides the tax bureaucrats with greater discretion, to the extent that the state can 'impose' its will over the public as the state's coffers are filled. This is noticeable especially in the manner in which the tax inspectors have been conducting audits. In 2005, the federal tax service deputy head, Tatyana Shevtsova, remarked that 'Every tax audit visit must be 100 per cent effective. Otherwise the inspector has merely wasted his or her time'. The comment provides a concise overview of how the tax service sees its own function, and it was interpreted by Russian tax experts as an explicit instruction for tax inspectors to increase the tax bill with each audit.[57]

The biggest issue with respect to audits is who is selected. Tax inspectors, pressed to reach target goals, mostly pursue legitimate taxpayers, who have all their paperwork together, rather than locate companies that are paying no taxes at all.[58] This was especially the case during the late 1990s, when more than half of local companies were bankrupt. The system even allowed unlimited time to return and do audits; multiple audits also could be conducted simultaneously.[59] Moreover, when looking at deductions during audits, the tax authorities lacked the ability to look through the substance and merit of a deduction, but instead often focused on paperwork – whether it was in order, completed, signed and stamped appropriately, in an attempt to throw out as many deductions as possible (and, most likely, try to reach the tax collection quota).[60] Before the tax code of 1999, there were many gaps in the legislation that were subject to interpretation, which enabled the tax authorities to interpret the legislation as they wanted it to be – sometimes in a very inconsistent manner within and between regions.[61]

However, following the Kremlin's 2003 assault on the Yukos oil company and its 'oligarch' chief executive officer and owner, Mikhail Khodorkovskii, who was charged with fraud and tax evasion in a move deemed to be political, businessmen have viewed the affair as giving tax bureaucrats the go-ahead to interpret tax laws as they like. Such arbitrary power combined with a lack of detailed knowledge on the part of tax inspectors regarding the firms and industries they audit has even allowed for the prosecution of taxpayers for 'bad faith'. Such a 'rationale' for prosecution has been seen as a creative necessity for the tax service officials given the fact that Yukos's efforts to reduce its tax liabilities before 2003 were deemed by the business community to be within the law.[62]

In the late 1990s, when audits were not adequate in raising extra revenue to meet a quota, some tax inspectors were said to have contacted good companies requesting payment in advance because of the regional budget crisis or because the tax collector had a target plan that needed to be reached for him to receive his bonus.[63] Furthermore, when a taxpayer went before a tax office with a view to paying arrears, some have even said that the tax inspector received 10 per cent of the extra revenue received.[64] Historically, tax authorities have had an informal relation with the taxpayers whereby each taxpayer was assigned to one person in the tax inspection office, which led to lots of issues being dependent upon personal relations. However, since the adoption of the 1999 tax code, which specified taxpayer rights, the relationship has been more formal than it used to be.[65]

As the new taxes were introduced throughout the 1990s, the tax authorities in Russia did not engage as much in public education campaigns as in Poland. According to some, the tax administration placed a low priority on educating taxpayers.[66] For example, there were few or no seminars between tax officials and taxpayers. While the 1999 tax code has allowed taxpayers to ask the tax authorities for explanations, the tax authorities are reluctant to provide them, and the responses are found by some taxpayers to be usually not very helpful.[67]

Proposed reforms during 2005–6 further illustrate ambiguity within the government as to how coercive and client-oriented the tax collection system should be. In 2005 Finance Minister Alexei Kudrin, whose ministry took control of the state tax administration in the previous year, proposed that each tax inspectorate should have a separate complaints department, an internal review for tax claims above a certain amount, and further restrictions on the types of tax investigations and methods used.[68] A further measure later suggested was the imposition of a limit to the number of tax audits performed on a taxpayer within a year.[69] Businesses were able to agree with the tax administration that there would be no more than two tax inspections per year, but the business community in mid-2005 was said to be unable 'to identify which official body will sanction additional inspections of large companies'.[70]

Other proposals, however, would not restrict the 'power' of the tax bureaucrats or require them to be particularly 'consumer-oriented'. In 2005, the government suggested giving the tax agencies the power to fine companies without a court decision, and in January 2006 such a law went into force, allowing fines to be levied provided that the penalty for each tax was no more than 5,000 roubles for entrepreneurs and 50,000 roubles for firms.[71] Furthermore, the tax authorities were said in 2005 to be turning to individual taxpayers and to be intentionally failing to inform citizens regarding property and car taxes, so that fines for unpaid taxes were 'accumulating like an avalanche'.[72]

Finally, there has been ambiguity as well with respect to whether the tax administration will still use tax collection 'targets' as a way of managing the activities of its tax inspectors rather than requiring tax inspectors to focus on seeking to ensure citizen compliance with the tax laws. Following President Putin's annual address to the nation on 25 April 2005, in which he renounced the use of such 'targets', the Federal State Tax Service stated four months later that it was now giving its inspectorates 'indicative indices'.[73] To muddle the issue of targets further, the Finance Ministry's draft budget for 2006 was said in August 2005 to assume that an extra $1 billion would be collected through additional inspections of businesses by the end of 2005, and that more than double that amount would be collected through additional corporate audits in 2006.[74]

Additional Structural Constraints to Prevent Corruption by Polish and Russian Tax Officials

Poland's tax system also appears at first glance to be designed in such a manner as to provide barriers to corruption better than that of Russia.

For example, within the tax chambers and tax offices, many people oversee particular cases. One team working on a case must transfer the paperwork to another unit; cases considered by employees require the director's signature; and taxpayers do not have direct access to the audit organs. In general, the system is designed in a manner that sacrifices some Weberian autonomy for the greater cause of uniformity and security. As one tax chamber department head put it, 'Corruption appears where the bureaucrat has discretion in making a decision'.[75] Moreover, the tax chambers conduct their own audits – complex or thematic – of the tax offices that they oversee, and undertake the complex audits every other year.

Another such barrier is the fact that tax allowances (exemptions) are no longer given out at the discretion of the tax offices in Poland. Back in 1995, NIK asserted that the decision-making process in the awarding of tax allowances was conducted in many cases incorrectly, with decisions made without an audit of the taxpayer who was receiving the exemption.

Moreover, a significant number of tax allowances, granted under the influence of recommendations from the ministry of finance, were not issued after careful research was conducted to justify such a decision.[76] NIK also found it problematic to conduct a review of the size and effect of these allowances owing to the lack of a register of such tax relief decisions, which NIK had earlier proposed that the ministry of finance should create.[77] Hence, a change in legislation on tax allowances prevents opportunities from arising whereby taxpayers try to influence tax administration employees to obtain such relief.

What is possible today, however, is that tax office employees have options for assisting those who incur tax arrears. On an individual basis, the tax office or the tax chamber (but not the tax control office) can change the terms of settlement periods so that the individual can pay in instalments, delay the date of payment, or amortize the debt, although the latter is very rare.[78] Although such assistance is checked by supervisors, NIK has found violations of this practice, suggesting that the structural constraints are not as strong as they should be.[79]

A final barrier for the tax bureaucrat with respect to his relation to taxpayers is that recently changed legislation stipulates that, unlike in Russia, a bureaucrat can no longer issue a fine or punishment to a taxpayer, but specifies rather that only a court can do this.[80]

In contrast to all these controls placed on a tax bureaucrat's work in Poland, Russia's tax system relied heavily throughout the 1990s on individual relations between tax inspectors and taxpayers. This practice, though, has been diminishing within the past couple of years. In the 1990s, a taxpayer would turn in his or her tax return to a single tax inspector who would review the accuracy of the documents – a situation that would provide an opportunity for collusion between the two parties.[81] Moreover, according to some, as mentioned above, when a taxpayer pays their tax arrears, the tax inspector receives a portion of the extra revenue received.[82] However, thanks to the 1999 tax code, a more formal relationship has developed in some parts of the country.[83]

Departments inside the tax administration and tax police departments in both countries do conduct internal audits and checks designed to examine corruption issues.[84] In Poland, an external organization that audits the tax collection process is the Supreme Audit Chamber (or NIK), mentioned above. As for analysing the different organs of the tax administration, NIK conducts thematic audits (analysing activities of the different tax bodies) as well as problematic audits (computerization of the tax organs, the collection of tax arrears, the collection of the personal income tax, and so on). Meanwhile, in Russia, the Accounts Chamber of the Russian Federation, accountable to the Federal Assembly, conducts mostly financial audits, but not performance audits. (On the basis of personal experience, I believe that NIK is a far more transparent organization accessible to outside researchers than Russia's Account Chamber.) The regional *upravlenie* (administration) was said to check the tax inspection offices about once every three years, while thematic checks could be ordered by the ministry of taxes and dues at the regional level.[85]

Conclusion

Such a discussion of the structural means to prevent the corruption of bureaucrats brings the topic back full circle to the Weberian ideals of a rational bureaucracy staffed by independent, professional employees. In comparing Poland's and Russia's tax administrations, we can look at how rational and society-oriented they are with respect to their *historical references, structures, human resources,* and *work philosophy.*

- *Historical references.* Poland's rational structural design draws upon its inter-war past for some of its current institutions whereas Russia appears lately to be drawing on some aspects of Soviet bureaucratic administration in an effort to obtain strong hierarchical control at the expense of bureaucratic autonomy.
- *Structures.* Poland's tax administration has maintained a structure that has direct lines of subordination between offices as well as within them. The uniquely separate, but integrated, position of the tax audit offices in Poland, though, does not always provide for smooth interactions with the other tax administration components, suggesting that the structure is not completely rational. Meanwhile, throughout the 1990s there appear

to have been insufficient barriers placed on Russia's tax inspectors as they interacted with taxpayers. Poland also has an external watchdog organization (the NIK) that actually produces critical financial as well as performance audit reports, available to the public (unlike Russia's Accounts Chamber).

- *Human Resources.* Poland's tax administration has utilized different employee training techniques to control how the new taxes were to work.
- *Work Philosophy.* The methods by which the Polish authorities work, as well as how they educate the public about tax procedures, appear to be more compliance-driven and less focused on reaching a monetary target than in Russia – a philosophy that tends to treat the taxpayers more as clients.

In short, in the model of Poland's tax bureaucracy – a mixture of successes and failures with respect to the use of its historical reference points, structures, human resources and work philosophy all oriented towards improving the trust that taxpayers have in the tax administration – combine to produce a case of partial bureaucratic rationalism. Meanwhile, a less successful mix of these Weberian components produced a lower level of bureaucratic rationalism on the part of the Russian tax administration in the 1990s, with some significant reform successes in the past couple of years. Poland has thus opted for *rationalizing* the tax bureaucrats whereas Russia has sought to *empower* them so that the state can be perceived as holding power over society – ordinary taxpayers and businesses alike.

Moreover, the Polish model also shows that a state agency need not only be internally strong and autonomous from outside groups in order to get the job done; it must also involve society by creating citizens' trust in the tax collection agencies through mechanisms such as 'audit-free' filings, tax office information booths and other means of public outreach. A strong structure alone does not produce effective implementation of tax collection policies. Nor should effective internal oversight or a unified *esprit de corps* be seen as preferable or contrary to being an outwardly focused state agency. The two approaches – internally and externally motivated – go hand-in-hand.

Finally, the fact that there has been significant progress in two Russian provinces suggests that Russian tax offices can perform in a rational bureaucratic manner once comprehensive reforms are initiated to overhaul the power relationship between tax bureaucrat and taxpayer, from one based principally on coercion to one based largely on trust through 'audit-free' filings. The Russians clearly are capable of building effective Weberian state agencies as well.

As the Polish and Russian paths and methods of governance diverged during the course of the transition – and became more distinct during the Putin era, comparing how bureaucrats collect taxes does help illustrate that a state that seeks to 'impose power' may not be as effective as one that engages with society on more equal terms. 'Empowering' bureaucrats so that the state will be 'strengthened' vis-à-vis society may not provide for as successful an implementation of state policy in the long run as an approach based upon 'rationalizing' the state.

NOTES

1. By way of comparison, 4 to 6 per cent has been the range typical for Canada, the United States and Australia: see International Monetary Fund (IMF), *Russian Federation: Selected Issues and Statistical Appendix*, IMF Country Report No. 02/75 (Washington, DC: International Monetary Fund, April 2002), p.61.
2. While evaluations of the size and scale of tax arrears is a better measure of tax collection as it incorporates what the state believes should be ideally collected, the most frequent method of reporting tax revenue statistics is to present the amount of revenue collected annually in terms of its percentage of GDP, even though the size of economies or tax rates may vary significantly across countries. In any case, in comparison to the average tax collection rates in terms of percentage of GDP for the OECD group of countries, Poland fared quite well with respect to its annual collection of indirect taxes from 1990 to 2002, rising higher than the OECD average with the introduction of VAT and then declining slightly over time to approach the OECD level. Specifically, Poland's annual collection of indirect taxes averaged 11.9 per cent of GDP while the OECD's averaged 11.4 per cent of GDP over the same period. From 1992 to 2003, Russia each year collected an average of 9.45 per cent of GDP in indirect taxes. With respect to collection rates for direct taxes, Poland has occupied a middle ground – not as high as the OECD states, but higher than those of Russia. Over the period 1990–2002, Poland's yearly collection of direct taxes averaged 10.3 per cent of GDP compared with an OECD average of 13.0 per cent. By contrast, Russia collected an annual average of 8.7 per cent of GDP in direct taxes from 1992 to 2003. Poland and OECD data from the OECD's *Revenue Statistics* (2004), available at <http://www.sourceoecd.org/>. All Russian data calculated by the author using data from the International Monetary Fund, *Russian Federation: Recent Economic Developments* (Washington, DC: IMF, Sept. 1999), p.67; IMF, *IMF Economic Reviews: Russian Federation* (Washington, DC: March 1995), p.91; IMF, *Russian Federation: Selected Issues* (Washington, DC: Nov. 2000), pp.79–82; IMF, *Russian Federation: Statistical Appendix* (Washington, DC: Feb. 2002), pp.24–8; IMF, *Russian Federation: Statistical Appendix* (Washington, DC: May 2003), pp.24–7; IMF, *Russian Federation: Statistical Appendix* (Washington, DC: Sept. 2004), pp.19–22.
3. Anton Oleinik, 'Introduction: Putting Administrative Reform in a Broader Context of Power', in this collection.
4. Michael Mann, *The Sources of Social Power: Volume II: The Rise of Classes and Nation-States, 1760–1914* (Cambridge: Cambridge University Press, 1993), p.444.
5. Michael Mann, 'The Autonomous Power of the State: Its Origins, Mechanisms and Results', in John A. Hall (ed.), *States in History* (Oxford: Basil Blackwell, 1986), p.135.
6. Valeri Ledyaev, 'Domination, Power and Authority in Russia: Basic Characteristics and Forms', and Oxana Gaman-Golutvina, 'The Changing Role of the State in the Context of Public Administration Reforms: Russian and Foreign Experience', both in this collection.
7. Interview with Tax Office Head, Warsaw, 20 Nov. 2001.
8. Interview with Tax Chamber Director, Warsaw, 15 Nov. 2001.
9. Antoni Z. Kamiński, 'Corruption under the Post-Communist Transformation: The Case of Poland', *Polish Sociological Review*, No.2 (1997), pp.91–117 (p.110); and Klaus H. Goetz and Hellmut Wollmann, 'Governmentalizing Central Executives in Post-Communist Europe: A Four-Country Comparison', *Journal of European Public Policy*, Vol.8, No.6 (2001), pp.864–87 (pp.874–5).

10. Najwyższa Izba Kontroli (NIK), 'Informacja o wynikach kontroli działalności urzędów skarbowych' (Information on the Results of the Audit of the Activity of the Tax Offices) (Warsaw, Oct. 1994), p.3.
11. Renata Wrobel, 'Tłok za biurkiem' (Pressed behind the Desk), *Rzeczpospolita*, 22 March 1999.
12. INDEM Foundation, 'Russia Anti-Corruption Diagnostics: Sociological Analysis', English edn (Moscow: INDEM Foundation, 2001), Part 4, pp.23–4.
13. Janusz Borkowski, *Jednostka a administracja publiczna po reformie ustrojowej* (Public Unit and Administration after the Structural Reform) (Warsaw: Instytut Spraw Publicznych, 2001), p.40.
14. NIK, 'Informacja o wynikach kontroli działalności urzędów kontroli skarbowej w latach 1992–1993' (Information on the Results of the Audit of the Activity of the Tax Audit Offices in 1992–1993), government report (Warsaw: Dec. 1994), p.4; and NIK, 'Informacja o wynikach kontroli działalności urzędów kontroli skarbowej' (Information on the Results of the Audit of the Activity of the Tax Audit Offices) (Warsaw: May 2000), p.3.
15. Rafał Zasuń, 'Czystka, potem reforma' (Purge, then Reform), *Gazeta Wyborcza*, 7 Dec. 2001, p.4.
16. Alexander Morozov, 'Tax Administration in Russia: Institutional Framework, Performance and Efficiency', manuscript in English, 1996, p.1; and interview with former head of the department of civil service and personnel, ministry of taxes and dues, Moscow, 8 Aug. 2003.
17. Interview with division head, department of international co-operation and information exchange, ministry of taxes and dues, 22 July 2003.
18. Interview with US Treasury official, Moscow, 3 June 2003.
19. Morozov, 'Tax Administration in Russia', p.4.
20. IMF, *Russian Federation* (2002), p.60.
21. World Bank News Release, 'Outcomes of the Russia Tax Modernization Project Supported by the World Bank and International Monetary Fund', 17 Nov. 2000; and World Bank, 'Project Performance Assessment Report: Russia – Tax Administration Modernization Project (Loan 3853)', 13 May 2003, Report No. 25915, p.6. As a comparison, in looking at data published by GosKomStat in the 2000, 2002 and 2004 editions of *Finansy Rossii*, the amount of tax arrears as a percentage of total tax income to the Consolidated Budget of the Russia Federation as a whole fell from 49.40 to 31.20 per cent from 1998 to 2000, a level of decline of approximately 37 per cent.
22. Interview with US Treasury official, Moscow, 3 June 2003.
23. World Bank, 'Project Appraisal Document on a Proposed Loan in the Amount of US$100 Million to the Russian Federation for a Second Tax Administration Modernization Project', Report No: 23565-RU (Washington, DC: World Bank, 19 Sept. 2002).
24. Interview with division head, department of international co-operation and information exchange, ministry of taxes and dues, 22 July 2003; Bureau of Economic Analysis, 'Chapter 2: Tax Policy', in *Review of Economic Policy for 2002*, manuscript (Moscow, 2003), p.5; and Vladimir Samoylenko, 'Russia Update', *ITIC Bulletin* (International Tax and Investment Centre), June/July 2004, pp.1–2, available at <http://www.iticnet.org/publications/ITIC%20Bulletin%202004%20June%20July.pdf>, accessed 2 Nov. 2007.
25. Interview with former head of a Moscow tax inspectorate, 5 Aug. 2003.
26. Michael Wines, 'Streamlining Government, Putin Creates New Anti-Drug Force', *New York Times*, 12 March 2003, p.A10.
27. 'Putin Cuts 13 Ministries and Almost a Dozen State Agencies', *RFE/RL Newsline*, Vol.8, No.46, Part I, 10 March 2004.
28. 'Sociologist Examines Administrative Reforms', *RFE/RL Newsline*, Vol.8, No.54, Part I, 22 March 2004.
29. 'Government Reform Reportedly Will Slow Work of Government ... As Analysts Continue to Mull Changes', *RFE/RL Newsline*, Vol.8, No.53, Part I, 19 March 2004.
30. Caroline McGregor, '20% of Civil Servants Face Axe', *The Moscow Times*, 2 April 2004; and 'Putin Reshuffles the Presidential Administration ... As Titles Change But Portfolios Appear to Remain the Same', *RFE/RL Newsline*, Vol.8, No.57, Part I, 26 March 2004.

31. 'Overhauling the Russian Government', *RIA Novosti*, 1 April 2004, in *Johnson's Russia List*, No.8148, 1 April 2004; and McGregor, '20% of Civil Servants Face Axe'.
32. Nick Paton Walsh, 'Putin Hikes his Pay to Fight Corruption', *The Guardian*, 17 April 2004, in *Johnson's Russia List*, No.8171, 17 April 2004; 'Civil Servants to Keep In-Kind Benefits Despite Government's Reform Effort', *RFE/RL Newsline*, Vol.8, No.142, Part I, 28 July 2004; and Boris Nemtsov and Vladimir Pribylovsky, 'The President, Simple and False: Ten Moments of the State's Lies; The Putin Regime is Based on Lies, Bureaucracy, and Corruption', *Novaya Gazeta*, 10 Feb. 2005, in *Johnson's Russia List*, No.9058, 12 Feb. 2005.
33. Konstantin Frunkin, 'Government Determined to Pursue Administrative Reform', *Izvestiya*, 2 Nov. 2005, in *Johnson's Russia List*, No.9286, 3 Nov. 2005.
34. Samoylenko, 'Russia Update'.
35. Ibid., p.1.
36. Ibid., p.2.
37. World Bank, *FY05 Report on the Status of Projects in Execution* (Washington, DC: World Bank, 2005), p.913.
38. Interview with former assistant to deputy head of Moscow city tax police, Moscow, 28 July 2003.
39. Ibid.
40. Alex Nicholson, '2 Tax Police Officers Caught Red-Handed', *The Moscow Times*, 26 March 2003.
41. Samoylenko, 'Russia Update', p.2.
42. Interview with manager, Moscow office of one of the 'big four' international accounting firms, Moscow, 13 Aug. 2003.
43. Interview with former assistant to deputy head of Moscow city tax police, Moscow, 28 July 2003.
44. Daniel A. Witt, 'Year-End Wrap-Up and Looking Ahead to 2005', *ITIC Bulletin*, 5 Jan. 2005, p.2, available at <http://www.iticnet.org/publications/ITIC%20Bulletin%202005% 20 Janury%20Special%20Edition.pdf>, accessed 12 Nov. 2007.
45. Interview with former assistant to deputy head of Moscow city tax police, Moscow, 28 July 2003.
46. Interview with former deputy head of regional tax directorate, 18 Aug. 2003.
47. Lawyer, Moscow office of a leading international law firm, Moscow, 11 Aug. 2003.
48. Head law partner, Moscow office of one of the 'big four' international accounting firms, Moscow, 28 July 2003.
49. Ibid.
50. NIK, 'Informacja o wynikach kontroli działalności urzędów skarbowych' (Information on the Results of the Audit of the Activity of the Tax Offices), April 1993, p.34.
51. NIK, 'Informacja o wynikach kontroli działalności Ministerstwa Finansów i urzędów skarbowych w zakresie poboru podatku od towarów i usług' (Information on the Results of the Audit of the Activity of the Ministry of Finance and the Tax Offices in the Scope of the Collection of Taxes on Goods and Services) (Warsaw: Oct. 1997), p.28.
52. Ibid., p.27.
53. Interview with a tax chamber vice director, Gdańsk, 26 Nov. 2001.
54. Interview with tax chamber director, Warsaw, 15 Nov. 2001.
55. Interview with tax office head, Białystok, 7 Dec. 2001.
56. Interview with tax chamber department head, Białystok, 3 Dec. 2001.
57. 'Tax Authorities Find "Yukos Effect" Beneficial', *Vremya novostei*, 10 Oct. 2005, in *Johnson's Russia List*, No.9263, 10 Oct. 2005.
58. Interview with head law partner, Moscow office of one of the 'big four' international accounting firms, Moscow, 28 July 2003; and lawyer, Moscow office of a leading international law firm, Moscow, 11 Aug. 2003.
59. Interview with partner, Moscow office of one of the 'big four' international accounting firms, Moscow, 28 July 2003.
60. Interview with head law partner, Moscow office of one of the 'big four' international accounting firms, Moscow, 28 July 2003.

61. Interview with partner, Moscow office of one of the 'big four' international accounting firms, Moscow, 28 July 2003.
62. Jason Bush, 'The Taxman Cometh – Again and Again', *Business Week*, 7 March 2005, in *Johnson's Russia List*, No.9079, 6 March 2005.
63. Interview with partner, Moscow office of one of the 'big four' international accounting firms, Moscow, 28 July 2003.
64. Interview with Aleksei A. Mukhin, director of the Centre for Political Information, Moscow, 23 May 2003.
65. Interview with lawyer at Moscow office of international legal firm, Moscow, 7 Aug. 2003.
66. IMF, *Russian Federation: Selected Issues and Statistical Appendix*, IMF Country Report No.02/75, April 2002, p.63.
67. Interview with lawyer at Moscow office of international legal firm, Moscow, 7 Aug. 2003.
68. Guy Faulconbridge, 'Kudrin Sets Out His Plans for Tax Service', *Moscow Times*, 10 Feb. 2005, p. 2.
69. Ekaterina Grigorieva and Konstantin Frumkin, 'Government in Instalments: President Putin delivers his budget address', *Izvestiya*, 26 May 2005, in *Johnson's Russia List*, No.9160, 26 May 2005.
70. Yana Yurova, 'Tax Reform in Russia: Business Is Happy, Unlike Ordinary People', *RIA Novosti*, in *Johnson's Russia List*, No.9148, 13 May 2005.
71. RosBusinessConsulting, 'Tax service reports on 2004 collections', 25 Jan. 2005, in *Johnson's Russia List*, No.9034, 26 Jan. 2005; and Yekaterina Dranitsyna, 'Tax Reforms Leave Business Unsatisfied', *St. Petersburg Times*, 11 Nov. 2005, in *Johnson's Russia List*, No.9293, 13 Nov. 2005
72. Yurova, 'Tax Reform in Russia'.
73. 'No More Plans for Taxmen', *Vedomosti*, 11 Aug. 2005, in *Johnson's Russia List*, No.9222, 11 Aug. 2005.
74. '06 Budget Sets Tax Collection Target', *Moscow Times*, 24 Aug. 2005, p.6.
75. Interview with tax chamber department head, Gdańsk, 26 Nov. 2001.
76. NIK, 'Informacja o wynikach kontroli wykonywania uprawnień przez resort finansów w zakresie wydawanych decyzji o zaniechaniu ustalania i poboru podatków' (Information on the Results of the Audit of the Carrying out of Entitlements through the Finance Department in the Scope of Completed Decisions regarding the Nonfeasance of Arrangement and Collection of Taxes) (Warsaw, May 1995), p.57.
77. Ibid.
78. Interviews with vice-director, department of the state budget, NIK, 8 Nov. 2001; manager of a department, tax chamber, Warsaw, 15 Nov. 2001; tax office head, Warsaw, 20 Nov. 2001; and tax control office director, Białystok, 4 Dec. 2001.
79. NIK, 'Informacja o wynikach kontroli działalności urzędów skarbowych' (Information on the Results of the Audit of the Activity of Tax Offices) (Warsaw, April 1993), p.6; and NIK, 'Informacja o wynikach kontroli działaności urzędów skarbowych w zakresie egzekucji i zabezpieczenia zaległości podatkowych' (Information on the Results of the Audit of Activity of the Tax Offices in the Scope of the Collection and Obtainment of Tax Arrears) (Warsaw, April 2001), pp.9–10.
80. Interview with tax office head, Białystok, 4 Dec. 2001.
81. Liam Ebrill and Oleh Havrylyshyn, *Tax Reform in the Baltics, Russia, and Other Countries of the Former Soviet Union* (Washington, DC: IMF, 1999), p.13.
82. Interview with Aleksei A. Mukhin (n.64); and Matthew Valencia, 'The Region's Tax Systems: Unclear and Severe', *Business Central Europe* (Sept. 1994), p.69.
83. Interview with lawyer at Moscow office of international legal firm, Moscow, 7 Aug. 2003.
84. Interview with former assistant to deputy head of Moscow city tax police, Moscow, 28 July 2003; interview with former head of a Moscow tax inspectorate, 5 Aug. 2003; and interview with former head of the department of civil service and personnel, ministry of taxes and dues, Moscow, 8 Aug. 2003.
85. Interview with former head of a Moscow tax inspectorate, 5 Aug. 2003.

Existing and Potential Constraints Limiting State Servants' Opportunism: The Russian Case

ANTON OLEINIK

Introduction: Methodological Remarks and Sources of Information

Classical studies of bureaucracy carried out in Western countries derive from the assumption that their subject does not significantly differ from other socio-professional groups. This allows the application of standard research methods. For instance, Michel Crozier builds his analysis of the bureaucratic milieu in France on two case studies.[1] Neither factual questions nor questions about values and beliefs seem problematic. The latter type contains particularly valuable information if one probes into intentions and justifications for their actions developed by actors. Social economists choose this perspective:

'The moral status of an act should not be judged by its consequences, the way utilitarians do, but by the "intention"'.[2]

Yet the present state of our knowledge about the inner life of Russian state servants does not allow us to proceed directly: the design of the most recent studies included neither in-depth interviews with office-holders themselves nor participant observation,[3] probably as a result of the extreme insularity of this milieu and the corresponding difficulties in obtaining access to it. The task of gaining access to a closed milieu is a necessary yet insufficient condition for understanding its constitution. A high risk of double-thinking – that is, 'an adherence *demonstrated publicly* to the ideals and norms which are accepted in society and which *may not correspond with* the internal convictions of individuals and *even contradict* their actual conduct'[4] – potentially questions the validity of data collected through in-depth interviews and questionnaires. Similar problems are encountered in studies of organized crime. The higher the probability that research subjects are involved in behaviour subject to public disapproval, the higher the risk of distortions due to double-thinking. The next-worst strategy would be to rely on secondary data, or to collect the data through participant observation. However, this prevents the collection of data relevant for studying the inner world of research subjects, namely their intentions and justifications.

Another option consists of asking indirect, projective and vignette questions by presenting the respondent with several scenarios of his or her behaviour in an imaginable situation. This manner of proceeding has an important advantage: it allows inquiry into intentions and justifications by asking the respondent to justify his or her eventual actions in a 'critical situation'. The critical character of the situation means that there are several socially acceptable justifications for the same act. With the variable of social approval or disapproval controlled, the respondent's choice reveals his or her preferences. A study of businesspeople presumably involved in extra-legal activities incorporated this research methodology.[5]

Still another alternative, also imperfect, involves adapting a 'black box' approach common in the discipline of economics. The researcher does not venture to look inside the black box of the phenomenon under investigation because of lack of information; he or she nevertheless aims to analyse factors influencing processes inside the black box. For instance, the firm was treated as a black box, or a 'shadowy figure', before the path-breaking analysis of its internal processes by Ronald Coase.[6] The input and the output were known, as was the situation in the market, yet the mere transformation of the input into the output remained obscure.

If projected on to studies of bureaucracy, the black box approach suggests that the researcher avoids making any heroic assumptions with regard to office-holders' values, interests and intentions. One 'soft' assumption consists in attributing self-interested behaviour to office-holders: if one lacks sufficient reasons for assuming their interest in the commonwealth (a word that can hardly even be translated into Russian), then they are presumably 'seeking self-interest with guile'[7] – that is, they may behave opportunistically. Opportunism can take two forms, group (seeking narrow group interests) and individual. In order to elaborate on this assumption, or to refute it, one needs to study factors that could limit office-holders' opportunism. The more we know about these factors, the narrower the 'shadowy' area that remains beyond the reach of our understanding. In the final analysis it might appear that office-holders do care about the common good – if there is no room for behaving opportunistically.

The research question can be formulated as follows: under what constraints do holders of offices in governmental bodies act in today's Russia? Constraints embedded in the institutional environment, as Anthony Giddens points out, are a double-edged sword: they limit the actor's freedom and let him or her pursue individual and group interests more successfully: 'Structure is always both enabling and constraining'.[8] The net balance between enabling and constraining, nevertheless, varies from one individual or collective actor to another. Some of them are more able than others to transform institutions into a partisan weapon by shaping them according to group and individual preferences. They manage not only to mobilize the 'bias of the system' but also to produce and strengthen it.[9] For others the balance is less favourable: institutions constrain their actions rather than help in achieving their objectives.

Constraints do not remain invariable over time because they are reproduced and changed by actors who aim to change the net balance in their favour. The changing configuration of constraints has taken especially manifest forms in the Russian case since the start of reforms in the second half of the 1980s. Dynamic aspects lie beyond the scope of the present analysis, which aims to show a snapshot of the situation in the Russian bureaucratic milieu in 2004–6.

Different balances of enabling and constraining influences result in particular configurations of power relationships: that is, they determine an actor's capacity to impose his or her will on other actors. The assumption of opportunistic behaviour combined with loose constraints (institutions enable actors to pursue their plans rather than constrain them) seems appropriate in the context of power as an end in itself, or, in Thomas Wartenberg's interpretation, domination: 'Power is exercised by the dominating social agent over the dominated social agent repeatedly, systematically, and to the detriment of the dominated agent'.[10] On the other hand, tight constraints limit the imposition of will in cases where it has an instrumental value and serves to achieve objectives endorsed by both the powerful and the subordinate. If power were a means to achieve other ends, then its uses – and even abuses – would be subject to some extrinsic imperatives. Being constrained in a particular way, office-holders take care about the common good, yet the researcher reaches this conclusion after showing that they have little room for discretion, rather than as a result of making heroic assumptions.

In what follows I refer to two types of sources. First, I use secondary quantitative data collected mostly by international organizations such as Transparency International or the World Bank. Second, I use primary qualitative data gathered in the framework of a current research project on particularities of power relationships in the post-Soviet context.[11] Thirty in-depth structured interviews were conducted in three regions of the Russian Federation (Moscow, Saint Petersburg and Kemerovo) with two types of interlocutors: (i) experts who have a good knowledge of the bureaucratic milieu but do not hold office in the state bureaucracy (former office-holders, journalists, academics) and (ii) low- and middle-ranking office-holders in governmental bodies at the federal and regional levels. Because of the closed nature of the milieu we were unable to interview high-ranking officials (ministers and their associates). So the subject of the analysis can be defined as a current configuration of constraints under which office-holders in Russian governmental bodies at the federal and regional levels act.

In part two, I outline potential constraints of office-holders' opportunism. The list derives from a taxonomy of power relationships constructed with the help of mechanisms for imposing will as a differentiating criterion. A tentative assessment of the hardness of these constraints in today's Russia is given in part three on the basis of various primary and secondary data. The concept of hardness of constraints, initially borrowed by János Kornai from mathematical programming, indicates the degree to which certain obstacles or conditions restrict activities and limit the number of choices available, in our case to power-holders.[12] The issues of strengthening the constraints are discussed in the Conclusion.

Constraints Limiting the State Servants' Opportunism

There exists a plurality of definitions of power because, as Wartenberg puts it, it is an 'essentially contested concept',[13] and accordingly there are several typologies of power relationships. For instance, Steven Lukes considers various forms of conflict of interest and links them to particular forms of power.[14] A number of scholars distinguish forms of power as functions of the source of the subordinate's submission to the power-holder; they highlight vehicles for imposing will – force, coercion, manipulation and so forth.[15] This approach focusing on technologies of power seems appropriate for studying the degrees of freedom available to office-holders. Technologies of power appear both enabling and constraining. On the one side, they provide the power-holder with a tool-box for imposing his or her will. In the case of the state bureaucracy, one can then speak of political technologies. On the other side, a set of available technologies defines what is feasible and places limits on the power-holder's potentially boundless desires. For instance, physical force can be used to support claims to power if obedience is achieved through 'the creation of physical obstacles restricting the freedom of another, the infliction of bodily pain or injury including the destruction of life itself and the frustration of basic biological needs'.[16] At the same time, one force can counterbalance the other force and so limit the scope of the latter.

A taxonomy of power relationships can be proposed using as a differentiating criterion the mechanisms for exercising control and imposing will (see Figure 1). It can easily be adapted for the purposes of an inquiry into the constraints of power by listing countervailing factors limiting the scope of uses of a particular technology.

The mechanisms for exercising control and imposing will are listed in association with the degree of violence each entails: they range from violence in its most manifest forms to persuasion by utilitarian arguments and a threefold process of justification. The strategy of coercing (b) refers to the threat of applying negative sanctions, such as force. Coercion differs from force (a), first, because it still leaves the subordinate a choice[17] and, second, because it makes the dominant figure worse off than he or she need be in the event that the tactic fails.[18] Manipulation (c) means 'any deliberate and successful effort to influence the response of another where the desired response has not been explicitly communicated to the other'.[19] Manipulation requires control over information flows and the ability to turn them on and off at will.

FIGURE 1
TAXONOMY OF POWER RELATIONSHIPS

Imposition of the will by

Violence, namely by | Rationalizing it, namely by | Legitimizing it, namely by

a. Applying force
b. Coercing (using threats)
c. Manipulating
d. Virtue of a constellation of interests
e. Structural bias of the system
f. Making obedience pay (giving promises)
g. Enforcing established rules
h. Sharing beliefs
i. Getting consent

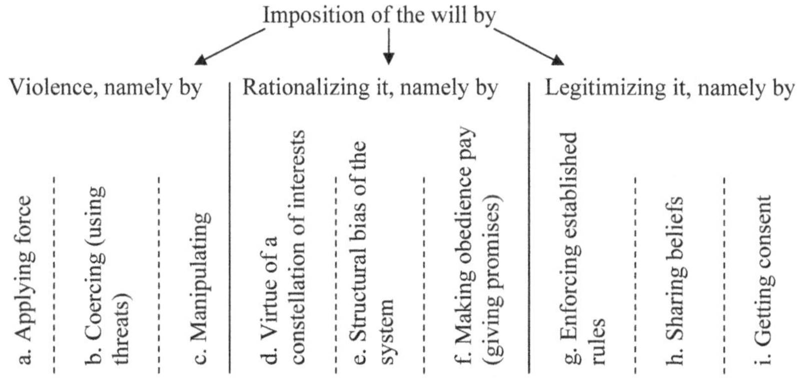

A combination of rational arguments and discretionary restrictions limiting choice makes feasible the next strategy for imposing will (d). Despite the appearance of free choice, the actor who is subordinated to the power of monopoly feels oppressed. 'Because of the very absence of rules, domination which originates in the market or other interest constellations may be felt to be much more oppressive than an authority in which the duties of obedience are set out clearly and expressly'.[20] The actor subjected to monopolistic power has only two options: either to accept the conditions imposed by the monopolist or to abandon the rational pursuit of his or her own interests.

The transfer of control by virtue of a constellation of interests (d) has a broader relevance than the case of economic monopoly. The imposition of will can result from mobilizing a bias of the system. Relationships can be structured in such a way that they systematically favour one party and place the other at a disadvantage: 'Changing the choice situation of people is ... an important way of altering their individual and collective power'.[21] Thus, it is pertinent to introduce a new technology for imposing will in the taxonomy, (e) structurally embedded power. This technology appears especially relevant to the study of bureaucracy: one of its functions consists of enforcing the rules of the game: that is, co-ordination procedures structuring interactions in the society as a whole.

The bias of the system takes at least two forms. First, the rules of the game provide one party with more options corresponding to his or her interests than the other party. In other words, the scope of room for manoeuvre might differ: 'The possessors of superior resources restrict the autonomy of others by limiting the range of relevant considerations and, therefore, the courses of action that they feel are feasible and desirable'.[22] Second, the mere interests and desires of the actor subject to power embedded in the structure can be altered and 'distorted' more than they would be in a 'counterfactual' situation when not being subject to power: '*A* may exercise power over *B* by getting him to do what he does not want to do, but he also exercises power over him by influencing, shaping or determining his very wants'.[23]

The strategy of making obedience 'pay' (f) derives from the model of rational choice in a pure form: a promise of positive sanctions made by the dominant increases the subordinate's gain if he or she transfers the right to control his or her actions. Finally, instead of combining moral, non-utilitarian mechanisms of persuasion (g, h and i) into a single case, I adapt David Beetham's approach to provide a more nuanced picture.[24]

In the proposed taxonomy of power relationships, a set of potential constraints corresponds to each of the nine mechanisms for imposing will that have been identified so far. This helps to systematize the existing and potential constraints of the state servants' discretion (see Table 1). The fourth column contains a tentative assessment of the hardness of each constraint that refers to the discussion in the next part of this study.

TABLE 1
CONFIGURATION OF THE CONSTRAINTS THAT CAN LIMIT THE STATE SERVANT'S DISCRETION

Mechanism of imposing will	Corresponding constraints	Level at which these constraints act	Hardness in today's Russia[†]
a. Applying force	a1. Hierarchical control	Group	+2
	a2. Peer control*	Group	−2
	a3. Other groups struggling for power	National	+1
	a4. Balance of power	International	+1
b. Coercing (threats)	b1. Brinkmanship	International	−1
	b2. Limited war	National/Internat.	−2
c. Manipulating	c1. Freedom of the press	National/Internat.	+1
d. By virtue of a	d1. Market competitiveness	National/Internat.	−2
constellation of interests	d2. Dependence of the economy on international markets	International	+1
e. Structural bias of the system	e1. Non-specific assets	National/Internat.	−1
	e2. Counter-hegemony	National/Internat.	−2
f. Making obedience pay (promises)	f1. Private property enforcement	National	−2
g. Enforcing established rules	g1. Bureaucratic traditions*	Group	−3
	g2. Rule of law	National	+1
h. Sharing beliefs	h1. Divine command (religion)*	National	−1
	h2. Tradition*	National	−1
	h3. Natural law	National	0
	h4. Scientific doctrine	Group/National	+1
	h5. *Volonté générale*	National	−1
i. Getting consent	i1. Charisma*	National	−1
	i2. Freedom of elections	National	+1

Notes: * constraints embodied mostly in informal institutions; [†] a tentative evaluation of the degree of hardness of this constraint; it varies from −3 (this factor only contributes to increasing the room for the state servants' discretion) to +3 (a hard constraint limiting the scope of discretionary behaviour) through 0 (a neutral or negligible impact).

A Tentative Assessment of the Hardness of Constraints

(a1) *Hierarchical control* operates within the state service. It helps to reduce the scope of the discretionary behaviour of individual state servants or small groups and coalitions of state servants, but it has only a limited impact on the scope of the discretion of the state servants as a whole group (the third column of Table 1 contains information concerning the level at which constraints of a particular type can be imposed). Since the end of the 1990s, policies intended to 'strengthen the vertical of power' have led to more efficient hierarchical control *within* the state bureaucracy: 'The Russian state under Putin is more responsible to its population, but not more accountable'.[25] The contrast is especially sharp with regard to the situation of the 1990s when state servants were not closely monitored by their superiors:

> They [state servants] do feel responsible, bear a responsibility to the ugly mechanism of the state, at least the people of my generation do. Our predecessors, apparently, did not. They managed to get away with so much! Sometimes they solicited us to do some foolish things too. They're like fools as far as I'm concerned. You'd be prosecuted immediately! They don't understand this: 'Come on, we went far further than this.' (male, 31–40, former head of a department at the federal level, Moscow)

> There are no such things as bribery in most manifest forms because everyone watches Criminal Russia [a TV show on criminal investigations] and is aware of possible provocations. (female, 31–40, head of a bureau in a federal ministry, Moscow)

Compared with the Soviet system of hierarchical control, the present situation nevertheless seems far inferior. In the former instance, subordinates' room for manoeuvre was narrower and disciplinary sanctions more severe.

> The minister in his industry commanded everyone, from Moscow down to the last rank-and-file worker. All his orders were immediately executed. Now it's not the same … There was a very rigid structure and any discretionary behaviour was immediately prosecuted. (male, 61-plus, associate head of a bureau in a federal ministry, Moscow)

Systems of electronic governance could potentially facilitate the task of monitoring and control by reducing associated costs. This is especially true in so far as A2A (administration-to-administration) systems allow monitoring of the circulation of electronic documents and the execution of orders.[26] The eventuality of increasing control explains several cases of resistance to the introduction of centralized computer systems for the circulation of documents in some post-Soviet countries. For instance, officials of Bulgarian customs did everything they could to postpone the installation of a new computerized system in the first half of the 1990s, presumably because it would have reduced their room for manoeuvre in collecting border taxes and fees, and hence opportunities to take bribes.[27]

Negative sanctions are never enough to induce state servants to behave in a less discretionary way. Negative sanctions can reduce the space for discretionary behaviour, but do not simultaneously prevent subordinates from behaving in this manner as long as that space does not completely disappear, which is possible only at the price of prohibitive costs for monitoring and control. This is why the efficiency of hierarchical control falls short of the maximum in both relative – compared with the Soviet period – and absolute terms (I put '+2' in the fourth column in Table 1).

> In the sphere where I'm competent to judge, vertical power exists only in a negative sense. [Superiors] have enough prerogatives to prevent [inferiors] from doing what [the former] don't want [the latter] to do. But [superiors'] prerogatives aren't enough to motivate inferiors to proceed in a way preferable for superiors. (female, 41–50, expert, Moscow)

(a2) *Peer control*. Mechanisms of control might also be embedded in horizontal structures. Peer groups can limit their members' individual discretion by imposing and enforcing group norms. Then instead of playing his or her own 'game' (pursuing narrowly defined self-interests) the member of a 'team' contributes to the group's well-being. Mechanisms of peer control have the same potential flaw as hierarchy: in the best case, they contribute to reducing the scope of an individual's lust for power while tending to be counter-productive as far as various forms of group discretionary behaviour are concerned. In the best case, peer control contributes to the transformation of non-systematic bribe-taking into systematic and organized corruption.

The expert interviews suggest that peer control functions in the world of Russian office-holders. Bureaucrats form groups whose boundaries do not necessarily coincide with those of their office – they call them 'teams' and 'benches' – on the basis of a common set of interests and values, or a common place of birth or study. Control within these groups reduces the scope of opportunistic behaviour with regard to fellow members and produces trust in relationships among them. Loyalty pays off because of increased chances of being promoted along with the team leader and the access to privileges distributed by him or her:

> Trust is a key word for a team ... A loyal member of the team has no interest in establishing new illicit contacts on his own because they'd jeopardize his status within the team ... This means it's generally expected that the leader provides the members with some long-term benefits. (male, 31–40, former head of a department in a federal ministry, Moscow)

In some situations, peer control reinforces the drift into power as an end in itself and extends the scope of the group of subordinates by extending it to fellow – yet less influential – state servants. In other words, one group within the state service intends to strengthen its domination at the expense of not only ordinary citizens, but other groups of office-holders as well. Peer control not only appears useless in fighting such forms of power lust; it changes into one of the driving forces of power lust by contributing to group cohesion. Anecdotal evidence indicates that a number of groups with strong internal cohesion struggle for domination in the Russian state service and hence in Russian society as a whole: the Moscow group, the Peter (Saint Petersburg) group, the power ministries group (*siloviki*). Peer group control functions efficiently within these groups and helps enforce the key principle of in-group solidarity:

> [The Moscow group] is built on the basis of personal loyalty one has demonstrated during previous work together. *How long it would take to build a good reputation?* Just the time needed to learn how to share [illicit profits] with your superiors. As soon as they see you can do it well, they accept you as a new member of their clan. (male, 41–50, expert, Moscow)

(a3) *Other groups struggling for power.* The potential for violence at the disposal of a group or an individual who controls the state can potentially be counterbalanced by the potential for violence of other groups and individuals struggling for power. Charles Tilly sees the *differentia specifica* of the state in 'eliminating or neutralizing their [the former group's] rivals inside . . . the territories in which they have clear and continuous priority as wielders of force'.[28] The three groups currently invested with power have been successful so far in eliminating potential challengers or reducing the level of resources at their disposal, which seriously undermines challengers' potential for violence. The list of eliminated challengers includes the group of so-called oligarchs – businessmen who made their fortunes during the 1990s (some of the members of this group have been sent to jail, others have been forced into exile), groups of former sportsmen who 'produce, promote, and sell private protection'[29] to businesspeople and who controlled a number of governmental bodies at the regional and federal levels in the 1990s,[30] and traditional organized crime[31] whose representatives also had some political aspirations. None of these groups had any interest in building a modern civil service. Nevertheless, their mere existence put limits on office-holders' discretion. From this perspective, their elimination has increased the room for behaving opportunistically: 'Parties to the bargaining process have absolutely unequal capacities to influence it. The bureaucrat has a strong position, businesses request a favour of him. He doesn't solicit a bribe, he is offered it' (male, 31–40, former head of a department in a federal ministry, Moscow).

One group that still represents a danger for power-holders is their former colleagues: members of the groups that had power in the 1990s but have since lost it. They are dangerous because they know the state machinery well from the inside and still have sympathizers at various levels of the state hierarchy. Conflict between members of the current and previous political elites inevitably emerges in Russia at the time of every succession to the 'throne'.[32]

> They [power-holders] don't fear the elections; they do fear succession to power, which is quite different. For this reason, for instance, they react so anxiously to Kasyanov [the former prime minister]. He is close to them; they understand the seriousness of his aspirations ... Kasyanov and Voloshin [the former head of the presidential administration] are friends. The latter is really fearsome, I worked for him. There is also Khodorkovskii [one of the oligarchs, now in jail], he [Voloshin] also worked with Khodorkovskii ... They [power-holders] fear people like Kasyanov, Khodorkovskii or Berezovskii [another oligarch, currently in forced exile in the UK], because they know these people and understand them. (male, 31–40, former head of a department at the federal level, Moscow)

(a4) *Balance of power.* Geopolitical theory provides us with some useful insights with regard to counterbalancing the potential for violence of the group invested with state power and its rivals outside national borders. In Tilly's terminology, war-making implies a continuous comparison of the potential for violence on an international scale. Randall Collins argues that geopolitical theory appeared to be a very efficient tool for predicting the collapse of the Soviet Union as a result of its over-expansion and geographic location in the middle of an inland region.[33] The last war that the Soviet Union pursued on foreign soil – the invasion of Afghanistan (1979–89) – ended in defeat on the eve of its fall. The fall of the Soviet Union contributed to the strengthening of the unipolar character of international relations and their restructuring around a country with the largest potential for violence, namely the United States.[34] It should be noted that since then the Russian Federation, the key successor to the Soviet Union, has faced few significant threats to its security at the international level.[35] References to a greater power limit the scope of office-holders' discretion in more or less 'peripheral' states:

> The power ministries group, at least those members who work for the FSB [Federal Counterintelligence Service], yet this particular subculture progressively spreads to the rest of this group ... They have fears of the West inherited from the past. If they keep their money offshore, this gives a lever over them to Western intelligence services. This is dangerous, unpatriotic and terrible. (male, 31–40, former adviser to top officials, Moscow)

(b1) *Brinkmanship.* Some strategies help to reduce significantly the need to rely on physical or mental violence, making force a support of the last resort. The first of these strategies, brinkmanship, is 'the deliberate creation of a recognizable risk of war, a risk that one does not completely control'.[36] In terms of contemporary politics, pressure applied from outside the country on the group invested with power may be as efficient, if not more efficient, in limiting the scope of its discretionary behaviour as a more obvious confrontation would be.

For various reasons (one group will be outlined briefly in d2 below), precisely the opposite happens in today's Russia. A number of representatives of the industrially developed states concentrated in the Western hemisphere express support for the Russian power elite (this takes especially obvious forms in the cases of Gerhard Schroeder, the former German chancellor, and Silvio Berlusconi, the former Italian prime minister) and prefer to 'close their eyes' to the potential dangers associated with power as an end in itself in national as well as international affairs. Being representatives of modern states, they are expected to demonstrate that their support has a legitimate character and not to refer simply to pragmatic considerations (such as the need to diversify energy supplies). To solve this dilemma 'they [may] act in ways that keep themselves intentionally uninformed. They do not go looking for evidence'[37] of the perverse effects of the reliance on the representatives of imposed power.

(b2) *Limited war.* The other strategy for playing with threats instead of applying force consists in substituting a small-scale, limited war for a full-scale war. 'One of the functions of limited war ... is to pose the deliberate risk of all-out war, in order to intimidate the enemy and to make pursuit of his limited objectives intolerably risky to him'.[38] The strategy of limited confrontation can be used within national boundaries and in international relations, both by rivals of the dominant group and by the dominant group itself. Limited confrontation, or confrontation with regard to particular policy issues, helps reduce the scope of the dominant group's discretionary behaviour only when applied by its rivals. In the Russian case, the strategy has been used more often by the group invested with power to achieve the opposite ends, namely to increase the scope of discretionary behaviour.

The two Chechen wars (December 1994–May 1996, August 1999 onward) illustrate this point. It is well documented that the first of the two wars resulted from a struggle (potentially large-scale – civil war) with internal rivals of the group – the Yeltsin 'family' – then holding power. 'According to O. Lobov, secretary of the security council of the Russian Federation, "we need a small victorious war, as in Haiti, to raise the president's ratings".'[39] Yet the wars have had important 'side-effects'. In particular, they contributed to the spread of terrorism and turned into a long-lasting military conflict whose scope can hardly be considered 'small'. As one interviewee commented, 'There are [in the power elite] widespread concerns and fears about the situation in Chechnya and the neighbouring regions' (male, 31–40, former head of a department at the federal level, Moscow).

Furthermore, the wars fuelled some criticism from external rivals. However, this criticism has not been intense enough to be considered an example of limited confrontation: international pressure has not produced significant changes in Russian policies in Chechnya so far.

(c1) *Freedom of the press*, if it exists, prevents the group invested with power from controlling information flows and distorting them for the purposes of manipulation. Reporters Without Borders (RWB), an international non-governmental organization, regularly releases press freedom indexes in most countries of the world. Every kind of violation directly affecting journalists (such as murders, imprisonment, physical attacks and threats) and news media (censorship, confiscation of issues, searches and harassment) are enumerated in these indexes. The Russian score systematically lies in the first quartile of the list, that is, in the bottom 25 per cent. Its score has varied from 48 in 2002 to 48.67 in 2005 (a score of zero corresponds to perfect freedom, the highest score to its lack).[40] Only four post-Soviet countries have a poorer record: Turkmenistan, Uzbekistan, Belarus and Azerbaijan (in 2005).

Emphasis is put on distorting information flows rather than on limiting them. Distortions contribute to the creation of a virtual world shaped according to the desires and interests of the group in which power is vested. 'The key to "virtual politics" is that authority is invented; political technologists stage the basic mythology of the state.'[41] It is worth noting that the task of manufacturing misinformation has always been one of the specialities of Soviet and Russian intelligence services.[42] They have elaborated numerous technologies of manipulation:

> The information available to the press is carefully crafted even if it's a presumably very open governmental body. (male, 21–30, associate head of a department in the federal service, Moscow)

> If a ministry is often subject to journalist investigations, it means they've got a bad PR expert who is not doing his job well. (male, 41–50, head of a department in the federal service, Moscow)

Control is tighter over television and relatively looser over the printed press. Criticisms of particular government policies do not necessarily cause the censors to feel anxious, as long as the model of power relationships as a whole remains unquestioned. The availability of the international press also increases the room for manoeuvre and reduces the scope for conscious distortions in information flows: 'In some cases one can use publications in the *Financial Times* as leverage. I know of several examples when *Gazprom* and some government bodies changed their decisions as a result of bad publicity in the West' (female, 41–50, expert, Moscow).

According to our experts' evaluations, control over the printed press seems tighter at the regional level and there are fewer alternative sources of information. At this level, the group invested with power often manages to turn the mass media into an additional mechanism for reproducing power as an end in itself. So the assessment in Table 1 ($+1$: a soft constraint) corresponds only to the federal press. At the regional level it may well be (-1):

> Speaking of [a region in Western Siberia], the press does not influence the process of decision-making. The regional authorities put all the mass media under control, none of them can be considered as oppositional. Even X. [a newspaper known for its independent editorial policies in the 1990s] has become much less critical ... What surprises me is that in public opinion, well, in the opinion of the political elite [*sic*] the leaders of the regions [with relatively tight control over the mass media] are weak. They've got an image of not being able to influence. (female, 31–40, expert, Kemerovo)

Russia does not figure on the RWB 'watch list' of censorship practices on the Internet.[43] However, the absence of apparent restrictions on the RuNet (the Russian segment of the Internet) does not preclude use of the above-mentioned technologies of manipulation. The virtual discourse appears saturated with voices whose origins are hardly identifiable and whose independence is highly questionable (for example, the same political technologist can run several Internet sites, which creates an impression of pluralism):

> No way to get reliable information. I was surfing on the net yesterday and found an interesting article on the situation in Yakutia. I know well all the guys whose names are mentioned and realize what is going on in reality. One group is struggling with the other for power. Yet it is pictured as a crime scene, the policemen make an arrest, etc. A lay person is happy: justice is rendered and corruption punished. This has nothing to do with the real situation. If before one was involved in siphoning budget moneys, now other people will do the same. The latter will spend their previously accumulated incomes on buying freedom out. The people are happy: look – they prosecuted a criminal! Good job, the policemen! (male, 31–40, former vice minister, Moscow)

(d1) *Market competitiveness.* The task of measuring power by virtue of a constellation of interests and its limits in the market requires references to macro-economic data. Economists assume that the closer the market is to a position of perfect competition – which implies a large number of buyers and sellers, a homogeneous character of traded goods or services, free entry to and exit and from the industry – the less room there is for any of the competitors to influence market price and extract rent, and vice versa. Such indicators as concentration ratio (CR_x – the share of the x largest firms in total output) provide us with a rough estimate of the strength of power by virtue of a constellation of interests. For instance, if values of CR_4 lie in the range of 25–50 per cent (that is, the four largest firms produce between 25 and 50 per cent of the total output in an industry), then each of these four firms has some market power and they form a loose oligopoly. Values above 50 per cent would seem to indicate a tight oligopoly. The closer the values are to 100 per cent, the closer the situation approximates to monopoly and the stronger is the market power.

At first sight, the situation in key Russian industries in the first few years after the new millennium was not so serious as to speak of monopolistic capitalism. Only in three industries out of ten – ferrous metallurgy (38.6 per cent), non-ferrous metallurgy (34.4 per cent) and the fuel industry (26.5 per cent) – does the CR_4 value suggests the existence of a loose oligopoly.[44] However, a closer look at the industry in which the lion's share of the Russian GDP is produced, oil and gas, provides a completely different picture. The gas industry is monopolized by Gazprom, whereas the oil industry has the characteristics of a very tight oligopoly (see Table 2).[45]

The non-competitive organization of industries gives business owners an important lever in pursuing their individual and group interests. These interests have an important political dimension: distortions in the structure of competition generated in the market can be protected and even strengthened by political intervention. '"Pure" economic monopolies are logically possible, but seem rare and unstable; on the other hand, monopolies based on political and economic power are common and stable.'[46] In these conditions the question as to who owns a business protected from competitive pressures becomes crucial.

Since 2005 the Russian government directly controls 50.01 per cent of Gazprom capital.[47] The state officially controls three of the eight largest oil

TABLE 2
CONCENTRATION RATIOS IN THE RUSSIAN OIL
INDUSTRY, 2004–6 (%)

	2004	2005	2006
CR_3	52.3	50.5	50.9
CR_4	65.3	64.1	64.5
CR_6	78.2	76.5	76.6
CR_8	87.7	86.9	86

Source: Calculated by the author on the basis of the official data of the Central Dispatching Office of the Fuel and Energy Complex (*TsDU TEK*; <http://about.onlinebroker.ru/news.asp?news_id= 110106.10&pg= 2>, retrieved 9 March 2007; <http://analit.online broker.ru/stock/intraday.asp?news_id=100107.11&pg=10>, retrieved 9 March 2007); the list of the eight biggest oil companies includes Lukoil, Rosneft, TNK–BP, Surgutneftegaz, Gazpromneft [former Sibneft], Tatneft, Slavneft and Yukos).

firms – Rosneft, Gazpromneft and Slavneft. All other key players act under the indirect yet tight control of state servants. One of the means of this control consists in the state monopoly on pipelines. The state servants turn the monopolistic structure of the oil and gas industry into a means to strengthen their hold on power, as witnessed by one of our experts:

> All oil companies are far from being saints. They pump more oil than official statistics show. They're encouraged to pump more, sell more, and then ... *share the profits?* No, the monies go to *Yedinaya Rossiya* [United Russia, the party that controls the federal and most regional parliaments]. It has a special budget. Up to three million tons of undeclared crude oil [annually[48]] are handled through a special firm that ships it by pipelines, sells it and transfers the money to the budget of *Yedinaya Rossiya*. These monies do not show up in any official budgets. (male, 41–50, expert, Moscow)

> As far as the oil and gas industry is concerned, all significant businesses are in fact under tight state control. They are managed by different clans in the [presidential] executive office. (male, 41–50, head of a bureau in the federal agency, Moscow)

(d2) *Dependence of the economy on international markets.* Another potential constraint of power as an end in itself derives from international markets. The more an economy is open to international trade, the fewer chances there are for state servants to control the options available to the subordinate and extract a rent. Yet the openness (measured, for instance, by the size of trade barriers) can play both a constraining and an enabling role with regard to the eventual opportunism of state officials. Their hold on the industry with one of the largest deposits of hydrocarbons in the world puts top Russian officials in a privileged position in international affairs and limits external pressures on them (see b1). They consistently decline any attempts to soften their quasi-monopoly over supplies of gas to Western Europe. For example, the Russian government has been refusing since 2000 to sign the Energy Charter Protocol on Transit that aims at promoting competition as a way 'to ensure secure, efficient, uninterrupted and unimpeded transit' of energy and at granting non-discriminatory access to transit facilities to all potential suppliers of hydrocarbons.[49]

The degree of economic dependence on international markets seems to predict better the behaviour of state officials. If the state enjoys a monopolistic position in the international market, which is the case of Russia at least in the European market for gas, the more open such an economy is, and the greater the opportunities of state servants for extracting rent and converting it into a resource for strengthening power as an end in itself. There is a correlation between the dynamics of world oil prices and Russia's economic growth since the second half of the 1990s.[50] Furthermore, revenues from the export of hydrocarbons are subject to heavy formal and informal taxation.[51] State officials redistribute these revenues and simultaneously lobby for Russia's admission to the World Trade Organization.

(e1) *Non-specific assets.* If the system has a structural bias then one of the interacting parties has significantly greater freedom than the other. This can result from the possession of specific assets. Economists call an asset specific if it has a limited 'redeployability', meaning that in any other combination it will yield less.[52] The owner of the specific asset tends to behave opportunistically: he or she threatens to withdraw it if the counterparts do not increase his or her share in the net profit, quasi-rent. By contrast, the less specific the assets, the more equal the repertoire of choices available to interacting parties.

Asset specificity takes several forms. One of these consists in physical specificity, if production requires a specific technological design or specific inputs. Thus, physical specificity influences the structure of the international market for oil. In fact, there are several segments of this market on which particular types of oil containing different quantities of sulphur are traded: Brent (a blend of oil from the North Sea and North Africa), West Texas Intermediate and West Texas Sour (WTI/WTS), Dubai, Iranian Light and Heavy, Urals (a blend of oil from Russia), and so forth. The level of sulphur determines the specifications of the equipment to be installed at oil refineries. This produces a 'lock-in' effect: after adjusting the equipment for a particular type of crude oil it becomes costly to adapt it to another type. Long-term customers of Urals crude oil then are in a weak bargaining position with the Russian government, which controls oil exports. For instance, the fact that the only Bulgarian oil refinery located in Bourgas has been using Urals crude oil indicates that some choices of the Bulgarian government are conditioned by the position taken by the Russian government.[53]

(e2) *Counter-hegemony.* The structural bias of the system can also take the form of hegemony. This concept, first introduced by Antonio Gramsci, refers to domination over formally independent actors who accept their inferior position because they believe that the associated benefits are greater than in alternative situations. It involves the evaluation of submission in terms of choosing the lesser of two evils, with independence considered as the greater.[54] In contrast to coercion, when the subordinate minimizes eventual losses, in the case of hegemony he or she expects some positive benefits. According to his or her perception of gains, he or she would be relatively better off by not challenging the power-holder and incurring relative (not necessarily absolute!) losses in the opposite case.

The situation in the region of Kemerovo (Western Siberia) illustrates the point. Businesses can work in the region and make profit as long as they accept the rules of the game set by the regional administration. Profit-making appears conditioned by the acceptance of the status quo. In this situation businesses cannot maximize profit because they are required to spend a part of it on various programmes launched by the regional administration – in addition to paying regular taxes. However, if they do not accept these rules of the game, businesses are pushed out of the region. In a sense, this case reveals further trends for the rest of Russia. The hegemony of office-holders consists in setting the rules of the game that protect their dominant positions. Those who accept them could be better off in relative terms; those who do not miss opportunities. No prospects for the emerging counter-hegemony which would allow reshaping rules of the game can be detected so far.

> Only those who take care of interests of the region can work here ... If you're an efficient owner and understand the interests of the region – go and work, good luck with it. If you don't – expect problems ... Here businesses have no choice but to be socially responsible. If they aren't, they'll lose their place. (male, 51–60, head of a committee in the regional parliament, Kemerovo)

> One side of the 'partnership' sets the agenda and shapes rules of the game; the other side accepts the subordinate position. If a business is OK with this, then it acknowledges that you're a boss, I'm a subordinate. (male, 31–40, former head of a department at the federal level, Moscow)

(f1) *Private property enforcement.* If the market approaches the conditions of perfect competition, then justification of state servants' power becomes possible primarily in terms of the exchange of public services in return for taxes. Subordinate economic agents, economists argue, are especially interested in establishing and enforcing exclusive property rights by the state because well-defined and protected property rights help to reduce uncertainty in interactions, create incentives for a more efficient use of resources and avoid the 'tragedy of the commons' – over-exploitation of open-access resources.[55] 'The creation of an infrastructure designed to specify and enforce a body of property rights entails the delegation of power to agents of the ruler.'[56] As a result, a constraint upon the discretion available to the dominant party emerges: the subordinate considers power relationships acceptable as long as the dominant party commits himself or herself to respecting and protecting property rights. In this situation, obedience does pay because it allows the individual to accumulate wealth and gain power over material objects.

The commitment of Russian state servants to keeping their promises respecting property rights raised serious doubts in the past and apparently continues to be problematic now. Power as an end in itself makes any property rights conditional. This gives rise to the phenomenon of power-property: power over human beings leads to power over material objects embodied in property rights:[57]

> Why do people often aspire to have power, not money? Because power helps make money. If you get a grasp on power, you'll get money ... Anyone who controls administrative resources has money. (female, 31–40, expert, Kemerovo)

> Now businesspeople seek positions in the state hierarchy precisely to redistribute the property, to get some stakes of this property. (male, 41–50, former adviser to a top official at the federal level, Moscow)

A series of empirical studies shows that violations of property rights committed by state servants represented the major obstacle to doing business in Russia in the early part of the present decade.[58] Clifford Gaddy and Barry Ickes argue that insecure property rights induce owners of resources to maximize short-term gains at the expense of long-term profits. In the oil industry, for instance, this leads towards the depletion of old oilfields and under-investment in new explorations.[59]

The Heritage Foundation assesses the security of property rights in a comparative perspective while calculating its annual 'Index of Economic Freedom'. A negative trend can be observed in the Russian case: the level of protection and enforcement of property rights by the government changed from '3' (on a scale of 5), which corresponds to a moderate level, in 1995–2001 to '4' (a low level: property ownership weakly protected, court system inefficient, corruption present and expropriation possible) in 2002–6.[60]

The *Yukos* case – the forced redistribution of property rights as a result of criminal charges brought by state prosecutors against the owners of the largest Russian oil company, Mikhail Khodorkovskii and Platon Lebedev – indicates that the dangers of expropriation are especially high in the oil and gas industry because of its importance for the reproduction of power as an end in itself. The two businessmen were arrested in October 2003; in September 2005 they were found guilty of tax evasion, fraud and a number of other economic crimes and sentenced to eight years in jail.[61] In the end, the key assets of *Yukos* were redistributed in favour of the state-controlled firm Rosneft. The former company has lost its leadership in the oil industry (it pumped the eighth largest volume of crude oil in 2006), whereas Rosneft changed from being an outsider (ranked eighth among the eight largest oil companies in 2004) to become one of the leaders (ranking second in 2006; the volume of pumped crude oil increased by 245 per cent between 2004 and 2005). The belief that 'the assault on *Yukos* has thus far been unique, both in form and content'[62] ignores the reputation of the Russian government with regard to using violence inherited from the Soviet predecessor. If the business community interprets a single exemplary prosecution as a credible threat, then state officials manage to increase the room for discretionary behaviour even without regularly carrying out the threat![63]

(g1) *Bureaucratic traditions*. Long-lasting bureaucratic traditions exist in Russia, but they contain very few, if any, elements of rational decision-making. 'Lasting patterns of thought and operation in Russian administration . . . exist in one country over a period of more than a century and under three or more very different regimes.'[64] This continuity of power as an end in itself, however, is not easily decipherable: the forms of state servants' discretion change repeatedly. An external observer gets the impression that no rules of decision-making exist at all and there is no point in guessing the outcomes of administrative deliberations. The lack of written job descriptions and specifications covering the circulation of documents further complicates the task of predicting the behaviour of bureaucrats:

> We attempted to work out regulations, algorithms for decision-making: if yes then one thing, if no then otherwise. This would reduce the impact of the human factor . . . Now we've got all of them although at the beginning there was no single regulation. Not only in our [federal] service, nowhere [in government offices]. (male, 51–60, associate director of a federal service, Moscow)

The lack of the continuity of 'rationalistic' bureaucratic traditions can be attributed to a high turnover at the lowest layer of the Russian bureaucracy (from the entry-level positions of experts up to associate heads of bureaus) combined with limited opportunities for vertical mobility and promotion to the middle and highest layers in the hierarchy (the former comprises heads of bureaus and associate heads of departments, the latter heads of departments, vice ministers and ministers). Seventy per cent of those who start their professional career in the state service do not expect to reach a position higher than the head of a bureau in the end.[65] They naturally have only short-term objectives concerning a bureaucratic career: to establish useful connections, to acquire particular know-how before applying for a job in business in three or four years:

> A maverick, somebody who is not well-connected, can reach at best the level of the head of a bureau. No chance to go further regardless of his qualities and efforts . . . At the lowest level the turnover is extremely high . . . People come, for example, to learn the basic accounting and then leave. (male, 21–30, associate head of a department in the federal service, Moscow)

> The key interest of applicants is to get a valuable experience, not necessarily related to the state service. They're interested in adding an entry to their CVs and establishing useful contacts with businesses. (male, 41–50, head of a bureau in the federal service, Moscow)

An attempt was recently made to establish new administrative traditions. Presidential decree No. 885 on General Principles of Professional Behaviour of State Servants (*Obshchie printsipy sluzhebnogo povedeniya gosudarstvennyh sluzhashchikh*) enacted on 12 August 2004 outlines a set of moral standards, including a top priority of the rights of the individual and citizen: respect for the law; impartiality; the need to avoid conflict of interest, and so on.[66] The decree does not specify any mechanism for enforcing these principles; instead it states that they are only voluntary (their breach does not figure among reasons for dismissing the state servant).[67] Thus, there is a high risk that these moral standards will be ignored in everyday life, as often happened with standards imposed from the top down in the past.[68] The real 'moral code' of the state service includes quite different ethical prescriptions and imperatives: pragmatism as a terminal value (the contradiction in this formulation is only apparent, taking into consideration the particularities of power as an end in itself by virtue of a constellation of interests); obedience to superiors coupled with ignorance of inferiors, Them (borrowing the Us/Them opposition from anthropology), and so forth.

> It seems to me that this [bureaucratic] culture is characterized by an incredible flexibility, the complete absence of values, any extrinsic criteria for judging behaviour. (female, 41–50, expert, Moscow)

> The only thing that unites the state servants is the love for Franklin [on US dollars]. Nothing else. (male, 31–40, expert, Moscow)

(g2) *Rule of law*. A rich body of both quantitative and qualitative data suggests that the legal framework does not place strict limits on the behaviour of state servants in Russia. For instance, Transparency International studies annually the perception of corruption in the public and political sectors in a comparative perspective. The Russian score has never been high: experts and business people, both resident and non-resident, do not consider the rule of law to be efficiently enforced.[69] As Vladimir Dal', Russian ethnographer and linguist, said in the second half of the nineteenth century, 'high authority is above the law'.[70] It is worth noting that the scores of some other post-Soviet countries, namely the Baltic States, do show a significant variability and progress towards a more law-bound civil service (for instance, the score of Estonia has improved from 5.7 in 1998 to 6.7 in 2006). Only five post-Soviet states had lower scores in 2006: Uzbekistan, Belarus, Tajikistan, Turkmenistan and Kyrgyzstan.

Our expert interviews confirm the loose character of the constraint related to the rule of law, but help bring out nuances in the picture. The low- and middle-ranked state servants adhere to the letter of the law, which can be verified and enforced relatively easily with the help of tight hierarchical control (a1). The task of hierarchically monitoring their adherence to the principles and general meaning of the law appears less feasible:

> The law does not count a lot, only the letter of the law. A decision has to adhere to the letter of the law, only to the letter, I'm afraid, not to its meaning. (female, 41–50, expert, Moscow)

> Let's consider the request for information made by a member of parliament. What really matters here is to send an answer before the deadline [set by the law]. We write the answer: Dear NN, as per your request we inform you that we do not have such information about X. Regards, data and signature. Formally speaking, the procedure was respected, the deadline wasn't missed. (male, 31–40, former head of a department at the federal level, Moscow)

Subordinates – ordinary Russians – have a very limited capacity to enforce the law from below. The number of litigations with state servants is a less telling indicator than the ratio of the cases that have been won. New opportunities related to submitting a case to the European Court of Human Rights increase the chances of success, yet the procedure is too time-consuming and costly to result in any radical changes in the situation:[71] 'I know several such cases [litigations with state servants]. Sometimes they can be successful enough. But such cases represent at best 10–15 per cent of their total number' (male, 41–50, expert, Saint Petersburg).

The law constrains top office-holders to an even lesser degree. They do not necessarily feel constrained even by the letter of the law: the scope of their power allows them to reshape the law, selectively applying and transforming it into a weapon. The law then should be considered as 'a form or dimension of social power'.[72] Instead of violating the law when it puts limits on office-holders' discretion, they prefer to reshape it according to their wishes by enacting new laws and revoking old ones. It can be done either through substituting decrees (issued by the executive) for laws, as in the 1990s, or by keeping the legislative branch under control of the executive. Top state executives in the current situation can do both: the ratio of the number of enacted laws to that of decrees in 2000–2003 increased compared with 1996–99, yet insignificantly (1.23 against 1.04);[73] the executive holds a majority in the Russian parliament through its proxy, the party *Yedinaya Rossiya*: 'In this country every group of office-holders [that attains power] practically re-writes all laws' (male, 41–50, head of a bureau in the federal agency, Moscow).

The law is selectively enforced in respect of the enemies of top office-holders who consider themselves above the law:

> Everything goes according to the Franco [the interlocutor most probably makes a mistake and means not the Spanish dictator Francisco Franco, but Oscar R. Benavides, President of Peru in 1933–40] principle: 'For my friends, anything; for my enemies, the law'. The legal constraint is tight only in this sense. (male, 31–40, expert, Moscow)

(h1) *Divine command (religion)*. In tsarist Russia religious faith was included in the repertoire of constraints on the ruler's discretion, at least at the discursive level. To continue the excerpt from Dal's definition of power, 'great authority [meaning high authority] derives from God. Any authority derives from God. Any authority reports to God'. It is questionable whether religious faith constituted an efficient constraint at that time (the state tightly controlled the Holy Synod, the Russian Orthodox Church's governing body), but during Soviet times the state, namely the KGB, increased its influence on all key appointments at the highest layers of the church hierarchy.[74] More recently, the increased economic dependence of the Orthodox Church on the state[75] (in the form of tax exemptions, for instance) prevents it from taking a more or less critical stance on issues related to state administration.

(h2) *Traditions* that exist at the level of the nation as a whole are functionally different from state service traditions. The latter refers to the enforcement of established rules, the former to a set of beliefs shared by both the dominant and the subordinate. Nevertheless, in the Russian case there is significant discontinuity in national traditions. Russians rank traditions rather low (usually the last or the next to last of 11 proposed alternatives) while speaking about their order of priorities, the constitution of an ideal society in Russia and that of the actual society, the resources and the conditions that they consider important for achieving their goals, and so forth.[76]

The results of a survey conducted in 2002 by FOM – Public Opinion Foundation on sources of shame and pride in the Russian national consciousness provides us with a more colourful picture of the discontinuity. The term 'great divide' seems appropriate indeed: Russians appear extremely ambivalent with regard to the history of their country in general and its different periods in particular (see Table 3). The period before the 1917 revolution gets 11.7 per cent of votes: it was mentioned by 7 per cent of respondents as a source of pride and by 2.7 per cent as a source of shame (if a characteristic was attributed to a longer period of time – for instance, 'the lack of respect for ordinary people' – then the percentage of votes was divided by the number of periods covered). Some 80.2 per cent of respondents mentioned Stalinism

TABLE 3
SOURCES OF PRIDE AND SHAME IN RUSSIAN HISTORY (PERCENTANGE OF
RESPONDENTS WHO MENTIONED THEM)

	The 2000s	The 1990s	The 1960 − 1980s	Stalinism	Before 1917
Sources of pride			Exploration of space (14) Achievements in sports (9)	Victory in WWII (41) Recovery after WWII (2)	The rule of Peter the Great and other events (9)
			The Soviet Union (13) Strong state (4) Achievements in science (4) Military–industrial complex (3)		
Sources of shame	The rule of Yeltsin and other events (10)	The rule of Gorbachev (3) The war in Afghanistan (6) The rule of Khrushchev (1) The rule of Brezhnev (1) Communism (3)	Stalinism (18) Revolutionary violence (4)	Slavery and other events (2)
		Undue behaviour of the country leaders (2)		
	Poverty (2)			
		The lack of respect for ordinary people (1)		

Source: FOM – Public Opinion Foundation, at <http://bd.fom.ru/report/cat/man/shame_pride/d020608>, retrieved 9 March 2007); N = 1,500 in 44 regions of the Russian Federation.

(+56/−24.2), 49.2 per cent the post-Stalin period (+35/−14.2), 11.7 per cent the 1990s (all in a negative sense). Besides the 1990s (the negative perception of traditions associated with this period bears a consensual character), all the other periods of time give rise to extremely ambivalent feelings. Thus, traditions are of little help in finding a set of beliefs shared by most Russians independently of their position in the state hierarchy.

It is worth noting that a negative tradition – the lack of respect for the individual – was attributed to all periods in Russian history, although only a small fraction of respondents made this observation. Most Russians in the early 1990s, according to the data of the All-Russian Centre for Public Opinion, endorsed the tradition of 'hierarchical egalitarianism': they used to reject only those inequalities that did not derive from established power.[77]

(h3) *Natural law.* A score of zero – indicating negligent impact on state servants' discretion – can be attributed to natural law as a basis for agreement in respect of the justification of power relationships. The doctrine of natural law, which considers power relationships as entailed by the nature of the world and of human beings, is deeply entrenched in the European school of thought, especially during the Age of Enlightenment.[78]

(h4) *Scientific doctrine.* A scientific doctrine popular among both state servants and ordinary people can reduce the scope of the discretionary behaviour of the former group: their power enjoys legitimacy as long as they act in accordance with scientific prescriptions. 'Scientific communism' is a well-known example but not the only one: according to some scholars, the rise of early capitalism in England was due to a large extent to the popularity of the writings of Adam Smith, Jeremy Bentham and Joseph Townsend among members of some groups in the English population and their representatives in the parliament as well as a particular configuration of powers in parliament.[79] Referring to a scientific doctrine to justify power relationships produces the rule of experts.

It is worth discussing subtle yet important differences between the rule of experts and rational bureaucracy. First, rational bureaucracy is 'value-free': it derives from respect for technical rules and procedures in decision-making (for this reason rational bureaucracy is compatible, according to Weber, with quite diverse political regimes), whereas the behaviour of experts can be better described in terms of value-based rationality. If bureaucrats are bound by procedures, experts are bound by the ideology embedded in a scientific doctrine. Second, experts do not necessarily commit themselves to the office and consider their job – sometimes temporary – as a vocation. Yet Weber places the vocation of office-holder (*Beruf*) at the centre of his analysis of bureaucracy.[80]

In the context of domination by virtue of a constellation of interests, the services of a special kind of experts – technocrats – appear to be in high demand. The technocrat is 'a policymaker who is motivated to pursue the objectives postulated by traditional *normative* economic analysis'.[81] Not surprisingly, the rule of experts was considered the most popular alternative to democracy in most East European and post-Soviet countries in the mid-1990s. The idea of the rule of experts, for instance, was endorsed by 56 per cent of Romanians and 90 per cent of Slovaks.[82]

Technocrats represent only a small fraction of the state service in Russia today. Most of them were recruited in the 1990s when the rhetoric of capitalist domination took on its most obvious forms. Their mere presence makes the state service more predictable on the basis of rational calculations, yet technocrats (or 'experts') are far from forming a dominant group in either quantitative or qualitative terms: 'I was hired through competition; I was a complete stranger who had no ideas about the functions of the state servant. I advanced quickly and I was not the only one. There existed a special procedure for supporting smart young people' (male, 31–40, former head of a department at the federal level, Moscow).

(h5) *Volonté générale*. Referendums and initiatives serve to make operational and concrete the abstract notion of *volonté générale*.

> Referendum means that laws and resolutions made by representatives must be submitted to the people for acceptance or rejection . . . Initiative

means that people have the right not only to vote on proposals but also to *initiate* the enactment of new laws or constitutional amendments, and alter or abolish old ones, if a certain number of people so request.[83]

According to Russian law, citizens and their groups do not have the right to initiate the enactment of new laws (for comparison, 51.4 per cent of 216 amendments voted in Switzerland between 1874 and 1985 were popular initiatives).[84] The constitution of the Russian Federation specifies the list of subjects entitled to take initiatives; it includes the president, the upper house of parliament, members of the upper and lower houses of parliament, the government and the regional parliaments in the 'subjects' of the federation (Article 104). The right of the constitutional court, the supreme court and the supreme commercial court to initiate new laws is limited to their jurisdictions.

On the other hand, Russian citizens can ask to have a referendum held on an important issue. The first law of the Russian Federation on referendum was enacted on 16 October 1990, the second on 10 October 1995 and the third on 28 June 2004 (the last version is currently in force). Each consecutive version of the law made the task of holding a referendum more difficult. To hold a referendum, the group of citizens who propose it has to get approval from a number of other citizens. The first law (Article 10) set this minimal requirement at the level of 10 million without establishing any requirements with regard to their place of residence. The second law (Article 8) increased the level to 20 million and stated that they should represent at least ten regions of the Russian Federation (out of 88). Article 14.1 of the third law does not change the minimum number of signatures but adds that they must be collected in at least 40 regions (and not more than 50,000 in each). It goes without saying that these developments narrow the scope of collective action from below. The need for large-scale co-ordination and organization implies that only proposals supported by the powerful elite have good chances of success:

> Decisions were initiated from below under Gorbachev's rule and at the very beginning of Yeltsin's rule. After 1993, well, even earlier, after 1992, one should forget about this. (male, 41–50, expert, Saint Petersburg)

> Popular protests played a very important role. In the 1990s they were common and had a broad, sometimes extreme scope. When miners, for instance, blocked the traffic on the Trans-Siberian railroad … this had an impact. (male, 41–50, former adviser of a top official at the federal level, Moscow)

The language of political technologies and administrative resources progressively takes the place of references – real or spurious – to the common will in political discourse. From this perspective the common will does not and cannot exist: it is simply a fiction, an empty abstraction. The population is then transformed into a meaningless aggregate subject to manipulation by different organized groups, mainly by groups invested with power: 'Almost every significant political force, and some insignificant ones, is subject to political manipulation'.[85] From the point of view of office-holders, mass protests can be anything but spontaneous; they assume that all mass actions are staged – either by themselves or by groups trying to challenge their power: 'Anyone who has money or power can stage public activities. Government bodies or pressures groups often inspire different "public" initiatives and proposals in order to lobby their own interests' (male, 51–60, head of a committee in the regional parliament, Kemerovo).

(i1) *Charisma*. The adjective 'charismatic', in Weber's classic explication, applies to 'the bearers of specific gifts of body and mind that [are] considered "supernatural"'.[86] The requirement that a charismatic leader has to possess these qualities and, furthermore, that they be recognized as such and acclaimed by the subordinate potentially limits the room for discretionary behaviour.

In the Russian case, causal relationships apparently work the other way around: power as an end in itself provides access to mechanisms of imposing will – for instance, manipulation – that help to persuade the subordinate of the dominant's supernatural qualities. Charisma appears compatible with plebiscitarian autocracy: 'instead of recognition being treated as a consequence of legitimacy, it is treated as the basis of legitimacy'.[87]

On the other hand, because charisma allows its bearer to have an independent source of legitimate power, it cannot be tolerated among low- and middle-ranked office-holders. In this perspective, the Russian state service does not look exceptional: 'Charisma is really harmful, because of potential competition. This is one of the worst qualities of the state servant' (male, 31–40, expert, Moscow).

(i2) *Free and competitive elections* held on a regular basis are often considered the single most effective constraint on the discretion of the powerful elite. At least the 'export' version of democracy promoted by international organizations and Western governments often takes a 'realistic' form: it is relatively easy to organize formally free elections and have them monitored by external observers. At the same time, if formally free elections are not complemented and reinforced by other constraints of power as an end in itself, there is a high risk of discrepancy between the form and the content. This is why 'realistic' democracy often turns into plebiscitarian autocracy.[88] Formally free elections are not enough to place hard constraints on the powerful elite: they are a necessary yet insufficient condition for achieving this result. The concept of guided democracy as its distorted or inverted – to use

Marxist terms – form provides us with some useful insights in this respect. It means that 'the organization of patronage within established vertical relationships ensures that the exercise of electoral choice by subordinate classes poses no threat to the dominant powers within society or state'.[89]

The task of 'guiding' democracy calls for so-called administrative resources as means for influencing voters' choices. The list of administrative recourses used in Russia, in particular, includes command–administrative methods (bosses demand that their subordinates vote for a particular party or candidate and apply administrative sanctions to those who do not obey); manipulation of election results (electoral fraud); budget financing for electoral projects supported by power-holders; turning lights and heating in flats on and off at will (that is, sending a signal that the level of comfort depends on voters' support for a particular party or candidate), and so forth.[90] 'Staged' political initiatives (see h5) also contribute to producing electoral results desirable for groups invested with power: 'Non-governmental organizations are our tool during elections' (male, 51–60, a top executive in the government in Moscow).

International observers characterize the elections that have been held recently in Russia as competitive but unfair. For instance, the Organization for Security and Co-operation in Europe (OSCE) Office for Democratic Institutions and Human Rights sent its observers to the presidential elections in 2004 and the parliamentary elections in 2003. In their opinion, the former were 'generally well administered but lacking elements of a genuine democratic contest', whereas the latter were 'well organized but failed to meet many international standards'.[91]

The Freedom House organization has been evaluating political rights and civil liberties throughout the world since the early 1970s. The results of its annual surveys provide a framework for judging the degree to which elections in a particular country are free *and* fair. Freedom House uses two indexes, one for political rights and another for civil liberties. The former includes a series of questions to establish whether there exist fair electoral laws, equal campaigning opportunities, fair polling, and honest tabulation of ballots; whether there is a significant opposition vote, de facto opposition power, and a realistic possibility for the opposition to increase its support or gain power through elections; whether the people have the right to organize in different political parties or other competitive political groupings of their choice, and the system is open to the rise and fall of these competing parties or groupings, and so forth. The combination of two indexes gives a good approximation of both the freedom and fairness of elections. In contrast to many other post-Soviet countries, specifically the Baltic States, Russia has not shown any progress since its independence in 1991. On the contrary, this country sees its score declining from 3.0 (a partially free political system) in

1992 to 5.5 (a system that is not free) in 2005–6, below the score of the Soviet Union in the late 1980s (4.5 in 1991, 5.5 in 1990 and 1989).[92] In 2006, only three out of 15 post-Soviet states – namely, Turkmenistan, Uzbekistan and Belarus – had a lower score than Russia.

Conclusion

The study of the existing constraints on power enables us to test the hypothesis about the character of power in a particular institutional context, namely post-Soviet Russia. The lack of constraints or their loose character means that one cannot rule out the hypothesis of office-holders' opportunistic behaviour. So long as more comprehensive information about values and the everyday behaviour of individuals and groups invested with power remains unavailable, we can assume that the model of *power as an end in itself* dominates in the Russian institutional context.

In the present situation the tentative assessment of elements of the institutional environment shows that most of them *enable* office-holders' pursuit of individual and group interests rather than *constraining* them. The potential constraints look quite weak: my very rough and preliminary estimate gives a total score of −10 on the scale ranging from −63 (absolute discretion on the part of state servants: 21 absolutely weak constraints transform into a partisan weapon in office-holders' hands) to +63 (absolutely hard constraints). The contribution of the elements that limit the discretion of groups invested with power was evaluated at +9, that of the factors enabling discretionary behaviour at −19.

What can actors contribute to strengthening each of the institutional constraints listed in Table 1? The actors at the international level – Western governments and corporations, international organizations and social movements – have limited leverage to influence the situation, even if they decide to do so (an unlikely possibility). In fact, they can influence the severity of only a few constraints: (a4), (b1), (b2) and (c1), and to a lesser degree (d1) and (d2). Furthermore, hopes for changes induced from above paradoxically further the logic of imposed power because they derive from the implicit assumption that 'the person over whom power is exercised is not usually as important as other power-holders'.[93]

Much more ought to be done from below. However, the proposed reasoning leads to an apparent contradiction: if power as an end in itself is embedded in existing institutional structures, how can one expect individuals and groups who act within these same structures to challenge it? To avoid this contradiction, we need to question deterministic assumptions in respect of human behaviour. To what degree is human behaviour determined by external constraints embodied, for instance, in institutions and to what degree can the actor go beyond institutionally prescribed roles? This age-old sociological question, which has not yet been answered satisfactorily, appears relevant in the context of post-Soviet transformations. No changes from below are imaginable if we stay within the limits of purely reactive and deterministic models of human behaviour. The history of modern countries teaches us that determinism is not absolute, and only the continuous struggles of collective actors representing the interests of subordinates for limiting the scope of power elites' discretionary behaviour has produced a configuration of power relationships usually associated with modernity. In other words, 'popular resistance to war making and state making made a difference'.[94] A crucial difference, one might perhaps add.

The other condition under which an escape from the vicious circle of institutionally embedded power becomes possible consists in convincing social and economic actors that other configurations of power relationships may be far more attractive for them. 'It is only from a standpoint outside given power relations that it is possible to understand the processes whereby their legitimacy is maintained and reproduced, and what are the forces at work eroding it, where such erosion is taking place.'[95] Yet, unfortunately, social surveys show that most Russians simply do not believe that any alternative to the current political regime is feasible. 'Since those with a preference for an alternative regime are a minority, most Russians appear resigned to accept it as "the only regime in town".'[96]

NOTES

1. Michel Crozier, *Le phénomène bureaucratique* (Paris: Editions du Seuil, 1963).
2. Amitai Etzioni, *The Moral Dimension: Toward a New Economics* (New York and London: The Free Press, 1988), p.12.
3. See, for example, Robert J. Brym and Vladimir Gimpelson, 'The Size, Composition and Dynamics of the Russian State Bureaucracy in the 1990s', *Slavic Review*, Vol.63, No.1 (2004), pp.90–112; Institute of Sociology of the Russian Academy of Sciences, *Byurokratiya i vlast' v novoi Rossii: pozitsiya naseleniya i otsenki ekspertov* (Bureaucracy and Power in New Russia: The Perception by the Population and Experts' Evaluations), final research report (Moscow: Institute of Sociology of the RAS, 2005); *Federal'naya i regional'naya elita Rossii: kto yest' kto v politike i ekonomike* (Federal and Regional Elites in Russia: Who is Who in Politics and Economy) (Moscow: Center for Political Information, 2004).
4. Alexander Khlopin, 'The Phenomenon of "Double-Thinking": Specific Features of the Role Behaviour', *Social Sciences* (Quarterly Review), Vol. XXV, No. 4 (1994), pp. 68–83 (p. 70).
5. Anton Oleinik, Natalia Aparina, Karine Clément, Eugenia Gvozdeva, Aleksandr Kashturov and Mikhail Minin, *L'Analyse socio-économique du blanchiment* (Paris: Institut National des Etudes de Sécurité, 2005).
6. Ronald H. Coase, *The Firm, the Market and the Law* (Chicago, IL and London: University of Chicago Press, 1988).
7. Oliver E. Williamson, *The Economic Institutions of Capitalism: Firms, Markets, Relational Contracting* (London and New York: Macmillan and the Free Press, 1985), p.30.
8. Anthony Giddens, *The Constitution of Society: Outline of the Theory of Structuration* (Cambridge: Polity Press, 1984), p.169.

9. The idea of the 'bias of the system' derives from a 'three-dimensional' view of power developed in Steven Lukes, *Power: A Radical View*, 2nd edn (Basingstoke and New York: Palgrave Macmillan, 2005). Nevertheless, Lukes does not link this bias to conscious actions: compare the opposition of power as a result of conscious actions with luck as a result of getting what one wants without acting in Keith Dowding, *Power* (Minneapolis, MN: University of Minnesota Press, 1996).
10. Thomas E. Wartenberg, *The Forms of Power: From Domination to Transformation* (Philadelphia, PA: Temple University Press, 1990), p.117.
11. This project is carried out by a team of researchers led by the author, composed of Prof. Svetlana Glinkina (Institute of Economy of the Russian Academy of Sciences), Evgenia Gvozdeva, Dr Karine Clément (Institute of Sociology of the Russian Academy of Sciences), Dr Natalya Aparina (Kemerovo State University) and Dr Galina Medvedeva (Sociological Institute of the Russian Academy of Sciences); it was funded by the Social Sciences and Humanities Research Council of Canada (award No. 820-2005-0004).
12. János Kornai, *Economics of Shortage* (Amsterdam: North-Holland, 1980), Vol.A, pp.25–6; Vol.B, pp.561–5.
13. Wartenberg, *The Forms of Power*, p.12.
14. Lukes, *Power*, p.36.
15. Dennis Wrong, *Power: Its Forms, Bases and Uses* (New York: Harper Colophon Books, 1980), Ch.2; Valeri Ledyaev, *Power: A Conceptual Analysis* (Commack, NY: Nova Science Publishers, 1997), Ch.12; John Scott, *Power* (Cambridge: Polity Press, 2001), Ch.1.
16. Wrong, *Power*, p.24.
17. Ibid., p.38; Wartenberg, *The Forms of Power*, p.100.
18. Thomas C. Schelling, *The Strategy of Conflict* (Cambridge, MA: Harvard University Press, 1960), p.123.
19. Wrong, *Power*, p.28; Ledyaev, *Power*, pp.190–93.
20. Max Weber, *Economy and Society: An Outline of Interpretative Sociology*, edited by Roth Guenther and Claus Wittich (Berkeley, CA: University of California Press, 1968), p.946.
21. Dowding, *Power*, p.24.
22. Scott, *Power*, p.72.
23. Lukes, *Power*, p.27.
24. See Anton Oleinik, 'Introduction: Putting Administrative Reform into a Broader Context of Power' (this collection).
25. Linda J. Cook, 'State Capacity and Pension Provision', in Timothy J. Colton and Stephen Holmes (eds.), *The State after Communism: Governance in the New Russia* (Lanham, MD: Rowman & Littlefield, 2006), pp.121–54 (p.144). Peter Solomon suggested that the word 'responsive' seems more appropriate in this context.
26. For an overview of different systems of e-governance see Vassilios Peristeras and Theodore Tsekos, 'e-Governance as a Public Policy Framework', UNTC Occasional Papers No.4 (Thessaloniki: United Nations Thessaloniki Centre for Public Service Professionalism, 2003), pp.4–10.
27. I am grateful for this example to Prof. Rumen Gechev, former deputy prime minister and minister of economic development of Bulgaria (1995–97).
28. Charles Tilly, 'War Making and State Making as Organized Crime', in Peter B. Evans, Dietrich Rueschemeyer and Theda Skopol (eds.), *Bringing the State Back In* (Cambridge and New York: Cambridge University Press, 1985), pp.169–91 (p.183).
29. Diego Gambetta, *The Sicilian Mafia: The Business of Private Protection* (Cambridge, MA and London: Harvard University Press, 1993), p.1.
30. See Vadim Volkov, *Violent Entrepreneurs: The Use of Force in the Making of Russian Capitalism* (Ithaca, NY: Cornell University Press, 2002).
31. See Anton Oleinik, *Organized Crime, Prison and Post-Soviet Societies* (Aldershot and Burlington, VT: Ashgate, 2003).
32. Vasily Klyuchevskii, 'Kurs russkoi istorii' (Lectures in Russian History), in Vasily Kliuchevskii, *Sochineniya* (Moscow: Izdatel'stvo sotsial'no-ekonomicheskoi literatury, 1958), Vol.4, pp.211–12; Yuri Pivovarov and Andrei Fursov, 'Pravopreemstvo i russkaya vlast'' (Succession and Russian Power), *Politiya – Vestnik fonda ROPC*, No.1 (1998), pp.68–80.

33. Randall Collins, 'Prediction in Macrosociology: The Case of the Soviet Collapse', *American Journal of Sociology*, Vol.100, No.6 (1995), pp.1552–93.
34. See, for example, Centre for Study of Globalization and Regionalization, *Democratizing the Global Economy: The Role of Civil Society*, research report (Coventry: University of Warwick, 2004).
35. Timothy J. Colton, 'Introduction: Governance and Postcommunist Politics', in Colton and Holmes (eds.), *The State after Communism*, pp.1–20 (p.8).
36. Schelling, *The Strategy of Conflict*, p.200.
37. Albert Bandura, 'Mechanisms of Moral Disengagement', in Walter Reich (ed.), *Origins of Terrorism: Psychologies, Ideologies, Theologies, States of Mind* (Washington, DC: Woodrow Wilson International Center for Scholars and New York: Cambridge University Press, 1990), pp.161–91 (p.189).
38. Schelling, *The Strategy of Conflict*, p.193.
39. Valery Tishkov, *Chechnya: Life in a War-Torn Society* (Berkeley, CA: University of California Press, 2004), p.127.
40. Source: <http://www.rsf.org/rubrique.php3?id_rubrique=554>, accessed 9 March 2007.
41. Andrew Wilson, *Virtual Politics: Faking Democracy in the Post-Soviet World* (New Haven, CT and London: Yale University Press, 2005), p.xvi.
42. Yevgenia Albats, *The State Within a State: The KGB and Its Hold on Russia – Past, Present, and Future* (New York: Farrar, Straus and Giroux, 2004), p.30.
43. Reporters Without Borders, *Internet under Surveillance* (2004), available at <http://www.rsf.org/rubrique.php3?id_rubrique=433>, accessed 9 March 2007. Several other post-Soviet countries were mentioned in this RWB report, including Armenia, Azerbaijan, Belarus, Kazakhstan, Kyrgyzstan, Turkmenistan, Ukraine and Uzbekistan.
44. Federal State Statistics Service, *Promyshlennost' Rossii: statisticheskii sbornik* (Industry in Russia: statistical yearbook) (Moscow: Goskomstat, 2002), p.56. But if one uses alternative indicators, for example the share of the total industrial output produced by the 200 largest Russian firms, there is clear evidence that the concentration has been rising since the second half of the 1990s, with the exception of the years 2002 and 2003. The value of this indicator increased from 35 per cent in 1996 to 58 per cent, the historical maximum for the post-Soviet period, in 2003: data of the Rating Agency 'Expert RA' <http://www.raexpert.ru/researches/> and the personal communication of Prof. Svetlana Avdasheva, the State University – the Higher School of Economics. The author is indebted to S. Avdasheva for providing him with this data.
45. A more precise estimate can be obtained if links within vertically integrated groups are taken into consideration. Not all links in these groups have a formal and transparent character. As a result, a formally independent unit may appear to be embedded in a vertically integrated group. For instance, CR_3 in the oil industry calculated according to the Federal State Statistics Service in 2001 was 32.5 per cent, whereas its adjusted value was significantly higher at 51.2 per cent: see Svetlana Avdasheva, Tat'yana Alimova and Guyzel Yusupova, 'Vozmozhnosti ispol'zovaniya statisticheskoi informatsii dlya identifikatsii gruppy lits' (On Uses of Statistical Data to Identify a Group of Persons), *Voprosy statistiki*, No.5 (2005), pp.9–17.
46. Etzioni, *The Moral Dimension*, p.227.
47. Gazprom, *Godovoi otchet* (Yearly Report) (Moscow: Gazprom, 2005), p.68.
48. In 2005 Russia produced in total 470.2 million tons of crude oil.
49. Energy Charter, *Energy Charter Protocol on Transit*, draft, Art.2.1 and 8.4, at <http://www.encharter.org/fileadmin/user_upload/document/CC251.pdf>, accessed 9 March 2007.
50. Clifford G. Gaddy, 'Perspectives on the Potential of Russian Oil', *Eurasian Geography and Economics*, Vol.45, No.5 (2004), pp.346–51 (p.347).
51. Clifford G. Gaddy and Barry W. Ickes, 'Resource Rents and the Russian Economy', *Eurasian Geography and Economics*, Vol.46, No.8 (2005), pp.559–83 (pp.563–7).
52. See Claude Ménard, 'Transaction Cost Economics: From the Coase Theorem to Empirical Studies', in Anton Oleinik (ed.), *The Institutional Economics of Russia's Transformation* (Aldershot, and Burlington, VT: Ashgate, 2005), pp.245–64 (pp.54–5).
53. I am indebted for this case to Prof. Rumen Gechev.

54. For a discussion of hegemony in different forms see Scott, *Power*, Ch.4.
55. Thráinn Eggertsson, *Economic Behavior and Institutions* (Cambridge and New York: Cambridge University Press, 1990), pp.84–91, Chs.8 and 9.
56. Douglass C. North, *Structure and Change in Economic History* (New York: Norton, 1981), p.25.
57. See Richard Pipes, *Property and Freedom* (New York: Knopf, 1999), Chs.2 and 4.
58. Timothy Frye, 'Credible Commitment and Property Rights: Evidence from Russia', *American Political Science Review*, Vol.98, No.3 (2004), pp.453–66.
59. Gaddy and Ickes, 'Resource Rents in the Russian Economy', pp.572–4.
60. Source: <http://www.heritage.org/research/features/index/indexoffreedom.cfm>, accessed 4 Nov. 2006.
61. The economic aspects of this case are discussed in more detail in Anton Oleinik, 'Institutional Traps in the Post-Privatization Development of the Russian Economy', in Oleinik (ed.), *The Institutional Economics of Russia's Transformation*, pp.xiii–xxviii.
62. Erika Weinthal and Pauline Jones Luong, 'The Paradox of Energy Sector Reform', in Colton and Holmes (eds.), *The State after Communism*, pp.225–60 (p.245).
63. See Schelling, *The Strategy of Conflict*, Ch.5.
64. Karl W. Ryavec, *Russian Bureaucracy: Power and Pathology* (Lanham, MD: Rowman & Littlefield, 2003), p.1.
65. Vladimir Gimpel'son and Vladimir Magun, 'Na sluzhbe gosudarstva rossiiskogo: perspektivy i ogranicheniya kar'ery molodykh chinovnikov' (In State Service: Prospects and Impediments to the Career of Young Bureaucrats), working paper WP3/2004/07 (Moscow: Higher School of Economics, 2004), pp.18–19.
66. Valeri Grazhdan (comp.), *Rossiiskaya grazhdanskaya sluzhba* (Russian Civil Service) (Moscow: Yurkniga, 2005), pp.117–18.
67. See the Federal Law on the Civil Service in the Russian Federation, enacted 24 July 2004, Art. 33 and 37.
68. See, for example, Vladimir Shlapentokh, *Public and Private Life of the Soviet People: Changing Values in Post-Stalin Russia* (Oxford and New York: Oxford University Press, 1989), pp.18–50.
69. See Figure 1 in my Introduction to this volume.
70. Vladimir Dal', *Tolkovyi slovar' zhivogo velokorusskogo yazyka* (Dictionary of Live Russian Language), Vol.I (Moscow: Gosudarstvennoe izdatel'stvo inostrannykh i natsional'nykh slovarei, 1955; originally Saint Petersburg: Wolf, 1880); entry *Vlast'*.
71. According to Luzius Wildhaber, the chairman of the European Court of Human Rights, Russia came in first in the number of complaints in 2005 (approximately 20 per cent of all complaints originate in this country) and this number keeps growing: see *Kommersant*, 27 Oct. 2006.
72. Austin T. Turk, 'Law as a Weapon in Social Conflict', *Social Problems*, Vol.23, No.3 (1976), pp.276–91 (p.276).
73. Thomas Remington, 'Democratization, Separation of Powers, and State Capacity', in Colton and Holmes (eds.), *The State after Communism*, pp.261–98 (pp.276–7).
74. Albats, *The State within a State*, pp.43–7; Michael Voslensky, *Nomenklatura: The Soviet Ruling Class* (Garden City, NY: Doubleday, 1984), p.75.
75. See for more details Nikolai Mitrokhin, 'Russkaya pravoslavnaya tserkov' kak sub"ekt ekonomicheskoi deyatel'nosti' (The Russian Orthodox Church as an Economic Subject), *Voprosy ekonomiki*, No.8 (2000), pp.54–70.
76. Oleinik, *Organized Crime*, pp.165–6.
77. Youri Levada, *Entre passé et l'avenir: L'homme soviétique ordinaire. Enquête* (Paris: Presses de la Fondation Nationale des Sciences Politiques, 1993), p.40.
78. See André-Jean Arnaud (ed.), *Dictionnaire encyclopédique de théorie et de sociologie du droit* (Paris: L.G.D.J., 1999), p.199.
79. Karl Polanyi, *La Grande Transformation: Aux origines politiques et économiques de notre temps* (Paris: Gallimard, 1995), pp.156ff.; North, *Structure and Change in Economic History*, pp.156ff.
80. Weber, *Economy and Society*, p.958.

81. Richard Rose and William Mishler, 'What Are the Alternatives to Democracy in Post-Communist Societies?', *Studies in Public Policy*, No.248 (Glasgow: University of Strathclyde, 1995), p.16 (emphasis in the original).
82. Ibid.
83. Reuven Brenner, *Labyrinths of Prosperity: Economic Follies, Democratic Remedies* (Ann Arbor, MI: University of Michigan Press, 1994), p.155 (emphasis original).
84. Ibid., p.156.
85. Wilson, *Virtual Politics*, p.38.
86. Weber, *Economy and Society*, p.1112.
87. Ibid., p.267.
88. On different political regimes, including plebiscitarian autocracy, see Richard Rose, William Mishler and Neil Munro, *Russia Transformed: Developing Popular Support for a New Regime* (Cambridge: Cambridge University Press, 2006), Ch.1.
89. David Beetham, *The Legitimation of Power* (Atlantic Highlands, NJ: Humanities Press International, 1991), p.174.
90. Wilson, *Virtual Politics*, Ch.4.
91. Source: <http://www.osce.org/odihr-elections/14519.html>, accessed 9 March 2007.
92. Source: Freedom House at <http://www.freedomhouse.org/uploads/fiw/FIWAllScores.xls>, accessed 9 March 2007. A free country has a rank between 1 and 2.5; a partially free one between 3 and 5; one that is not free 5.5 and below.
93. Arthur L. Stinchcombe, cited in Tilly, 'War Making and State Making as Organized Crime', p.171.
94. Ibid., p.183; see also Pipes, *Property and Freedom*, pp.146–58.
95. Beetham, *The Legitimation of Power*, p.110.
96. Richard Rose, William Mishler and Neil Munro, 'Resigned Acceptance of an Incomplete Democracy: Russia's Political Equilibrium', *Post-Soviet Affairs*, Vol.20, No.3 (2004), pp.195–218 (p.204).

Basis for Regime Legitimacy: Study of Attitudes Toward Privatization in Ukraine

NATALIA POHORILA

Economic Interests as a Component of Regime Legitimacy

The aftermath of the presidential electoral campaign in the autumn of 2004, known as the Orange Revolution, received significant attention from analysts within Ukraine and throughout the world. Irregardless of varied hypotheses about the driving forces behind this national outburst, it is difficult to contest the statement that the key question of revolution was legitimization of the ruling power. If we define 'legitimate power' as that which people obey because they think it has a moral right to expect compliance,[1] then we can identify the power of that moment, which was termed 'kuchmism' after the power-holder, President Leonid Kuchma, as illegitimate. On the eve of the 2004 presidential campaign, 'kuchmism' was perceived as more corrupt, non-transparent and non-reciprocal than ever before.[2] It is true that public protests were initiated four years in advance of the Orange Revolution, in 2000 and 2001,[3] but they reached an unprecedented scale when the incumbent power decided to falsify the elections of 2004.

It cannot be said that the protests were exclusively headed and initiated by the political opposition, which was supporting its candidate Viktor Yush-chenko. Adherents of Viktor Yanukovych, his opponent, were also determined in their decision to defend their choices. It seems that both parties were demanding a transparent electoral campaign and an honest contest between candidates. Without questioning the legitimacy of the political regime, voters protested against the way Kuchma implemented its goals, and his rating was abysmally low on the eve of the elections.

However, the relationship between power and legitimacy has a longer and deeper story than that of electoral campaigns and political repressions in Ukraine. The conviction that the power-holders have been robbing the country since it obtained independence in 1991 was heard long before kuchmism. It seems that the principal reasons are unsuccessful economic reforms and, in particular, an ineffective and corrupted process of privatization.

For the first three years after obtaining national independence, Ukraine saw no economic reforms other than the introduction of national currency. In 1994 the voucher privatization programme was launched.[4] This is now defined by economists as a tool for achieving the political goal of prompt privatization rather than as an economic tool.[5] But mass privatization did not bring immediate increase in salaries, financial middlemen were untrust-worthy, and redemption of enterprises' stocks often ended in their capture by the former directors. Although at the end of 1999 most of the small and medium-sized companies were privatized, continued economic recession called forth the necessity of 'large privatization' as was documented in 'The national programme of privatization' adopted in 2000. This programme aimed to solve the fiscal problem by selling control stocks of the largest enter-prises at the commercial price in open contests. Although this goal was partially achieved, and GDP growth was secured after 2000, the programme also provided previously unknown opportunities for corruption. State bureaucrats exercised much freedom in manipulating conditions to make privatization poss-ible only for select financial-industrial groups supported by political power. Fictitious bankruptcy, legislative collusion and creation of joint ventures followed by asset tunnelling were typical mechanisms of individual privati-zation, as disclosed in the spectacular example of *Kryvorizhstal'* the largest steel works in Ukraine. The Fund of State Property issued a special condition for prospective buyers: the presence of stable coal production in Ukraine in exchange for the elimination of foreign bidders. As a result *Kryvorizhstal'* was sold below market value to one of the largest financial-industrial groups.

Although most corrupt transactions could not be prosecuted by the law because of their formal allegiance to the law, truth and fantasies about scan-dals around privatization attracted wide public attention and caused a strong drop in support for large-scale privatization in 2004–5.[6] The notorious case of *Kryvorizhstal'* became 'the symbol of oppositional fight against the ruling regime'.[7] The presumption that the government of Yulia Tymoshenko, appointed in 2005, was occupied with the re-privatization of *Kryvorizhstal'* and other companies during the first three months of its rule is the best proof of the importance of 'fair privatization' as the main instrument of legitimization of the power of the 'Oranges'.

The process of re-privatization, which escalated after 2005, was referred to as 'political process' by the politicians of the new opposition and in fact it had little in common with lawful 'restoration of fairness'. The Oranges were starving for legitimization and this made them more prone to value-loaded statements than the rule of law. Lena Kolarska-Bobinska, concerning the first generation of reformers in Poland, defined this type of legitimacy as based on 'the mission of the new system's building'[8] which, adjusted to the Ukrainian situation, can be rephrased as the 'mission of fight with oli-garchs' system'. The critics of re-privatization stated that the whole burden of blame in corruption fell onto the shoulders of those who purchased the enterprises, omitting those officials who were responsible for the transaction under unfair conditions. The political character of re-privatization contributed to a new round of corruption within the new government. Acute confrontation between Tymoshenko and other interested parties led to the dismissal of her government in the summer of 2005 (she returned to the office in late 2007).

The present situation with privatization is still observed as an extremely politicized process in which decisions on privatization of each large public asset depend on political compromises among the ruling coalition's parties.[9] This situation can hardly be understood without pointing to the most important social transformation, the merging of state bureaucracy and private capital in one force, which greatly contributed to the alienation of the general population from privatization and, as a consequence, from the ruling power.

Significant Actors of Legitimization

A brief overview of the history of privatization in Ukraine propels the con-clusion that it was conducive to enlarging the distance between the power and the masses. Survey data collected since 1994 show not only low trust for politicians but also businesspeople, banks and directors of state-owned enterprises.[10] The important observation is that the level of trust after summing up the answers 'completely trust' and 'rather trust' did not exceed 13 per cent before 2005 but, in February of 2005, three months after the elec-tion of Yushchenko and a month after the appointment of Tymoshenko's gov-ernment, the level of trust in the power structures was extremely high. However, a year afterwards it had decreased again, although not to the 2004 level. Unsolved economic and social problems and political scandals within the ruling party contributed to this disappointment. Unsuccessful emphasis on re-privatization and inefficient privatization of large enterprises probably affected the attitudes.

It should be said that the level of attitudinal support does not exhaust the question of legitimization. As David Beetham pointed out, power is legitimate not because people think it is legitimate, but because it is grounded in common beliefs shared by both the power-holder and the subordinate.[11] People provide legitimization for the regime through their everyday activities: taking decisions about their financial investments, employment, spending for consumption, family planning and general coping strategies. People may think that privatization and business development are generally positive because they contribute to the common good; however, if they do not invest their money in the domestic economy, do not grow as potential customers of domestic products or companies and do not take any initiatives in the private sphere, they hardly provide support for the economic system based on the open market. If people do not believe that the economic system can provide solid ground for their personal growth, they tend to 'capsulate' their resources, both human and material: withhold from investing money or labour in the domestic economy, reduce family growth so as not to have excessive needs, abstain from business initiatives in order to avoid risk and so on. And still this does not mean that people will call the legitimacy of the economic system into question. Referring to privatization, one can speak about two sets of values: moral justification and instrumental value. The latter enables practical adjustment to the system. It is possible that people will think the economic system is legitimate even though they cannot derive gain from it. And the opposite situation is also theoretically possible: people can be sceptical about the regime although they have the opportunity to benefit from it.

In the literature these combinations are known as different levels of legitimization.[12] Full legitimization of the regime or ideal normative agreement is possible when citizens share the basic values of the regime and are able to act successfully in it. Instrumental acceptance – individuals comply despite not giving the regime a moral endorsement because there is an advantage for them in the long run. Finally, normative agreement is the situation when people perceive regime as moral even if they cannot benefit from it.

In the case of privatization, ideal normative agreement means support for private property rights and at least attitudinal readiness to function within the private economy: to work in business, to invest in the domestic economy, to launch start-ups. Instrumental acceptance is typical for those who can use the advantages of privatization, and normative agreement exists when people believe that a given regime is able to protect a common good even though they cannot benefit from it.

The question is how these levels of legitimization vary across different social groups. If privatization is indicated as one of the ways to legitimize power in Ukraine, it is important to know which social groups are the most interested and ready to participate in the private economy. Since the distance between the power and the people is a problematic issue, and a consequence of an ill-developed process of privatization, these groups can be defined as 'potential bridges' over this gap. In this part of the present study, socio-occupational groups are chosen as units of analysis, since they are the closest proxy of economic interests that can be measured in a sociological survey.

It is rare in Ukrainian social science to consider the events of the Orange Revolution in terms of class or economic interests. However, there are theoretical assumptions about the role of an emerging middle class,[13] younger generations of businesspeople and students in the social sciences and humanities,[14] as a driving force of the events. It is argued that these 'new' social groups developed their own economic interests during the period of national independence; and that the existing oligarchic system and shadow relationship restrained their economic growth. One can also hypothesize that for the Oranges the support of the 'old' social groups was important as well, although maybe for different reasons. The group of intellectuals or professionals, for example, who were considered as a driving force of systemic transformation in the 1980s, also could be 'potential bridges', even if they express only 'normative agreement'.

'New' and 'old' social groups differ in the amount and quality of resources which they are able to invest in the economy. Some may be interested in the private economy or privatization process as a coping strategy in the face of losing other sources of income; employees of state-owned enterprises could be such a group. These would provide 'instrumental agreement'. And, finally, social groups vary in their level of ongoing engagement in the privatization process if they already own private business, work for it or control the process of privatization. Directors who have contacts with large masses of people as their subordinates, and state officials who contact their clients and represent the 'face of the state' for them, can be seen as 'opinion leaders' in this respect.

By and large these groups can be defined as 'socially significant actors of legitimization'.[15] It can be hypothesized that those who gained either economic or political liberties due to the introduction of the new regime, the so-called 'winners of transformation', will be the most committed actors of legitimization in the privatization sphere. Numerous studies proved that the incomes of better educated professionals increased after the introduction of market rule in comparison with those of the less educated workforce.[16] This aligned their economic interests to market reforms; and there is ample empirical evidence that position in the occupational hierarchy is closely connected with acceptance of market reforms and privatization: highly skilled professionals definitely approve changes much stronger than labourers.[17]

Managers and state officials can be simultaneously considered as actors of both legitimization and de-legitimization. By their strategic position they are the closest to the 'political class', as it was described by David Lane, because in the market economy they have no property for the means of production, but have control over access to various resources.[18] We would expect from managers and officials general loyalty to privatization, since for many of them it provided new opportunities to control previously inaccessible resources. For example, directors received relative independence from state intervention in their business and an opportunity to legalize the assets which they actually already owned. State officials, in turn, received an opportunity to control the privatization process and to make profit from their position.

On the other hand, this group is expected to have normative allegiance to market norms, because they occupy an intermediary position between the power-holders and the ordinary people, and actually serve the political regime which is supposedly responsible for and interested in the loyalty of the employees. However, it is probable that normative support is not correlated with economic interest of this group. State officials do not have a chance to get a second job, and not all of them have an opportunity to make profit from their control of privatization. Managers may have more opportunity to benefit than officials. However, there is a relatively high risk of downward mobility for the older part of the directorate. Empirical studies in Poland showed that managerial groups, the former nomenklatura were fairly susceptible to downward mobility in the early 1990s.[19] Irrespective of the strength of social capital, a director in the case of bankruptcy can no longer enjoy the guaranteed support of the state in return for his/her loyalty.

The working class is believed to be a bearer of paternalistic interests. Even though the working class made up the core *Solidarność*, anticommunist movement in Poland, it was recognized as the group whose interests are against, rather than for, market reforms.[20] According to evolutionist theory, the economic interests of the working class are subject to change, as are the interests of any other groups. Experiencing different stages of reform, the workers may have recognized that most reforms contravene their interests, prompting them to redefine their economic interests in response to the changing social or economic environment.

Regional Differences

It can be said that the types of legitimacy are extremely unevenly distributed throughout the territory of Ukraine: one can risk an assumption about the prevalence of normative or axiological agreement in the West and pragmatic in the East. At the referendum for national independence of Ukraine on 1 December 1991, extensively Russified eastern oblasts' support for independence was unexpectedly high – above 83 per cent. This is explained by the fact that the Easterners were promised that the regional industrial product of coal mining, which was previously driven by Moscow, would be left for Ukraine, making Donetsk oblast the most affluent region of energy-poor Ukraine. Bohdan Krawchenko and Alexandr Motyl discuss pragmatic legitimization of national independence in this part of Ukraine in contrast to axiological motivation of the Westerners, who voted for cultural and economic independence from Russia.[21]

For a decade and a half after obtaining independence, sociologists reported disappointment and political apathy in Eastern region, which survived strong economic and cultural depression despite still very powerful industrial potential.[22] However, the political victory of Eastern party 'Regions' in the 2006 parliamentary elections, and that of Yanukovych as a Premier-Minister, could have changed the situation. Easterners received economic protection which, although not openly declared by Yanukovych, was expected by his electorate, concentrated mostly in Donetsk oblast. Easterners' pragmatic orientation could have caused their consolidation on an economic basis and more active disposition to practical privatization. In contrast, the Westerners who became disappointed after the year of the 'Orange' rule, could probably have partially lost their normative support which was very high until 2005.

Dispositions Towards Political Regime and Political Culture

The variable 'occupational group' may have a secondary importance for explaining the support for privatization. The ill-developed process of privatization could have caused the misalignment of social inequality and corresponding social interests along professional lines. Support to or opposition for the political regime of 'kuchmism' unites people across occupational groups, which provides a relevant explanation for the level of support for privatization. A tricky question is whether support for 'kuchmism' is correlated positively or negatively with support for privatization. Market orientation was declared as a major blueprint of policy endorsed by both President Kuchma and Yushchenko, his political opponent. However, if it is true that private entrepreneurship was handicapped due to abuses of power associated with 'kuchmism', those who were apt to start businesses of their own would be opposed to the government and mistrustful of Kuchma as president.

Another consideration is political culture, known from Gabriel Almond and Sidney Verba's book *The Civic Culture* as the concept of civic competence.[23] Disposition to start business in a country with a weak tradition of private initiative implies a great deal of self-confidence, readiness to protect one's interests, political awareness and ability to mobilize. One can assume that these abilities are accumulated in 'civic competence' – a belief that one can influence the situation if power-holders take an unfair decision.

Both civic competence and desire to start one's own business are qualities of a committed social actor. They imply a disposition actively to protect one's political or economic interests. This means that a declared readiness to protest in defence of one's interests is a correlate of the disposition to start business, especially if it is perceived that those interests are being violated. Consequently, this correlation is expected to be stronger before the Orange Revolution.

Data Description

The present analysis applies the data collected in a nationally representative self-administered questionnaire, 'Ukrainian Society', in February of each year since 1994. In total, 1,800 adults are selected in a stratified random sample with quota selection at the last stage. It is conducted by the Institute of Sociology of the National Academy of Sciences of Ukraine, field work is done by the Center for Social and Political Investigations SOCIS. This is the only long-term observation of Ukrainian public opinion which covers the most important social problems and attitudes. It was initiated in 1994 by Ukrainian sociologists Yevhen Golovacha and Natalia Panina to monitor changes in social well-being. In presenting the data in dynamics, we consider the full sample of 1,800 cases.[24] Annual differences higher than 5 per cent are statistically significant at 1 per cent. In the analysis of occupational groups we used only respondents currently employed in the labour market. Since the research interest was in changes after the Orange Revolution, we grouped together two available datasets, 2005 and 2006, comprising of 1,724 respondents. In order to provide a comparable basis we merged two data files, 2003–4, that comprised 1,654 respondents who were in the labour force. This allowed us to compare two samples of approximately the same size. From the point of view of annual changes, this is the most appropriate method of data grouping since most variables of social well-being stopped changing after 2001. This suggests some stabilization of attitudes; until 2000 many variables of social well-being were steadily worsening.[25] The distribution of respondents in occupational groups is presented in Table 1.

TABLE 1
NUMBER OF INTERVIEWEES IN THE MERGED DATA FILES,
2003–4 AND 2005–6

	2003–4	2005–6
Managers and state officials	53	100
Professionals	378	384
Semi-professionals	273	264
Businesspeople (big and small)	158	153
Manual workers	792	823
Total	1654	1724

In order to display smaller groups we merged five datasets from the 2001 to 2006 annual waves (Table 2). This dataset is extremely important since it enables the consideration of occupational groups – managers, state officials and big business – which are normally very small in a representative survey.

Support for Privatization and Economic Interests

As the data show, general support for business development in Ukraine is stable: since 1996, 51 to 54 per cent definitely support and rather support development of private business. However, support for privatization of some particular sectors is lower and is decreasing. Thus, privatization of small enterprises, which was supported by roughly half of the population in the 1990s, in 2006 has 43 per cent support; support for privatization of land has dropped three times since 1992 and support of large enterprises by 2.5 times. In 2006 support for privatization of land composes 24 per cent and

TABLE 2
NUMBER OF INTERVIEWEES IN THE MERGED
DATA FILE, 2001–6

Managers	55
State officials	73
Professionals-technical	508
Professionals-humanists	471
Semi-professionals	590
Military	87
Big business	59
Small and medium business	336
Manual workers	2016
Students	361
Pensioners	2520
Unemployed	1622
Total	8698

of large enterprises, 11 per cent. It can be concluded that although the population is very critical towards the strategy of privatization of state property, it does not resist privatization per se, which is stably supported by half of the population. Juan Linz and Alfred Stepan call this phenomenon a 'legitimacy-efficacy gap' to describe individuals' ability to distinguish between the blueprint and the implementation of the plan in practice.[26]

The desire to work for private business was initially as high as the support for business development. However, in 2002 strong proponents of hired labour for private companies decreased suddenly from 40 to 16 per cent of the able-bodied respondents. At the same time, the share of Ukrainian citizens who would not mind starting their own business has been relatively stable and is approximately as high as the support for private business development.

Wladyslaw Adamski also observed in Poland in the early 1990s the diminishing attractiveness of hired labour for private companies and the relatively stable and high preference for owning a business instead of being employed by a private entrepreneur, if respondents are theoretically given a choice.[27] Simultaneously he observed a growing attractiveness of working for state-owned enterprises, an option which was not given in the Ukrainian version of the questionnaire. The analysis of dynamics of these preferences within occupational groups in Poland showed significant trends, which allowed Adamski to interpret the results in terms of constant redefinition of group interests. The finding was that skilled workers and semi-professionals ('mixed manual and non-manual labour' in the Polish classification) are responsible for two opposite tendencies: an increased disposition to work for state-owned companies and, simultaneously, a growing interest in starting businesses of their own. Professionals showed the opposite propensity: increased desire to work for a private employer rather than state-owned companies or their own business. It was only the group of unskilled workers who showed the undoubted preference to work at state enterprises (a leap from 40 to 60 per cent in 1995). Adamski explains that initially statist-oriented skilled manual workers are interested in protection of the workplace and they perceive state-owned enterprises as a more stable employer. However, at a certain point, supposedly after the closure of many state enterprises, some of them have recognized private business as a way of improving their economic lot.

As far as professionals are concerned, it could be assumed that some of them probably reassessed their economic interests after the experience of market reform in Poland showed them difficulties with running their own business, about which they were so enthusiastic at the beginning of reforms in the 1990s. Perhaps this can be explained by the fact that initially most businesses in Poland were engaged in trade activities, which are not considered prestigious by better educated layers of the population.

TABLE 3
DISPOSITION TO WORK FOR A PRIVATE ENTREPRENEUR AND OCCUPATIONAL
GROUPS, UKRAINE, BEFORE AND AFTER THE ORANGE REVOLUTION

'Would you like to work for private entrepreneur?'	2003–4			2005–6		
	'Yes'	'No'	Difference	Yes	'No'	Difference
Managers and state officials	9.4	13.2	−3.8	14.0	43.0	−29.0
Professionals	10.3	13,5	−3.2	19.8	27.4	−7.6
Semi-professionals	8.1	17.9	−9.8	23.3	26.3	−3.0
Manual workers	11.1	17.2	−6.1	25.3	26.2	−0.9

The Ukrainian data presented in Table 3 are somewhat different from Adamski's findings. The difference is that the time period is the early 2000s, more than 10 years after the Polish study. It can be hypothesized that the reconsideration of interests may be motivated by the aspirations raised by the events of November 2004.[28]

Although all occupational groups showed an increase in negative answers, in the groups of manual workers and semi-professionals the scale of increase of positive answers is larger than that of negative, while professionals, especially managers, displayed the opposite tendency. So, it can be said that at least some manual workers and semi-professionals reassessed their economic interests in favour of private rather than state-owned companies after 2004. Perhaps this is the result of some partial success of the Oranges to legitimize power by efforts to reform privatization principles. The remaining negligible difference in earnings in the two sectors of the economy speaks in favour of this assumption.

An obvious fact is that managers, 80 per cent of whom in our sample work for state-owned enterprises, and state officials reassessed their interests, but not in favour of private companies. If we merge together five waves of the monitoring 'Ukrainian Society' (years 2001 through 2006), we get a large enough group of managers to draw the conclusion that they comprise the biggest portion, except pensioners, of those who are not interested in working for private business – 39 per cent compared with 29 per cent of the national sample.

Formally the situation of managers is understandable: it is not advantageous to be employed by private business if you are in the prestigious position of being a manager. However, an interesting fact is the rapid growth of negative attitudes in this group and that of state officials after 2004: by 25 points according to Table 3. It seems that state officials and directors of state-owned plants perceive a worsening of working conditions in private enterprises and consider them as an unreliable or unbeneficial employer, which may have some accuracy since these two groups are in a way 'insiders of the process'.

It can be summarized that since 2005 we observe the growth of two polar categories, noted in the definite 'Yes' or 'No' responses to work for private companies. It seems that manual workers and semi-professionals are the most split group (the difference between 'Yes' and 'No' answers is minimal, Table 3). It can be hypothesized that the split is explained by age: younger workers of whatever level of qualifications may be more 'pro-private' and more willing to take risks to try to get higher incomes in unstable conditions, and their human capital is more in demand than that of the older generations.

However, survey data (Table 4) show a different scenario. Indeed in 2005–6 the youngest respondents comprise the highest percentage of those who would like to work for a private entrepreneur, and this grew by 10 points after 2004. However, in the other two groups, except the oldest one, the number of proponents of private companies has doubled. But at the same time, we also see that the number of opponents has doubled. This means that the two middle age groups are at least as divided in relation to working for private companies as occupational groups, with the strongest divide observed in the 26–40 year-old group.

Interestingly, education has little effect on the choice of employment sphere in Ukraine, although the studies show that the young and the better educated benefited the most in incomes. Some variations among the regions of Ukraine are observed, but they cannot be compared with variations and dynamics observed in occupational groups.

Further analysis has convincingly shown that semi-professionals and manual workers displayed higher dynamics of readiness to start businesses than professionals (Table 5). This conforms with Adamski's findings. Manual workers and semi-professionals showed higher growth of approval (by 12 per cent, difference is statistically significant at the level of 1 per cent) than professionals. As a result we can see that the desire to start one's own business changed from 'class-based' interest in 2004 (first column of

TABLE 4

DISPOSITION TO WORK FOR A PRIVATE ENTREPRENEUR AND AGE, UKRAINE, BEFORE AND AFTER THE ORANGE REVOLUTION

'Would you like to work for private entrepreneur?'	2003–4			2005–6		
	'Yes'	'No'	Difference	'Yes'	'No'	Difference
18–25	19.7	7.7	12.0	31.4	15.5	15.9
26–40	12.6	11.7	0.9	25.3	22.9	2.4
41–60	8.0	21.2	−13.2	16.5	39.3	−22.8
61 and older	4.4	38.2	−33.8	6.6	57.9	−51.3

TABLE 5

DISPOSITION TO START ONE'S OWN BUSINESS AND OCCUPATIONAL GROUPS
BEFORE AND AFTER THE ORANGE REVOLUTION

'Would you like to start your own business?'	2004			2005–6		
	'Yes'	'No'	Difference	'Yes'	'No'	Difference
Managers and state officials[1]	n.d.	n.d.	n.d.	32.0	24.0	8.0
Professionals	27.2	15.7	11.5	29.9	20.3	9.6
Semi-professionals	20.0	15.6	4.4	32.6	16.3	16.3
Manual workers	17.8	21.3	−3.5	30.4	23.8	6.6

[1]Since the question was asked only in 2004, the number of observations is not sufficiently large to allow consideration of the results.

Table 5) to 'class independent' variable in 2005–6: positive attitudes prevail over negative in all main occupational groups and do not vary much among groups. The same can be said about negative attitudes. Thus, excluding the group of top managers, we can further develop the hypothesis about ongoing polarization of occupational groups into proponents and opponents of business initiative.

The role of age and education are specific for this variable. The share of those pro-business is maximal within the youngest group of 18–25 years: 47 per cent in 2003–4 and 50 per cent in 2005–6. Since 2004, significant growth (by 10 points) was observed among 26–40 and 41–60 age cohorts that made up 37 and 25 per cent of positive replies, respectively. In terms of education, the growth of pro-business attitudes was observed in all groups (7–8 points), although the highest growth (12 points) was observed in the group with less than secondary education, which had a minimal interest in business ownership in 2004 (difference between years is statistically significant at the level of 1 per cent). This means that besides social groups which are traditionally defined as supporters of privatization – the young and educated – other groups, somewhat older and less educated, also exhibited interest in starting their own businesses after 2004.

Earlier we discussed the role of regional differentiation in Ukraine as an explanation of attitudes towards privatization. The different economic structure of Ukrainian regions may have consequences for perceptions towards business. Perhaps these regionally different perspectives are responsible for the growth of pro-business intentions within the older, less educated and worse positioned labour force. This would be evident if a region demonstrates growth in some specific sectors not requiring high levels of education (real estate operations or recreation businesses).

Table 6 makes it visible that in 2001 Western region showed the strongest disposition to running one's own business. This could be explained by strong

TABLE 6
DISPOSITION TO RUN OWN BUSINESS AND REGIONS, PERCENTAGES

Answers definite 'Yes'	West	Center	South	East	Ukraine
2001	47.9	33.0	33.3	25.3	34.1
2004	25.8	16.4	24.5	20.3	20.7
2005–6	28.6	28.2	32.5	25.4	28.1

normative support for the market economy in Western cities and villages during the whole period of independence, where the preference for pro-reform and pro-Western development was well-documented.[29] However, this enthusiasm had dramatically dropped in 2004. Other regions also showed disappointment in 2004, probably connected with deepening de-legitimization during Kuchma's rule. But in Central oblasts interest in private business has quickly regained in 2005–6 (difference between years is statistically significant at the level of 1 per cent), while Western Ukraine has not shown significant revival of this interest. In 2005–6 the values are approximately similar in all regions. It can be hypothesized that in Central region the motives for business participation are more pragmatic; although we would have expected this for the Eastern region instead. The detailed analysis provides evidence for this assumption: disposition to start business grew first of all in rapidly developing tourist business and resort areas with growing real estate values: Kiev city from 17 to 28 per cent, Poltava oblast from 9 to 37 per cent.

In Table 7 we present the results of the ordinary least squares (OLS) regression analysis which summarizes our findings concerning political, civic orientation, socio-demographic and geographical variables in relation to the desire to work for a private entrepreneur and readiness to start business.

The data indicate clearly that the age of respondent is a crucial explanative variable for both dependent variables under study: it has an inverse linear effect on the desire to work for a business and even more on the readiness to start business, which by far exceeds all other influences. This means that career opportunities associated with private economy and business are perceived as the forte of younger people. The consequence for delineation of actors of legitimization is obvious. This is explained by the fact that the opposite alternative to the private economy, however distorted, is a planned economy with low salaries and income levelling, associated with communist rule and its substantially older age cohorts.

Another characteristic of 'winners' in transformation, education, plays an important role in explaining the definite desire to start one's own business. Interestingly, the 'professionals' group is correlated negatively with this

TABLE 7
ORDINARY LEAST SQUARES (OLS) REGRESSION ON DESIRE TO WORK FOR
PRIVATE COMPANY AND TO RUN OWN BUSINESS BEFORE AND AFTER THE
REVOLUTION OF 2004, BETA STANDARDIZED COEFFICIENTS

	Desire to work for private company		Desire to run business	
	2003–4 $N = 3,562$	2005–6 $N = 3,572$	2004 $N = 1,778$	2005–6 $N = 3,576$
Age (18+)	−0.32**	−0.33**	−0.43**	−0.44**
Gender (1–0)	0.03*	0.06**	0.04	0.066**
Education (1–3)	0.02	0.04*	0.09**	0.10**
Trust in the government (1–5)	0.06**	0.06**	−0.06**	−0.04**
Estimation of president (1–10)[1]	0.07**	0.04**	0.08**	0.03*
Local civic competence (1–3)[2]	0.07**	0.055**	0.10**	0.09**
Readiness for protest (1–3)[3]	−0.06**	0.01	0.10**	0.05**
Western region (1–0)	0.06**	0.02	0.065**	0.01
Eastern region (0–10)	−0.06**	−0.00	−0.01	−0.03*
Professionals (1–0)	0.03	−0.01	0.03	−0.05**
R square adjusted	15.0	13.7	27.3	27.0

*significance at 5 per cent level
**significance at 1 per cent level
[1] In 2003–4 the question was about the activity of Leonid Kuchma and in 2005–6 about Viktor Yushchenko.
[2] The question was 'Imagine local authorities have issued a decision that is against your interest. Can you do something against this decision?'
[3] The question was 'Imagine that a mass-meeting or protest march against deterioration of living standards or breaking of rights will take place at your living unit, will you take part?'

dependent variable. This means that people with higher education, other than professionals – students, officials, military and businesspeople – are more positive about a career in business than professionals, on average. Noteworthy is the growth in the category of gender: after 2004 males are slightly more prone to work for private business and to start one's own business.

Estimation of Kuchma as a president is positively correlated with both the desire to work for business and to start one's own business. As in the case of age, it can be explained by the fact that the only perceived alternative to the market economy is a planned economy, so the communist electorate provide lower grades for Kuchma, who in fact started economic reforms in 1994. However, the correlation has weakened since Yushchenko was elected to the highest office.

Noteworthy is that those who want to start businesses tend to trust government less than those who do not; the opposite happens with the desire to work for business. It should be remembered that although two variables under analysis are closely correlated (Pearson's $r = 0.424$), still coincidence is not perfect and those who want to work for business and start their own business are different people in many cases. Among those who definitely want to work for business 61.5 per cent would like to start business, and among those who want to start their own business only 38.2 per cent want to work for business. Those who want to start their own business are on average better educated and younger than those who agree to work for somebody else's private business. One can imagine that these two categories are driven by different motives that are not irrelevant to the question of power. Those who want to work for private business are attracted by higher salaries in private companies. It can be hypothesized that they are aware of informal arrangements that business owners normally make with local authorities to proceed. However, since they are not supposed to participate in these arrangements themselves, proponents of hired labour reveal fewer grievances to the government than other categories. On the contrary, those who would like to start businesses themselves are aware that they will be forced to make such arrangements with power-holders, and this awareness manifests in stronger grievances with power. In a way, the perceived balance of costs and benefits in the case of hired labour has positive results for the trust in government, and a negative result in the case of potential businesspeople. Table 8 depicts that exactly the portion of those who want to start businesses, but reject working for business, exhibit the lowest average trust in the government, while those who accept the idea of working for business exhibit the highest. Different signs of coefficients on readiness to protest indicate the same difference: those who wanted to start businesses in 2004 were more oriented to protest than those who wanted to work for business.

Readiness to operate one's own business is associated more strongly with an active civil position – civic competence and readiness to protest against unfair decisions by the local power – than with loyalty to the

TABLE 8

AVERAGE SCORE OF TRUST IN GOVERNMENT (SCALE 1–5), WITHIN GROUPS THAT ARE ORIENTED TOWARDS PRIVATE BUSINESS

'Would you like to work for private entrepreneur?'	'Would you like to start your own business?'			
	'No' and 'rather no'	Difficult to say	'Yes' and 'Rather yes'	Total
'No' and 'rather no'	2.68	2.61	2.44	2.61
Difficult to say	2.63	2.67	2.48	2.59
'Yes' and 'rather yes'	2.80	2.58	2.67	2.68
Total	2.69	2.62	2.58	2.63

regime, which again witnesses an instrumentality of this type of legitimization. Coefficients for the regions support the inferences made above: belonging to Western region became less relevant for the support of working for and owning business. However, coefficients for occupational groups were very small and, with the exception of professionals, insignificant. This does not depreciate the findings demonstrated above, since they were focused on the dynamic of attitudes within groups. Occupational groups are traditionally considered as social and political actors of change. Younger, educated people and those with an active political position seem to be better candidates as such group actors. Nevertheless, without considering even minor changes within occupational groups it was impossible to note such a shift on the social scene.

Social Attitudes and Political Representation of Interests of Social Groups

If 'rising interest in privatization' is a sociological fact, 'strengthening legitimization' of power after the Orange Revolution is an assumption. Our findings leave unanswered the following question: whether growing practical interest in privatization means growing legitimacy of the new political power that came after the Orange Revolution. This question definitely exceeds the scope of this essay. However, it is possible to sketch the picture of public opinion towards some social and political issues on the eve of and after the Orange Revolution in order to speculate on the type of ongoing legitimization in the areas that do not concern privatization.

Probably one of the most problematic issues with understanding the Orange Revolution is the interpretation of the year that followed the Orange events, 2005. Many political scientists and journalists in Ukraine announced general disappointment with the new power, stating that the political elite had betrayed public trust. These judgements are most frequently not supported by any solid set of time comparable data and as such impede the understanding of the Orange Revolution's consequences. One should acknowledge that the population learned a positive lesson from the Orange Revolution, a lesson of communication with power, understanding its motives and intentions, and learning how to bargain one's interest.

A set of variables from 'Ukrainian Society' that concerns attitudes towards power refute the above 'disappointment hypothesis'. First of all, some attitudes indeed increased in 2005, after the Revolution, but have dropped in 2006 to the level of 2004. These are: belief in the necessity of a multiparty system and trust in government. There are also two variables that dropped before the Orange Revolution: support for a pluralistic political system in favour of 'strong leaders that can bring order to the country' and the desire to work for a business owner. Disregard of the multiparty system can be seen as a very serious problem for legitimacy of the regime, since it undermines the very basis of democracy. Corruption and strong merging of politics and the capital could have caused erosion of trust in the multiparty system. Linz and Stepan noted a decrease of belief in the multiparty system in Eastern Europe in the early 1990s.[30] A growing stance towards 'strong hand' power, up to its acceptance by two-thirds of the population, can be seen as an even more anti-democratic attitude. More variables should be included in the analysis to see if this wish means growing favour for authoritarianism in the Ukrainian population. For example, Jadwiga Koralewicz and Marek Ziolkowski, in their multidimensional analysis of attitudes towards power, interpreted the desire for a 'strong hand' in the Polish population of the late 1980s as an appeal to put an end to illegal relationships, unfair pay and corruption.[31] The most disturbing sign, of course, is diminishing trust in government, which was abysmally low before the Revolution, and has never exceeded 10 per cent since the monitor started in 1994.

The following variables showed substantial growth in 2004–5, and have dropped in 2006, though not to the extent of 2004: estimation of Ukraine's economic situation, interest in politics, confidence in the existence of politicians who are able to rule the country (from 28 per cent in 2004 to 50 per cent in 2005 and 43 per cent in 2006), trust and estimation of work of the president (from 2.7 score for Kuchma to 5.6 for Yushchenko in 2005 and 3.8 in 2006, on a 10-point scale), trust in parliament (from 2.2 in 2004 to 2.9 in 2005 and 2.5 in 2006, 5-point scale) and national pride (from 38 per cent in 2004 to 54 per cent in 2005 and 45 per cent in 2006). Despite a strong drop in 2006, one should recognize that from 1994 to 2004 neither trust in politicians, nor national pride had attained the level of 2006.

And there are variables that showed irreversible growth in 2004–6: disposition to start one's own business (from 21 per cent in 2004 to 29 per cent in 2006), trust in state banks of Ukraine (11 to 21 per cent), confidence in the existence of political parties and movements that are able to execute power (from 25 per cent in 2004 to 43 per cent in 2006), tendency to identify oneself as a 'citizen of Ukraine' costing advance of local and Soviet identities (from 44 to 55 per cent), confidence in one's ability to do something against unfair decisions by local power, trust in the police and speaking out against the death penalty. And still some variables stayed at the 2003–4 level: attitude towards private business development, state intervention in the market, trust in the legal system (14 per cent), local power (17 per cent), businesspeople and directors (18 per cent each) and confidence that one can do something against unfair decisions by central power.

This brief overview enables us to state that at least some variables exhibit some improvement. Public interest in politics and politicians, stronger national feeling, and disposition to start businesses and to save money at national banks are more or less directly indicative of the strengthening of legitimization of power after the Orange Revolution. One can interpret the effect of the Orange events as advancing political education and increasing confidence of the polity in general.

It is also true that the absolute level of trust in power structures is low, as well as in separate significant groups of the population like businesspeople and managers. Most people still feel helpless against the unfair exercise of power, yet they prefer strong power to a pluralistic system, as indicated by their low level of support for parliament. The only variable that illustrates the 'disappointment hypothesis' is the fall of trust in government which, although it is important, is not the single indicator of power de-legitimization.

The two variables, interest in politics and confidence about the existence of trustworthy political parties, show clear growth in 2005–6. This could be regarded as a result of the Orange Revolution. If before this event Ukrainian voters were seen as emotionally oriented towards personalities, not parties, the Orange events permitted them to discover political forces which address interests of different social groups (Figure 1). Supposedly, this contributed to a growing interest in politics in these very groups.

The detailed analysis showed that interest in politics increased to the strongest extent in the group of manual workers (Figure 2), although in the group of businesspeople and semi-professionals the increase is also statistically significant at the level of 1 per cent. Similarly, confidence in the existence of

FIGURE 1
POLITICAL PARTIES WORTHY OF TRUST

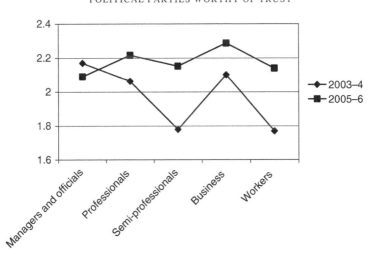

FIGURE 2
INTEREST IN POLITICS

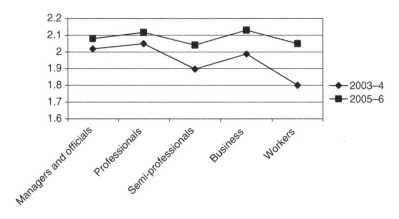

trustworthy political parties in the group of semi-professionals and, again, of manual workers increased the most (increase is significant in the group of businesspeople, but only at 5 per cent level). This could support an argument for ongoing legitimization of power in these two groups: after 2004 they feel more interest in privatization probably because they discovered political forces that are ready to defend their interests. At least the revolutionary event forced them to choose their political identity, to support their candidates actively. This definitely cannot be stated about managers and officials.

People were even more enthusiastic about the existence of political leaders who can rule the country: in 2005 this figure doubled, but had dropped somewhat in 2006. Public opinion studies rarely provide an opportunity to see such dramatic changes in such a short period of time that are revolutionary per se. Since 1999, Ukrainian voters have observed more and more politicians acting as independent leaders not in direct affiliation with party politics: Viktor Yushchenko, Yulia Tymoshenko, Petro Poroshenko, Olexandr Zinchenko. In the electoral campaign of 2004 these politicians acted first of all as personalities and only secondly as representatives of their political parties.

The analysis showed that confidence in efficient political leaders has increased the most within groups of semi-professionals and professionals, and to a lesser extent among manual workers, although all annual differences are significant at the level of 1 per cent, and in the group of businesspeople at 5 per cent.

Conclusion

The analysis of the data enables us to say that we have observed the signs of legitimization of political power in Ukraine since 2004. Trust in politicians and in separate significant social groups is still low and volatile, and criticism about the consequences of the events is too strong to allow us to estimate the changes in public opinion as unambiguously positive. Mass protests in autumn 2004 were directed against non-transparent, mafia-type relationships within power elites and unresponsive relationships of the power to its subjects. Corruption in the area of privatization was one of the hottest issues of public discourse and the strongest argument of opposition politicians. Promises by the opposition and attempts by the new government to stop unfair, corrupt privatization were the principle due to which the opposition and, later, new power were seeking to legitimize their power. One can assume that these promises corresponded to voters' expectations, as illustrated by mass support for the new government of Tymoshenko.

Two years after the Orange events show the growth in numbers of those who would like to start businesses of their own, and those who trust key political bodies (except government) and national banks, which allows us to make inferences about signs of legitimization. Statistical analysis revealed that the young are the most consistent adherents of private business. This coincides to some extent with civic activity: confidence in one's own ability to defend one's own interests. The correlation between support for hired work in a private company with trust in government and estimation of president was higher in 2003–4 than afterwards. This means a stronger correlation of this variable with the capitalist reforms' orientation than with sympathy to Kuchma. However, the desire to start one's own business is inversely correlated with trust in government, which probably means more decisive opposition against corruption and informal regulation in Ukrainian business. Those who would like to be business owners are also more willing to protest, which serves as proof of the hypothesis that the proto-middle class was a driving force of the Orange Revolution.

The detailed analysis of attitudes towards privatization within different social and occupational groups and regions of Ukraine at two points in time propels the interpretation about different kinds of legitimization: based on instrumental motives and normative agreement. It seems that those younger and better educated, semi-professionals, officers of the army, students, officials, and residents of Central Ukraine exhibit instrumental legitimization. Inhabitants of Western Ukraine exhibited more normative support in the recent past; however, the desire to start business is significantly weaker since 2001, and has probably become more instrumental.

Professionals are possibly not the first in line among those who strive for business activities. This group shows strong adherence to democratic values and pro-Western foreign policy, and therefore show more normative legitimization. Professionals are firmly interested in politics and do not tend to be easily disillusioned by political leaders. Despite this positive estimation about economic changes in the country, they plan less and less to start businesses of their own. A possible explanation that needs testing is that the reason lies not so much in disappointment in attempts to do this, but in a rational expectation that their education and training will be better compensated if they hold positions as experts with high salaries.

Analysis also has shown that those who are ready to defend their interests against unfair decisions by power-holders are also more interested in privatization. What about power-holders themselves? Managers of enterprises and state officials, who are supposed to be actors of legitimization, leave more doubts than confidence that they actually can be so, especially in the new political context. Their negative assessment of working for private enterprises and reluctance to start businesses of their own is much stronger after than before the Orange Revolution. Perhaps this means that they were quite satisfied with their standing and gains from unfair privatization and, therefore, perceive re-privatization as a threat to their position in the power structure.

In this chapter we concentrated on the labour force, because the question of private business concerns those who have some human capital and opportunity to invest in private business. At the same time, both the hottest proponents and opponents to private business are located outside the labour force: these are students and pensioners. Survey data show that students demonstrate the strongest support for business initiatives and democratic institutions. Pensioners are the least interested in privatization. This confirms their reputation as reform oppositionists. On the other hand, Ukrainian pensioners are strongly politically engaged: they are interested in politics and ready to participate in it. The percentage of those pensioner-respondents who see political parties able to take power increased by 22 points after 2004, while in the group of manual workers it increased by 14 points. This means that despite low interest in practical privatization, pensioners have an opinion towards privatization and, possibly, strong political representation of their interests. This also could mean that the history of Ukrainian privatization strongly affected the attitudes of pensioners who, through their political participation, can have their say in legitimization or rather de-legitimization of the regime.

NOTES

1. Andrzej Rychard, 'Komu jest protrzebna legitymacja?' (Who Needs Privatization?) in Andrzej Rychard and Antonij Sułek (eds), *Legitymacja: klasyczne teorie i polskie doświadczenia* (Legitimacy: Classic Theories and Polish Experience) (Warsaw: PTS UW, 1988), pp.301–19.
2. According to the data collected by the company SOCIS (Center of Social and Political Investigations) in October of 2004 (national representative sample, $N = 1000$) 14 % of those interviewed believed that the presidential elections would be honest and 17 % observed the electoral campaign as honest and fair in relation to all candidates.
3. The beginning of the movement 'Ukraine without Kuchma' was launched following the disappearance of the opposition journalist Georgiy Gongadze in the year 2000.

 4. Voucher privatization was carried out as follows: the value of all national assets was approximately estimated and this amount then divided by the number of all inhabitants of Ukraine, which gave the price of an individual voucher certificate – 10,000 Roubles. These certificates were granted to every citizen of Ukraine, who then had the right to invest it in stocks or to buy shares of enterprises.
 5. Olexandr Paschaver and LidiaVerchovoda, *Privatizacia do i posle Oranzhevoy revolucii* (Privatization before and after the Orange Revolution) (Kiev: CASE Ukraine, 2005).
 6. The data of yearly Ukrainian monitoring, which is described in detail in 'Data description'.
 7. Paschaver and Verchovoda, *Privatizacia do i posle Oranzhevoy revolucii*, p.11.
 8. Lena Kolarska-Bobińska, 'Vplyv korupciji na vladu v novych demokratiach' (The Influence of Corruption on the New Democracies) in Stephen Kotkin and Andras Sajo (eds), *Politychna korupcia perechidnoji doby* (Political Corruption in the Transitional Period) (Kiev: K.I.C., 2004), p.280 (pp.276–86).
 9. Elena Struk, 'Unesennye privatizatsiej' (Taken away with Privatization), *Delovoy*, Vol.12 (40) (2006).
10. Natalia Panina (ed.) *Ukrains'ke suspil'stvo 1994–2004: sotsiologichnyi monitoring* (Ukrainian Society in 1994–2004: Sociological Monitoring) (Kiev: Zapovit, 2004).
11. David Beetham, *The Legitimation of Power* (Atlantic Highlands, NJ: Humanities Press International, 1991), p.11.
12. David Held, *Political Theory and the Modern State: Essays on State, Power, and Democracy* (Cambridge: Polity Press, 1989), p.14.
13. Andrey Yermolaev, *Kogda nastupit god Ukrainy v Ukrainie?* (When will the Year of Ukraine come to Ukraine?) (Kiev: Center for Social Research 'Sofia', 2005).
14. Paschaver and Verchovoda, *Privatizacia do i posle Oranzhevoy revolucii*, p.25.
15. Tatiana Alekseeva, 'Legitimnost' vlasti v perechodny period' (Legitimacy of Power in the Period of Transition), in Tatiana Zaslavskaya (ed.), *Kuda idet Rosiia?* (Where does Russia go?) (Moscow: Moscow High School of Economic and Social Sciences, 1997), pp.142–8.
16. Henryk Domański, 'Merytokratyczna dystrybucja i zmiany mobilności: Polska i kraje Europy Środkowo-Wschodniej' (Meritocratic Distribution and Changes in Mobility: Poland and the Countries of Central-Eastern Europe), in Andrzej Śićiński (ed.), *Do i od socjalizmu: dwa przelomy w ciagu polwiecza w Polsce* (With and Without Socialism: Two Radical Turns in Fifty Years in Poland) (Warszawa: Instytut Filozofii i Socjologii Polskiej Akademii Nauk, 1998), pp.13–31; Natalia Pohorila and Kazimierz M. Slomczynski, 'Individual Income Gains and Losses in Ukraine, 1993–1996: A Test of the Human Capital and Mental Adjustment Hypothesis', *International Journal of Sociology*, Vol.29, No.4 (2000), pp.54–76.
17. Kazimierz M. Slomczynski and Shabad Goldie, 'System Transformation and the Salience of Class Structure in Eastern Central Europe', *Eastern European Politics and Societies*, Vol.11, No.1 (1997), pp.160–77.
18. David Lane, *The Rise and Fall of State Socialism: Industrial Society and the Socialist State* (Cambridge: Polity Press, 1996).
19. Slomczynski and Goldie, 'System Transformation and the Salience of Class Structure in Eastern Central Europe'.
20. Jadwiga Staniszkis, 'Stabilizacja bez uprawomocnienia' (Stabilization without Legitimization), in Andrzej Rychard and Antonij Sułek (eds), *Legitymacja: klasyczne teorie i polskie doświadczenia'* (Legitimacy: Classic Theories and Polish Experience), (Warsaw: PTS UW, 1988), pp.215–38.
21. Alexandr Motyl and Bohdan Krawchenko, 'Ukraine: from Empire to Statehood', in Ian Bremmer and Ray Taras (eds), *New States, New Politics: Building the Post-Soviet Nations* (Cambridge: Cambridge University Press, 1997), p.259 (pp.235–75).
22. Ihor Pas'ko, Yaroslav Pas'ko and Hennadiy Korzhov, 'Plavilny basejn Donetskoji identychnosti' (Melting Pot of Donetsk Identity), *Krytyka*, No.9, (2006), pp.2–5.
23. Gabriel Almond and Sidney Verba, *The Civic Culture* (Princeton: Princeton University Press, 1963).
24. Panina, *Ukrains'ke suspil'stvo 1994–2004: sotsiologichnyi monitoring*.
25. Ibid.

26. Juan Linz and Alfred Stepan, *Problems of Democratic Transition and Consolidation: Southern Europe, Southern America and Post-Communist Europe* (Baltimore, Johns Hopkins University Press, 1996).
27. Wladyslaw Adamski, 'The Evolution of Acquisitive and Threatened Interests in the Process of Ownership Transformation', in Wladyslaw Adamski (ed.), *System Change and Modernization*, (Warsaw: IFiS Publishers, 1999), pp.167–82.
28. We analyzed enlarged categories of answers ('No' + 'Rather no', 'Yes' + 'Rather yes'), as opposed to the original distribution of answers coded on a 5-point scale, because this distribution has been extremely abnormal and volatile over time: in some years more than 50 per cent of cases were concentrated on the poles (firm 'Yes' and 'No'), in other years frequencies were distributed more or less equally among five categories. This is why using the arithmetical mean is problematic; it shadows the polarization of the responses.
29. Valeriy Khmel'ko and Andrew Wilson, 'Regionalism and Ethnic and Linguistic Cleavages in Ukraine', in Taras Kuzio (ed.), *Contemporary Ukraine: Dynamics of Post-Soviet Transition,* (Armonk, N.Y.: M. E. Sharpe, 1998), pp.60–80.
30. Linz and Stepan, *Problems of Democratic Transition and Consolidation*.
31. Jadwiga Koralewicz and Marek Ziołkowski, *Mentalność polaków: sposoby myślenia o polityce, gospodarce i życiu społecznym* (The Mentality of the Poles: the Way of Thinking about Politics, Economics and Social Life) (Warsaw: Collegium Civitas Press, 2003).

The Role of the State in Catch-Up Modernization: The post-1789 Reforms in the Germanies and the Russian 'Great Reforms' in Comparative Perspective

JOACHIM ZWEYNERT

Introduction

In historical literature, parallels are often drawn between German, especially Prussian, and Russian catch-up development. In particular, it is often stressed that the emancipation of serfs in Russia followed the Prussian example.[1] However, there is scant literature comparing the reforms of Heinrich Friedrich Karl vom Stein and Karl August Hardenberg in early nineteenth-century Germany and those put through under Alexander II in Russia in the 1850s and 1860s. Certainly, Alexander Gerschenkron in his famous work *Economic Backwardness in Historical Perspective* (1962) compared German and Russian catch-up modernization in much detail, but he focused on industrialization processes in the late nineteenth and early twentieth centuries. Without returning to the fairytale of official Soviet historiography that Russia entered the capitalist age in the 1860s, I will argue that the foundation of the 'Great Transformation'[2] of Germany and Russia into capitalist societies was laid in the reforms undertaken between 1806 and 1819 in the Germanies and between 1861 and 1866 in Russia. Therefore, in order to understand the processes and associated difficulties of industrialization and political modernization[3] in these countries, it is this reform era we should be particularly interested in.

In my view, it would be rather misleading to restrict this comparison to Russia and Prussia. In order to understand what 'went wrong' in these countries it is instructive also to pay attention to the reform processes in the South-Western Germanies[4] which started under similar conditions as in Prussia but were more successful. As it is impossible to compare fully the political, economic and social transformations that took place in three different countries over a significant period of time in the scope of this chapter, this analysis should be taken mainly as a prolegomenon to an in-depth study raising some of the issues that would have to be looked at in more detailed research. In this essay, I will concentrate on an issue that is especially relevant in view of today's developments in Russia: the question of the relation between state and society and, in particular, the 'appropriate' degree of society's participation in politics during processes of catch-up modernization. My comparison is based on two theoretical pillars: first, on some elements of Max Weber's sociology of power[5] and, second, on the more recent idea of the transfer or transplantation of institutions.[6]

The essay is organized as follows: first I will outline the theoretical framework, and then briefly examine the historical background of the reform processes in the three analysed 'countries'.[7] A very general comparison of the reform processes in the South-Western Germanies, Prussia and Russia will then follow. The next section will compare the post-totalitarian experience of Germany and Russia, and in the final section I will draw some conclusions for today's Russia.

The Theoretical Framework

In the fifteenth and sixteenth centuries, the continental European sovereigns shared their power with the church, the nobility and the cities. Private and public rights had not yet clearly differentiated, and the power of the sovereign was patrimonial in nature.[8] The political development of the seventeenth and eighteenth centuries was marked by the attempt of the sovereigns to accomplish a monopoly of power against their competitors. In continental Europe, the modern nation-state emerged in a kind of double movement. In a first step, traditional society's participation through corporate bodies had to be repressed by the absolutist state. However, once the state had accomplished its monopoly of power and a clear borderline had been established between 'state' and 'society', the latter started to call, and indeed struggle, for political participation. If the traditional estates managed to regain power, the emergence of the modern state was threatened. Only where the power of the traditional forces – especially the nobility – had been broken, could there emerge the kind of participation we know in modern, Western societies: that of individual citizens or, to use a fashionable term, 'civil society'. Comparing the cases of the South-Western Germanies on the one hand and Prussia and Russia on the other, we find that the former were much more effective than the latter, both in crushing the old and paving the way for the new.

Up to the present day, historiography is mainly occupied with the history of nation-states.[9] However, in order to understand catch-up development, it is crucial to be aware that countries almost always encounter political, military and economic competition from other states or groups of countries. In the societies we are concerned with here, reforms started as a reaction to foreign occupation (some of the South-Western Germanies) or military defeats (Prussia 1806, Russia 1856). It is typical for historical latecomers that reforms are set off by external political shocks and subsequently modelled on foreign examples. The term 'transplantation of institutions' indicates the main problem connected with such attempts: the imported, formal institutional settings developed in a different political, historical and cultural context are transplanted to a different 'soil' which economists – following Douglass C. North[10] – usually call 'informal institutions'. In this essay, I will mainly concentrate on the dimension of thought, that is, on ideology.[11] The basic idea is that 'unfitting' institutions that are transplanted from one society to another in the short or long run will either be adapted to make them fit the domestic habits of thought, or they will be completely pushed off so that the old institutions 'survive' their replacement with imported transplants.

In the relevant literature, it is sometimes supposed that in a first step formal institutions are fully taken over, before in a second step they start to strike roots (or fail to do so) in the informal institutional settings of the receiving country. In reality, however, even in the reception of ideas or reform concepts by the relevant political actors, one can clearly observe the role played by domestic 'shared mental models'[12] – and these models are particularly instructive in understanding the reaction of the politically active strata of the population in the receiving country. Catch-up development is always connected with the problem of *non-simultaneity* of social development. If social and economic developments are imitated with temporal delay, the countries which serve as examples may in the meantime already have entered a different developmental stage, and this can undermine the acceptance of already 'outdated' reform concepts.

According to Max Weber's sociology of power, the main task of the German and Russian latecomers was to finish the process of the monopolization of state power and, in so doing, to pave the way for the emergence of modern political participation through civil society. The model case for this process had been provided by France after the Revolution of 1789.

If we understand catch-up modernization as a process of institutional transplantation, we have to focus on the following questions:

1. How strong was the exogenous pressure to import foreign reform concepts?
2. What were the ideological convictions of the key political actors, who were mainly bureaucrats, and how did they relate to the convictions of other parts of the executive?
3. How did the politically active strata of the population react to the modernization process of their societies?

Although I will be much concerned with ideological issues here, I should like to stress that I do not see a contradiction between 'idealist' and 'materialist' explanations of institutional change. The connection between economic and cultural determinants of institutional change was succinctly expressed by Max Weber as early as 1920: 'Not ideas, but material and ideal interests directly govern men's conduct. Yet very frequently the "world images" that have been created by "ideas" have, like switchmen, determined the tracks along which action has been pushed by the dynamic of interest.'[13]

The theoretical framework applied here is also Neo-Weberian in the sense that it is assumed that reform-minded bureaucrats do not pursue their own interests, but those of their country. More precisely, the motivations of the actors are not taken into account at all – at least not systematically. I am proceeding this way not because I hold that motives and interests are irrelevant to understanding the problems I am concerned with.[14] Rather, as an economist I am trained in the method of 'isolating abstraction'. The interpretation I am delivering here is consciously one-sided and does not claim to convey the full picture.

The Historical and Cultural Background

The key to understanding the parallels between Prussian and Russian development is 'enlightened absolutism', a political strategy of the economically backward countries of Central and Eastern Europe aiming at catching up with the West.[15] The German historian Theodor Schieder very aptly characterized Prussia, the model case of enlightened absolutism, as a 'kingdom of contradictions', for the conflict between the individualist-liberal ideals of enlightenment and autocratic rule in a *Ständegesellschaft* (society of estates) was irresolvable.[16] Yet this was not the only contradiction of 'enlightened absolutism'. In order to find support for their economic and military modernization programmes, the sovereigns of both Prussia and Russia in the sixteenth and seventeenth centuries had to make considerable concessions to the nobility. This led not only to a strengthening of serfdom, but also to a significant loss of power. This was particularly the case in Russia. As Richard Pipes wrote about the epoch of Catherine the Great: 'As a price for maintaining autocratic prerogative under conditions where it no longer made sense, the crown had to surrender most of its title to the country'.[17] In both instances, the modernization programme of enlightened absolutism, aimed at catching up with the West, resulted in developments that set these countries further apart from the Western nations in certain respects.

In comparison not only to France, but also to Prussia, the South-Western Germanies in 1789 seemed to be desperately backward: they remained a small, calm world of stagnating imperial towns, tiny knighthood territories and clerical estates. The building of the modern state had not even yet begun when the South-Western Germanies found themselves tangled in European policy in the 1790s – and as we will see, in some respects this gave them an important advantage over Prussia and Russia. Another advantage was that they were located nearer to the epicentre of the French Revolution. Some of them were even occupied by Napoleon, and this made it quite difficult to resist change.

Even though in all three 'countries' reforms were implemented as a reaction to external political shocks, the people and ideas behind these reforms did not 'spring out of nowhere'. Rather, it can be shown for each of the 'countries' that reforms were initiated by bureaucrats who had long since been thinking about possible ways to modernize their homeland. The degree to which they could implement such changes depended significantly on the acceptance of their ideas both within the bureaucracy and in the politically active strata of society. An important point in this argument is that the reception of social ideas depends on the cultural context. Following a Weberian approach, I hold that religion forms the deepest stratum of culture and therefore is also of particular relevance to understanding secular ideas.

If we compare our three 'countries' in this respect, we find that the South-Western Germanies were mainly shaped by Catholicism, Prussia by orthodox Lutheran Protestantism and Russia by Russian Orthodoxy. In an almost completely forgotten essay, Franz Borkenau put forth the thesis that the usual confrontation between Catholicism and Protestantism is misleading. Instead, he argued, the modern Christian world was divided by Catholicism and Calvinism, and by Lutheran Protestantism and Russian Orthodoxy as pre-modern versions of Christianity. In his view, Lutheran Protestantism, with its mainly contemplative asceticism and extreme emphasis on obedience to political authorities, could be seen as a conservative reaction against Western cultural influences emerging, not by accident, in the most backward region of Germany, the North–East.[18] Whereas Lutheranism was the decisive source of political authoritarianism, the key feature of the Orthodox tradition is the ideal of an 'organic' society not being fragmented into different subsystems.[19] This idea stands in direct contradiction to the path of Western modernity which is based on increasing division of labour between the different parts of society.

Without reference to Borkenau, Hans Rosenberg traced back the Prussian 'prolonged concentration of political leadership in the responsible central executive, the adoration of state power, and the far reaching political and intellectual influence of the irrational teachings of German Romanticism'[20] to the Lutheran tradition. That said, I in no way want to argue that the Lutheran and Orthodox traditions were insurmountable obstacles to the Westernization of these countries. But I hold that the way in which Western ideas were received in the three countries cannot be understood if the dimension of 'habits of thought' or 'shared mental models' is not taken into consideration.[21]

Nineteenth-Century Reforms in the South-Western Germanies, Prussia and Russia in Comparative Perspective

History shows that advanced countries exert pressure on 'backward' nations to imitate their patterns of political, military and economic development; that is, to import their structure of formal institutions. This dimension is usually not taken into account by those authors who emanate from the idea of path-dependence in long-term development.[22] In the path-dependence literature, it is often assumed that patterns of social life are determined by certain 'cultural legacies' reaching far back into the history of a people and thus are often regarded as exogenous factors.[23] The paradigm of the transfer of institutions tries to do justice to both the influence of external pressure and to that of domestic cultural traditions. 'Backward' countries certainly develop under political, military and economic pressure from 'advanced' nations. But the way in which ideas and institutions are interpreted and implemented, and the way in which the politically active stratum of the population reacts to reforms, significantly depend on the cultural legacies carried over from a country's historical past.[24]

The External Shock

It is out of the question that the spurt of modernization that took place in continental Europe in the first half of the nineteenth century started with the French Revolution in 1789. The impact of this event on the three 'countries' we are concerned with here was not only of different strength, it even worked in different directions. The South-Western Germanies simply were unable to oppose the French territorial extension under Napoleon. After Prussia's defeat in 1806 under French pressure, the so-called *Rheinbund* (Rhine Union) was formed in the South-Western Germanies.[25] The tiny princedoms now were transformed into a number of larger states, and this also meant that the free cities and ecclesiastical domains were integrated into the emerging larger units. Certainly, this was an important step towards the development of a modern state. However, maybe even more important was the implementation of the *Code civil*, representing a level of formal rationalization, abstraction and systematization unknown not only in the previous code of laws in the South-Western Germanies, but also in the relatively modern (and post-revolutionary) Prussian *Allgemeine Landrecht*. However, as much as the adoption of the *Code civil* at first glance may look like a prime example of purely 'forced institutional transplantation', in fact it can be shown that it was significantly modified as a reaction to the different social structures of the receiving states, to its interpretation by bureaucrats who had been educated in a different tradition and, last but not least, as concession to public opinion. Therefore, newer German historiography speaks of the 'reception' of the *Code civil* rather than of a simple takeover.[26]

The defeat of the Prussian troops in Jena and Auerstadt in 1806 hit a country that in the century before had risen to become not only the major German, but even a European power. Although the labelling of Prussia as the 'Sparta of the North' gives evidence that its rise was mainly due to its military strength, the self-esteem of its political elites was also based on the achievements of its artists and intellectuals. While military self-confidence suffered a significant loss in 1806, the same was not true of the 'cultural' self-esteem of its ruling stratum. Even though the elite had to appreciate the country's inferiority, and thus grudgingly accepted the necessity to imitate French patterns to a certain degree, its members were determined to search for their own way of putting through reforms. In this context it was important that the Prussian elite saw the cultural tradition of their country in sharp contrast to that of 'the West'. The military defeat threatened Prussia's status as a European nation, but it did not have to fear occupation. Compared with the South-Western Germanies, Prussia encountered significantly less external pressure, and this widened not only the space of the political actors, but also increased the relevance of the domestic habits of thought.

It would be wrong to say that Russia remained untouched by the French Revolution of 1789. As the example of Alexandr Radishev's famous *Journey from St. Petersburg to Moscow* (1790) shows, it had a stimulating impact on Russian intellectual life. In political terms, however, it had just the opposite consequences than in the German States, as it put a quick end to Catherine's enthusiasm about French enlightenment and caused a conservative turn in her policy. Again, in intellectual, military and – although to a lesser degree – also in political terms Russia participated in the upheaval that took place in Western Europe in the first decades of the nineteenth century. But then the 'half-hearted demonstration'[27] of the Decembrists marked the end of a more or less liberal period of political development in 1825. Sergei Uvarov's famous trinity of 'Orthodoxy, Autocracy and Nationality' was a last attempt to return to the basic pattern of Russia's eighteenth-century policy: to import only those elements of the Western political order that did not threaten autocracy. This attempt to cling to eighteenth century principles widened the gap between Russia and Europe. Similar to the case of Prussia, the military defeat that marked the beginning of the 'great reforms' threatened Russia's status as a great power, but neither British nor French troops had any intention to occupy Russian territory. Therefore, compared with the South-Western Germanies, external pressure was relatively low in Russia.

The Political Ideas

The reform processes in the three countries were set off as a result of external political shocks, but in all of them there had been bureaucrats who, in the decades before, had carefully studied the political and administrative order of advanced countries to ascertain how to apply it to their own country. This is well known of Stein and Hardenberg, both of whom had long since worked in the civil service and did not have to experience military defeat to be convinced of the necessity of reforms.[28] For a long time the reformers in the South-Western Germanies were regarded to have reacted passively to the political needs of the time. Only newer research has shown how fundamentally the French Revolution shaped the political views of Maximilian Josef Montgelas, the key figure behind the reforms in Bavaria. Even less was known about the background of the Russian reformers, before W. Bruce Lincoln in 1982 published his detailed study *In the Vanguard of Reforms: Russia's Enlightened Bureaucrats 1825–1861*. He argued that the ideas behind the Russian reforms of the 1860s had their roots in the reign of Nicholas I when – in the 1830s and 1840s – a group of young bureaucrats started to discuss the need to pursue economic and legal reforms.

We have thus established that the beginning of reforms was preceded by the spread of ideas – but what was the nature of these ideas? The intellectual impact of the French Revolution was most direct in the case of Montgelas. 'What a great spectacle' he noted, 'given that we will manage to profit from it'.[29] He agreed with all German reformers that benefit was only possible if one drew lessons from the French Revolution in order to prevent a revolution in Germany. At the heart of his reform concept – both in theory and in practice – was what he himself called 'civil freedoms'; equality of all citizens before the law, equality of taxation independent from estates, and the rule of law. Although in his 1796 manifesto he had emphasized the role of political rights; that is, the issue of participation in and control of public affairs by the citizens, as Bavarian minister he did little to promote the latter. Whether this was due to a shift in ideas or to practical political needs is not entirely clear up to the present day. An important difference between Montgelas and the Prussian reformers, namely Hardenberg, is that economic freedom played a fairly subordinate role in his ideas, and indeed the emancipation of serfs took place later in most of the South-Western Germanies than in Prussia.

Very much has been written about the political ideas of Stein and Hardenberg; particularly about the differences between the key actors of the Prussian reforms.[30] For decades the liberal conservative Stein – and this says much about path-dependence in ideas – was the 'hero' of German post-war historians, who saw his main merit in that he did not 'slavishly' follow the French example, but rather developed a more or less independent reform concept, 'organically' combining German traditions with imported Western influences. The decisive characteristic of Stein's political thought is that he was critical about the emergence of a sharp distinction between state and society in post-revolutionary France. The fact that he criticized the *Code civil* for 'disordering all civil conditions' (zerüttet alle bürgerlichen Verhältnisse) shows that his understanding of 'civil conditions' was somewhat opposed to that prevailing in Western Europe. Being concerned that the Prussian state – which he thought to be strong – threatened to 'choke' society, he aimed for participation of the nation in the reform process through self-administration of the estates.[31] On the one hand, Hardenberg, who in 1810 replaced Stein as State Chancellor, was more positive about the achievements of the French Revolution. Similar to Montgelas, he was determined to accomplish the monopoly of state power. On the other hand, he agreed with Stein that the division between state and society had to be attenuated by organs of self-administration of the estates. This conviction was basic for Prussian reforms in general, and it proved to be a fatal misconception. To let the estates participate in policymaking, in a situation in which the state had not yet fully accomplished its monopoly of power over the nobility, bore the risk that the latter was able to find a compromise with the bureaucracy and then to build a coalition against any further reforms.

As indicated in the previous section, the ideas of Russia's 'enlightened bureaucrats' (W. B. Lincoln) were shaped under the reign of Nicholas I in the 1830s and 1840s. In 1848 Konstantin Kavelin wrote to the liberal professor of history Timofei Granovskii, 'I believe completely in the necessity of absolutism in present-day Russia, but it needs to be progressive and enlightened'.[32] Certainly, this reads very much like a definition of enlightened absolutism, and statements like this may well have contributed to the idea that the views of the Russian reformers had been decisively influenced by the Prussian model. However, if we look at the ideas of Nikolai A. Milyutin, the key figure behind the emancipation of serfs and other reforms, we find that he and his circle oriented much more on the French than on the Prussian example. Not by accident, Otto von Bismarck, who had made the acquaintance of this group during his Petersburg mission (1859–62), remembered its members as 'haters of nobility' and 'progressives' who dreamed of a state 'according to Napoleonic patterns'.[33] Very much in line with the French example, they understood the state as an arbitral authority standing above the classes and saw the traditional estates, especially the privileges of the nobility, as an outdated social model. Although deeply influenced by Western liberal ideas, they were quite aware that premature participation of society would make any far-reaching reforms impossible. Thus, they welcomed autocracy as an instrument to accomplish their social model against the will of what they saw as impeding forces.

The Opposition

The views of the key actors of reform did not go unchallenged in the countries compared here. Indeed, some of them, including Stein in Prussia and Milyutin in Russia, were in office for a relatively short period of time. When looking at opposition against the reformers' ideas we should distinguish between resistance from within the state apparatus, from the politically active parts of the population, and from the nobility. In the South-West Germanies, resistance was significantly weaker than in Prussia and Russia. According to the information we possess – relatively little research has been done on this issue so far – the population in the South-Western Germanies was more supportive of reform than that in Prussia and Russia.[34] There was some conservative opposition from within the bureaucracy, but its protest set in only after key reforms had already been put through. Both in Bavaria and in Baden the liberal wing of bureaucratic opposition, which demanded even more far-reaching reforms, proved to be more effective than the conservative opposition party.[35] The protest of the nobility represented the greatest threat to the reform process in the South-Western Germanies, but it remained weaker than in Prussia for a number of reasons: first of all, the reformers had quickly deprived the nobility of its previous privileges; second, the new establishment of territorial states undermined solidarity within the nobility; and third, after a decade of more or less permanent war the strong desire for peace reduced what we would today call rent-seeking activities.

In Prussia, the attack on the privileges of the nobility began only with the appointment of Hardenberg as State Chancellor in 1810. Accordingly, opposition by the nobility started only at this time. It has to be stressed, however, that only a small party within the nobility fought for a full return to the previous state of affairs. While Hardenberg had been able to imprison his most radical noble critics temporarily in 1811, the monarch soon started to turn away from the reformers – mainly due to foreign political influences,[36] but also because he feared a destabilization of his power. As a result, the reformers were more and more excluded from important decisions. Although at the height of reform there had been little open opposition from within the bureaucracy, it quickly became clear that many conservative bureaucrats had kept calm during the reform period and now captured or regained key positions in the state apparatus.

Obviously, in Prussia the group of reformers had always been a minority that gained power as a result of an external political shock and lost its position as soon as this shock had been more or less absorbed. In contrast to the South-Western Germanies, there does not seem to have been a liberal party of any significance within the bureaucracy. Another important difference between the South-Western Germanies and Prussia is the strong opposition by the politically active parts of the population. In this respect, Prussia was more similar to Russia than to the South-West of Germany. The rather small group of liberals, many of whom had been inspired by the ideas of Adam Smith, saw themselves confronted with the vigorous critique of romantic writers and publicists. Certainly, the romantic thinkers expressed the interests of the estate owners, and one of the key figures of the romantic camp, Friedrich August Ludwig von der Marwitz, was himself a *Junker*. But this alone can hardly explain the lasting impact of romantic ideas on Prussian/German political discourse.[37] In my view, the holistic demand of the romantic camp to maintain the 'unity' of society and to avert its fragmentation (which was seen as typical for the 'West') also had its roots in Northern-Eastern German cultural traditions that had been shaped under the influence of Orthodox Protestantism. If this thesis is correct, it might also provide a partial explanation why the distribution of power within Prussian bureaucracy was less favourable for the reformers than it was in Bavaria or Baden.

In contrast to the South-Western Germanies, reforms in Russia could not aim at depriving the nobility of its privileges. The reason for this was quite simple: the enhancement of state power meant that the state had to take over the administrative tasks of the estates it had deprived of power. In Russia, the state apparatus was too weak to cope with this task, and hence it was dependent on the participation of the nobility.[38] It is understood that the serf-owning nobility opposed the liberation of serfs but, while it was generally successful in accomplishing convenient conditions for itself, it proved unable to prevent the reform. The nobility was, all in all, ambivalent about the creation of *zemstva*, the organs of communal self-administration.[39] On the one hand, it deprived them of traditional privileges; on the other hand they hoped that these organs would increase their political influence. In particular, these hopes found expression in the constitutional campaign of 1861–3, in which 'noble liberals' called for a division of competence between the central government and the organs of self-administration. All in all, Russia's nobility was not well enough organized to fight successfully for political participation. If it regained many of its privileges after 1881, this was not so much due to its strength but rather an expression of the weakness of the state.

Basically the same seems to have been true for Russian as for Prussian bureaucracy: the 'enlightened bureaucrats' formed but a small minority whose leading position was grudgingly accepted as long as they were supported by the emperor. However, as soon as external pressure started to decrease, more conservative – not necessarily reactionary – civil servants entered key positions. Also the reaction of the politically active part of the population shared common features with that in Prussia. As is well known, the discussion about the abolition of serfdom saw a strict separation between Western-minded liberals on the one hand and *Slavophiles* on the other, with the former demanding to abandon the village commune in order to pave the way for the Westernization of Russia, and the *Slavophiles* – very much in the spirit of the German romanticists – warning against the 'atomization' of society and thus calling for maintaining the *obshchina*, the traditional Russian peasant commune. 'Non-simultaneity' of social development proved to be a serious problem for Russia's reformers. This was because Russian reforms set in after Western Europe had already seen the revolutions of 1830 and 1848. As a consequence, a portion of the politically active sector of the population raised demands that were completely incompatible with the autocratic order, and this certainly did not strengthen the position of the reformers. However, it is interesting to see that although the political ideas of the leftist intelligentsia were inspired by Western thought, they met with the *Slavophiles* in their demand to maintain the *obshchina*. As a result, the traditional order was defended by a coalition of romanticists and pre-Marxian socialists against a very small number of Western-minded liberals. This constellation in my view can only be understood if it is taken into account that the individualization of the citizens was a Western European idea that stood in potential conflict with the holistic-organic patterns of thought dominating in the minds of the vast majority of Russian intellectuals.[40]

The Results

Let us now compare the results of the reforms in the three 'countries' this essay is concerned with. It is understood that we cannot go through all of the changes in the different reform areas, but will instead concentrate on the degree to which reforms achieved – or failed to achieve – decisive steps toward modernity in the sense defined here. In this respect, there is no doubt that the reforms in the South-Western Germanies were by far the most successful. Of the three countries, they were the only one to introduce a constitution that clearly defined the borderline between state and society and the ways in which society could participate in political decision-making. As Paul Nolte and other German historians argue,[41] the main reason for the success of reforms in the South-Western Germanies is that reformers started with a rigorous centralism. This enabled them successfully to accomplish the monopoly of power. Only after it had achieved a position of strength could the state return power to 'society' without risking to lose its dominant position. This reform sequence can be detected as a basic pattern in all the South-Western Germanies.

Much speaks in favour of the thesis that the relative strength the Prussian state had achieved at the outset of reform proved to be an obstacle on the path to constitution. Yet certainly it was also due to their sceptical attitude toward 'Western' patterns of social development that both Stein and Hardenberg wanted to prevent the emergence of a gap between state and society. To them, participation of the nation was not only a target of reform, but they held that the 'nation' should already participate in the *realization* of reforms. The main problem with this approach was that the Prussian state abstained from completing its monopoly of power, even though it was in a far better starting position to do so than the South-Western Germanies. Instead, it not only permitted, but even prematurely stimulated, participation and it is no surprise that this participation was mainly exerted by the nobility. Now why was this an obstacle on the road to constitution? First, participation in a situation in which the state did not have a firm monopoly of power weakened the state to a degree that made additional concessions in the direction of increased political participation even more difficult. Second, bureaucrats and the nobility started to form a coalition in which neither of them was particularly interested in being controlled by the public. This resulted in what Hans Rosenberg called 'bureaucratic absolutism': 'under bureaucratic absolutism the *Junkers* regained ... though in altered forms, the substance of the political *Ständestaat* privileges which had been expropriated from them in the age of royal dominance'.[42]

As strong as state power may have looked under Nikolay I, when it came to the emancipation of serfs it became clear that the state apparatus was simply unable to take responsibility for 20 million peasants who had been previously under the power of the land-owning nobility.[43] As the Russian state apparatus was unable to match the responsibilities of a truly absolutist state, it also could not convincingly claim a monopoly of power. Milyutin and his like-minded comrades were keenly aware that noble participation seriously threatened the provision of reforms – but how could the government abstain from noble participation when this was the only way to maintain the functions of the state? Certainly, as in the case of Prussia, it has to be emphasized that the reformers represented only a small minority within the bureaucracy, and also within the politically active parts of the population the share of those who called for following the example of the West was rather small. The best illustration is the debate about the *obshchina*, in which the small number of Western-minded liberalists came under the crossfire of the romanticist and socialist camps. However, the case of the Russian rural commune also clearly shows how difficult it is to discern whether ideas or material interests are the decisive forces in institutional change. The maintenance of the *obshchina* was in accordance with the political preferences of most educated Russians. It also made taxation much easier and, in this sense, was another expression of the weakness of the state.

Summarizing the comparison, we may say that

1. In the South-Western Germanies the external 'Western' influence was significantly stronger than in Prussia, and it seems to have been weakest in Russia.
2. The reform concept in the South-Western Germanies closely followed the Napoleonic pattern of strong centralization and consequent accomplishment of the monopoly of state power. This strength enabled it to participate in a second phase of reform. In Prussia participation was admitted at an early stage of reform. This later became an obstacle for the introduction of a constitution. In Russia, the state was too weak to accomplish a monopoly of power. Even if the government had made stronger efforts, it would have had no chance to cope with its administrative task without relying on the nobility.
3. In the South-Western Germanies, there was no strong resistance against the reforms either within the bureaucracy or in the public. Only the nobility tried, unsuccessfully, to defend its rights. In Prussia, there was strong resistance by a romantic camp against the reforms, and within the bureaucracy reformers represented only a small minority. Much the same is true for Russia, but here the romanticists' protest was partly accompanied by the socialist camp, and the resistance within bureaucracy is likely to have been even stronger than in Prussia.
4. All in all it can be said that the ideas imported from the West met with little opposition in the South-West Germanies but, in contrast, with fierce resistance in both Prussia and Russia. There were a number of reasons for this, but certainly the prevailing organic-holistic patterns of thought did not play the smallest role in preventing the emergence of an individualist civil society.
5. Historical experience shows that the modern state with its extremely high concentration of power can efficiently be constrained only by a civil society. While the South-Western Germanies managed to pave the way

to its emergence, both in Prussia and in Russia bureaucracy lacked any effective constraint and thus managed to gain too much independence from state and society. Therefore, the second stage of the modernization process, in which the strong state is controlled by an equally strong civil society, failed to develop in the latter countries.

Post-War Germany and Russia in the 1990s

In 1998 the German historian Heinrich August Winkler published a history of Germany since 1806 under the apt title *The Long Path to the West*, stating that although it had always more or less directly participated in Western European political and cultural development, Germany finally arrived in the Western world only after 1945. Simplifying matters a bit, one might be tempted to say that obviously this country, unable to produce revolutions on its own, could only permanently import Western European political and economic institutions with the help of foreign occupation, as was the case in the South-Western Germanies in the nineteenth century. The import of Western institutions was made much easier as the political ideas that provided the background to Germany's *Sonderweg* (culminating in the Third Reich), as well as the former political elite, were lastingly discredited. At the same time, it should not be overlooked that the reformers could rely partly on the works of German liberal social scientists and economists who had outlined a political and economic post-war order during the Nazi-Dictatorship.

The most famous examples are the works of the Freiburg resistance circles.[44] Among others, Walter Eucken, a German economist and founder of the so-called theory of economic orders that was basic to the German Social Market Economy, had participated in these circles.[45] What is striking in the political reform programme of the circles is the call for a strong state that would stand as a neutral instance above social interests. This was mainly a reflection of the experience of the Weimar Republic, when a weak state had come under the influence of powerful interest groups. As authoritarian as the political style of the first German post-war government may look from today's perspective, it was committed to the task of 'taking along' the population on the path of reform. For example, the German monetary reform of 1948 was put through against the will of the majority of the population in an authoritarian fashion. But the government, especially the minister of economics, Ludwig Erhard, thereafter did everything possible to explain the reform to the population.[46] Although democratic rules were quickly established after 1945, it took much more time for Germany to become a true democracy. Participation of citizens in political affairs did not set in before the late 1960s; about 20 years after the start of political and economic post-war Westernization. Obviously, what proved to be efficient here was a mixed strategy of, first, intense attempts to take society along by explaining reforms to the population and, second, precluding it from premature political participation. Indeed there is evidence that premature participation might have prevented the German economic miracle given that, as opinion polls showed, the vast majority of citizens of Western Germany were against the monetary reform of 1948,[47] which was basic to quick economic recovery.

The fact that Bonn, a relatively small West German city, was chosen as the capital of the Federal Republic of Germany was definitely not an accident. The political elite of post-war Germany chose it as a symbol of the end of Prussian dominance and their ambition to set Germany on the Western track of development again – a track, they thought, the South-Western Germanies had been following when they had come under Prussian (that is, Eastern) dominance after 1871. There is also much evidence that Konrad Adenauer, the first German chancellor, was not really interested in a quick re-unification of Germany that was allegedly promised by Josef Stalin if the unified Germany remained neutral. Like many of his contemporaries he feared that Germany might all too easily be pushed away from its 'path to the West'.

By the end of the 1980s, Russia clearly had lost both the Cold War and economic competition with the West. But the country was not occupied, nor were the former rulers – with the exception of Stalin – regarded as criminals. In short, external pressure certainly was not strong enough to become the engine of far-reaching change, and the old elite was not so discredited as to be vulnerable to attack from within. From the approach represented in this essay, the primary misconception of the Boris Yeltsin government in the 1990s was that the main political and economic issue was 'destatization'. This idea was based on the implicit or explicit assumption that the state was still strong and thus restrained individual initiative. However, by 1990 the Soviet Union had turned itself into a rent-seeking society with the *nomenklatura*, the power elite in the party-state, being able to block reform processes efficiently. According to the scheme presented here, the first task would have been to restore state power by depriving the old economic elite of its privileges before thinking about decentralization and privatization.

Very much in accordance both with the findings of modernization theory and with historical experience, the way in which 'democratization' was put through under president Yeltsin led to the 'capture' of an extremely weak state by businesspeople having transformed their *nomenklatura* relations into economic power.[48] As a result, at the end of the 1990s Russia had still not overcome its feudal structure, as neither the border between state and society had been clearly defined, nor was it possible to distinguish clearly between political and economic affairs.[49] This diagnosis then leads us directly to the question with which I will conclude this essay.

Conclusion: Everything all right with Mr Putin?

From the perspective outlined in this chapter, at first glance it looks like the answer to this question has to be a clear 'yes'. If it is true that in a situation in which the state has not firmly established a monopoly of power, rigorous centralization is the only means to establish the prerequisites for admitting political participation, the strengthening of the 'vertical of power' seems to be just the right thing to do. Indeed, in general there is nothing wrong with the attempt to roll back the influence of the 'oligarchs', and there also seem to be good reasons for partly restraining the power of the regional administrations (which in my view, however, is not a justification for abolishing elections at the regional level).

It is sometimes argued that one of Vladimir Putin's major problems is that he has a professional bureaucratic background. Therefore, the argument goes, it is not to be expected that he will be able to restrict the power of the bureaucracy. At least from the perspective of this essay, this argument is hardly convincing. Many reform processes have been initiated by individuals who came out of previous careers in the state service, and one should be careful when taking for granted a close relation between belonging to a class or social group and practical policy. In particular due to high oil prices, external political pressure on the Russian government is extremely low at the moment. Neither is it constrained by a functioning civil society. This may not be the worst starting condition for paving the way to a functioning democracy. As a comparison between the South-Western Germanies and Prussia shows, an authoritarian style of reform can sometimes be more efficient than one which tries to let society participate at a premature stage of reform. However, especially in a situation where there is little pressure from without, whether such a path to reform will indeed lead to more political participation in the end decisively depends on the ideological convictions of the reformers.

Considering this question in regard to today's Russia gives only reason for pessimism. Russia's educated strata had been extremely ill-prepared for the task of Westernization. Our historical comparison has shown that liberal reforms usually are preceded by intellectual movements taking place decades before reforms are implemented. In contrast not only to Germany after 1945, but also to the Central European countries where there had been a lively liberal underground discourse at least since the end of the 1960s, the vast majority of Russian intellectuals being critical of the Soviet state in the 1960s, 1970s and even 1980s could hardly be labelled as liberals in the Western sense.[50] Therefore, the country lacked a decisive prerequisite for the import of Western ideas and institutions. As Western liberalism has not yet gained a foothold in Russian society, the centralization of the Putin government is very unlikely to contribute anything to future democratization. Thus, in my view, a Western-type political and economic order is extremely unlikely to emerge in Russia within the next two or three decades. However, if the recent developments continue, Russia in the medium or long run will again fall behind the West in economic terms, and this will sooner or later lead to an increased external pressure. Such an external stimulus will, I think, be a prerequisite for far-reaching changes in Russia. But it will not work if Western ideas do not gain a stronger foothold, so that the reform forces will have at least a minimum backing within both the bureaucracy and the general population.

NOTES

1. See e.g. Andrei Anfimov, 'Prusskii put' razvitiia kapitalizma v sel'skom khoziaistve i ego osobennosti v Rossii' (The Prussian Path of the Development of Capitalism in Agriculture and its Peculiarities in Russia), *Voprosy istorii*, Vol.40, No.7 (1965), pp.62–76; Günter Mühlpfordt, 'Der Übergang vom Feudalismus zum Kapitalismus auf dem "preussischen Weg". Eine Gemeinsamkeit der russischen, polnischen und deutschen Geschichte', in Günter Mühlpfordt (ed.), *Beiträge zur russischen, polnischen und deutschen Geschichte* (Halle: Niemeyer, 1956), pp. 135–70.
2. Karl Polanyi, *The Great Transformation: The Political and Economic Origins of our Time* (Repr. New York: Octagon Books, 1975 [1944]).
3. The focus of this chapter is on catch-up adaptation of 'backward' countries to patterns that formed the basis of the economic and military success of the Western world. Therefore, there is no need to enter the twisted debates on the concept of 'modernity' in the social sciences. Rather, with Shmuel Eisenstadt, I define modernization simply as 'the process of change towards those types of social, economic, and political systems that have developed in Western Europe and North America from the seventeenth century to the nineteenth and have spread to other European countries in the nineteenth and twentieth centuries to the South American, Asian, and African countries' (Shmuel N. Eisenstadt [ed.], *Modernization: Protest and Change* [Englewood Cliffs, NJ: Prentice-Hall, 1966], p.1). It is worth mentioning, however, that this process has not led to a unification of societies but to 'multiple modernities', each reflecting the specific conditions of different societies or cultural regions; see the contributions in Shmuel N. Eisenstadt, *Multiple Modernities* (New Brunswick, N.J.: Transaction Publishers, 2002).
4. I refer to the South-Western Germanies as comprising the sixteen South- and South-Western German States which signed the *Rheinbundakte* on 12 and 16 July 1806.
5. Max Weber, *Wirtschaft und Gesellschaft: Grundriß der verstehenden Soziologie* (5th edn, Tübingen: Mohr, 1972 [1956]), pp.583–98; 617–34.
6. See e.g. Bertrand Badie, *The Imported State: The Westernization of the Political Order* (Stanford, Calif.: Stanford University Press, 2000); Viktor M. Polterovich, 'Transplantat-siia-ekonomicheskikh institutov' (The Transplantation of Economic Institutions), *Ekonomicheskaia nauka sovremennoi Rossii*, No.3 (2001), pp.24–50; Simeon Dyankov *et al.*, 'The New Comparative Economics', *Journal of Comparative Economics*, Vol.31, No.4 (2003), pp.595–619; Anton Oleinik, 'The More Things Change, the More They Stay the Same: Institutional Transfers Seen Through the Lens of Reforms in Russia', *Journal of Economic Issues*, Vol.XL, No.4 (2006), pp.919–40.
7. Of course the South-Western Germanies represented not one, but a number of states; and in view of today's unified Germany it looks rather odd to speak of Prussia as a country. Nevertheless for the sake of simplification I will use this terminology.
8. Weber therefore spoke of a *ständisch-patrimonialen* state.

9. If it pays attention to relations between the nation-states, it does so mainly in the context of the history of foreign relations and of military history. However, recently the discussion about 'transnational historiography' is intensifying. See e.g. Gunilla Budde (ed.), *Transnationale Geschichte: Themen, Tendenzen und Theorien* (Göttingen: Vandenhoeck & Ruprecht, 2006).

10. Douglass C. North, 'Institutions', *The Journal of Economic Perspectives*, Vol.5, No.1 (1991), pp.97–112.

11. This seems to be more justified as Gerschenkron explicitly emphasized that 'the "spirit" or "ideology" differed considerably among advanced and backward countries', but did not systematically deal with this problem in his book; see Alexander Gerschenkron, *Economic Backwardness in Historical Perspective: A Book of Essays* (Cambridge, Mass.: Belknap Press of Harvard University Press., 1962), p.7.

12. This term was introduced into the economics discourse by Arthur T. Denzau and Douglass C. North in their paper 'Shared Mental Models: Ideologies and Institutions', *Kyklos*, Vol.47, No.1 (1994), pp.3–31.

13. Max Weber, *From Max Weber: Essays in Sociology*, edited by Hans Heinrich Gerth and C. Wright Mills (New York: Oxford University Press, 1958), p.280.

14. For an approach towards catch-up development and the transfer of institutions focusing more on interests and constraints see e.g. Anton Oleinik, 'The More Things Change, the More They Stay the Same'.

15. Karl Otmas Aretin (ed.), *Der Aufgeklärte Absolutismus* (Köln: Kiepenheuer & Witsch, 1974).

16. Theodor Schieder, *Friedrich der Große: Ein Königtum der Widersprüche* (2nd edn, Frankfurt a. M.: Ullstein Propyläen, 1983). For an in-depth analysis of the antinomy embedded in the notion and practice of 'enlightened absolutism' see Leonard Krieger, *An Essay on the Theory of Enlightened Despotism* (Chicago: University Press, 1975).

17. Richard Pipes, *Russia under the Old Regime* (London: Weidenfeld and Nicolson, 1974), p.114.

18. Franz Borkenau, 'Luther: Ost oder West?', in Franz Borkenau, *Drei Abhandlungen zur deutschen Geschichte* (Frankfurt/Main: Klostermann, 1947), pp.45–75.

19. See Joachim Zweynert, 'Die "ganzheitliche Gesellschaft" und die Transformation Rußlands', in Hans Hermann Höhmann (ed.), *Wirtschaft und Kultur im Transformationsprozeß* (Bremen: Themmen, 2002), pp.10–35.

20. Hans Rosenberg, *Bureaucracy, Aristocracy and Autocracy: The Prussian Experience 1660–1815* (Cambridge, Mass.: Harvard University Press, 1958), pp.22–3.

21. Yuri Levada remarked that the notion of Orthodox Lutheranism contradicted the fact that it was the Catholic Bavaria from which the national socialist movement spread over Germany. This is true, but on the other hand it is also a well-established fact that it was the Protestant North East that soon became the region with the highest political support for National Socialism.

22. For overviews see Ulrich Witt, *Path-Dependence in Institutional Change* (European Study Group for Evolutionary Economics, Freiburg 1993); Daniel Kiwit, 'Path-Dependence in Technological and Institutional Change: Some Criticisms and Suggestions', *Journal des économistes et des étues humaines*, Vol.7, No.1 (1996), pp.69–93; James Mahoney, 'Path Dependence in Historical Sociology', *Theory and Society*, Vol.29 (2000), pp.507–48.

23. A typical example is Douglass C. North, who surprisingly – given his careful analysis of the links between cognition, culture and institutional change – speaks more than once in his recent book of 'the cultural heritage' of societies as if this was something homogeneous and unchangeable. E.g., North writes: '... we can see that the cultural heritage provides the artifactual structure – beliefs, institutions, tools, instruments, technology – which not only plays an essential role in shaping the immediate choices of players in a society but also provides us with clues to the dynamic success or failure of societies through time'; see Douglas C. North, *Understanding the Process of Economic Change* (Princeton: Princeton University Press., 2005), p.36.

24. This idea is developed in more detail in Joachim Zweynert and Nils Goldschmidt, 'The Two Transitions in Central and Eastern Europe as Processes of Institutional Transplantation', *Journal of Economic Issues*, Vol.40, No.4 (2006), pp.895–918.
25. Michael Rowe, *From Reich to State: The Rhineland in the Revolutionary Age. 1780–1830* (Cambridge: Cambridge University Press, 2003).
26. See the contributions in Werner Schubert (ed.), *200 Jahre Code civil: Die napoleonische Kodifikation in Deutschland und Europa* (Köln: Böhlau, 2005).
27. Israel M. Lubin, *Zur Charakteristik und zur Quellenanalyse von Pestels "Russkaja Pravda"* (Hamburg: Augustin, 1930), p.14.
28. See e.g. Wolfgang Treue, 'Die preußische Agrarreform zwischen Romantik und Rationalismus', *Rheinische Vierteljahresblätter*, Vol.20, No.2 (1995), pp.29–54.
29. Quoted in Paul Nolte, *Staatsbildung als Gesellschaftsreform: Politische Reformen in Preußen und den süddeutschen Staaten 1800–1820* (Frankfurt: Campus Verlag), p.114.
30. For an overview see Walter Demel, *Vom aufgeklärten Reformstaat zum bürokratischen Staatsabsolutismus* (Oldenbourg: München, 1993).
31. This idea found its clearest expression in the idea of the 'order of cities' (*Städteordnung*) in which many historians see his major achievement.
32. Quoted in Dietrich Beyrau, 'Reformen und soziale Beharrung im ländlichen Russland', in Gottfried Schramm (ed.), *Handbuch der Geschichte Russlands*, Vol.3, I (Stuttgart: Hiersemann, 1983), pp.14–67 (p.31).
33. Quoted in: Boris Nolde, *Die Petersburger Mission Bismarcks 1858–62: Rußland und Europa zu Beginn der Regierung Alexander II* (Leipzig: Lamm, 1936), p.185.
34. Eberhard Weis, 'Bayern und Frankreich in der Zeit des Konsulats und des ersten Empire (1799–1815)', *Historische Zeitschrift*, Vol.237 (1983), pp.559–95 (p.563).
35. Walter Demel, *Vom aufgeklärten Reformstaat zum bürokratischen Staats absolutismus* (Oldenbourg: München, 1993), pp.150–4.
36. After the murder of the Russian consul general August von Kotezbue by a member of a liberal-nationalist student league on 23 March 1819, it was decided (at a secret conference held from 6–31 August 1819 in Karlsbad under the aegis of the Austrian Minister of Foreign Affairs) to implement a restrictive policy regarding freedom of the press and the autonomy of universities.
37. One just has to take a look at the vast debate about 'Agrarian versus Industrial State' at the end of the nineteenth century to see how deeply the romantic protest against the spread of capitalism was rooted in the minds even of German economists.
38. W. Bruce Lincoln, *The Great Reforms: Autocracy, Bureaucracy, and the Politics of Change in Imperial Russia* (Dekalb, IL.: Northern Illinois University Press, 1990), p.91.
39. In detail see Terence Emmons (ed.), *The Zemstvo in Russia: An Experiment in Local Self-Government* (Cambridge: Cambridge University Press, 1982).
40. Joachim Zweynert, *Eine Geschichte des ökonomischen Denkens in Rußland: 1805–1905* (Marburg: Metropolis, 2002), pp.203–4.
41. Paul Nolte, *Staatsbildung als Gesellschaftsreform*; Hans-Ulrich Wehler, *Deutsche Gesellschaftsgeschichte*, 2 vols (München: Beck, 1989).
42. Rosenberg, *Bureaucracy, Aristocracy and Autocracy*, p.226.
43. Lincoln, *The Great Reforms*, p.94.
44. Ulrich Kluge, 'Der Freiburger Kreis 1938–1945: Personen, Strukturen und Ziele des kirchlich-akademischen Widerstandsverhaltens gegen den Nationalsozialismus', *Freiburger Universitätsblätter*, Vol.27, No.2 (1988), pp.19–42.
45. Rainer Klump, 'Der Beitrag der Freiburger Kreise zum Konzept der Sozialen Marktwirtschaft', in Nils Goldschmidt (ed.), *Wirtschaft, Politik und Freiheit: Freiburger Wissenschaftler und der Widerstand* (Tübingen: Mohr Siebeck, 2005), pp.383–401.
46. Joachim Zweynert, 'Shared Mental Models, Catch-Up Development and Economic Policy-Making: The Case of Germany after World War II and its Significance for Contemporary Russia', *Eastern Economic Journal*, Vol.32, No.3 (2006), pp.457–78.
47. Philip Herder-Dorneich, *Ökonomische Systemtheorie: Eine kurzgefaßte Hinführung* (Baden-Baden: Nomos, 1992), p.111.

48. Joel S. Hellman, 'Seize the State, Seize the Day: State Capture and Influence in Transition Economies', *Journal of Comparative Economics*, Vol.31, No.4 (2003), pp.751–73.
49. Richard E. Ericson, 'The Russian Economy: Market in Form but "Feudal" in Content?', in Michael P. Cuddy and Ruvin Gekker (eds), *Institutional Change in Transition Economies* (Aldershot: Ashgate), pp.3–34.
50. Jan Kubik, 'Cultural Legacies of State Socialism: History Making and Cultural-Political Entrepreneurship in Postcommunist Poland and Russia', in Grzegorz Ekiert and Stephen E. Hanson (eds), *Capitalism and Democracy in Central and Eastern Europe: Assessing the Legacy of Communist Rule* (Cambridge: Cambridge University Press, 2003), pp.317–51.

Index

For Product Safety Concerns and Information please contact our EU
representative GPSR@taylorandfrancis.com Taylor & Francis Verlag GmbH,
Kaufingerstraße 24, 80331 München, Germany

Printed and bound by CPI Group (UK) Ltd, Croydon, CR0 4YY
01/05/2025
01858453-0001